False Mystics

Engendering Latin America

EDITORS:

Donna J. Guy
Ohio State University

Mary Karasch
Oakland University

Asunción Lavrin
Arizona State University

FALSE MYSTICS

Deviant Orthodoxy in Colonial Mexico

Nora E. Jaffary

University of Nebraska Press • Lincoln and London

Acknowledgments for the use of
copyrighted material appear on
page xv.
© 2004 by the Board of Regents
of the University of Nebraska.
Manufactured in the United
States of America
⊗
Library of Congress
Cataloging-in-Publication Data
Jaffary, Nora E., 1968–
False mystics : deviant orthodoxy
in colonial Mexico / Nora E. Jaffary.
p. cm.—(Engendering Latin
America)
Includes bibliographical references
and index.
ISBN 0-8032-2599-7 (cl. : alk. paper)
ISBN 978-0-8032-1840-6 (pa. : alk. paper)
1. Inquisition—Mexico—History.
2. Mysticism—Mexico—History.
3. Mexico—Church history.
I. Title.   II. Series.
BX1740.M6J34 2004
272'.2'0972—dc22
2004010511

Set in Minion by Kim Essman.
Designed by R. W. Boeche.

For Ann and Karl

Contents

Illustrations

Preface

Since I began working on this book I have often been compelled to explain my interest in the group of one hundred Mexican "false" mystics whose stories lie at its core. One scholar to whom I outlined my project (then in its incubation stages) many years ago remarked, "Well, that sounds fine if you don't care about the lives of 97 percent of the population." At the time I had no ready answer. But over the course of researching and writing *False Mystics: Deviant Orthodoxy in Colonial Mexico* I have discovered that its scope, in fact, encompasses the history of many sectors of colonial Mexican society and confronts issues of tremendous importance to the people who lived in this context, as well as to those living in many other times and places, including our own.

The first and most basic reason why I chose to examine Mexican pseudo-mystics is that the Inquisition trial documents recording their histories tell good stories. I was captivated by the details of the trial and biographical portrait of one eighteenth-century *ilusa*, Ana de Aramburu, from the first moment I encountered a published transcript of her hearing. These documents are filled with intimate details about the spiritual, economic, and gendered lives of the humble people who populated New Spain's urban centers. Readers will likely respond with a range of reactions to the accounts of these mystics' religious expressions. I have perceived them variously as bold, clever, devout, humorous, perplexing, and unknowable, and I have accepted that no one of these (or many other) individual labels suffice to qualify who they were or what their religious practices signified.

Besides my enjoyment of a good story, my other initial attraction to studying the history of Mexican pseudo-mystics was that when I first learned of them, I concluded they must have been a group of transgressive rebels. I read of women who vomited reliquaries, denounced the viceroy, and masturbated in church, and I concluded that I had happened upon a group of people who purposefully sought to subvert their society's dominant paradigm: patriarchal Catholicism. The Mexican Inquisition and I did not differ greatly in what we thought these people were trying to do; we just had very different reactions to their objective.

As I pursued their history in greater detail, however, I discovered that focusing on these mystics' rebelliousness meant ignoring significant elements of their spiritual and social conventionality. As in all historical contexts, the analysis of the figures a society labels "deviant" (or virtuous) reveals a great deal more about the anxieties, values, and modes of perception pertaining to the administrators of deviancy and sanctity than it does about the people attributed with these qualities.

While I was completing my research on *False Mystics* in July 2002 in the penitential fourth gallery of Mexico's National Archive (the building, a former prison, is a panopticon), the motorcade of Pope John Paul II passed by the archives' front doors en route to the airport. The pope had just canonized Juan Diego, the Indian to whom the Virgin of Guadalupe appeared in 1531. It was an incredibly popular event, and traffic was stalled for hours in a two-mile parameter from the pope's transit routes. People camped out overnight in front of the basilica to catch a glimpse of His Holiness entering or exiting the building. Women appeared on television screaming, fainting, and sobbing. (They might have been described as ecstatic, hysterical, or epileptic in an earlier age).

The canonization ceremonies blended traditional sacraments and Catholic rituals with elements of the early twenty-first century's ideas of indigenousness. The scent of copal filled the basilica. A troupe of men in native costume proceeded to the altar accompanied by drummed rhythms and chanting. Priests prayed in Nahuatl. Outside on the sidewalk, however, street vendors sold plastic plates, key chains, and coffee mugs emblazoned with images of Juan Diego, evoking a different set of connotations. Set against a hazy yellow background, John Paul II stretched out his hand, on these plastic icons, to a pale-faced, bearded man who looked, as the pages of *La Jornada* indignantly observed, more like Jesus Christ or Hernán Cortés than someone who might be mistaken for the Mexican Indian Juan Diego. In a very different historical setting from seventeenth- and eighteenth-century New Spain, the Vatican appeared receptive to the incorporation of Indian traditions in Juan Diego's canonization ceremony, but the mementos that people purchased in markets and took home to treasure in remembrance of the event canonized an iconographically Europeanized Indian saint.

A variety of opinions swept Mexican newspapers, talk shows, seminar rooms, and subway cars about Juan Diego's canonization. Was it a cynical effort to pacify Mexico's sizable indigenous population, which remains the most economically marginalized sector of the country's population? Was it really the result of political finagling between various groups within Mexico's ecclesiastical hierarchy? Had the Vatican finally recognized the heroic virtue and miraculous import of an indigenous Christian, something it had resisted acknowledging since the first decades of the Spanish presence in Mexico? Many Mexicans expressed their indifference to cynical interpretations of the event as they concentrated on celebrating Juan Diego's canonization. Yet popular reactions to—and participation in—the construction of this new symbol of spiritual pride will continue to have important ramifications on the shaping of national identity and racial attitudes in contemporary Mexico, just as they did in the colonial period.

Acknowledgments

I wish to acknowledge my gratitude to the many individuals and institutions that provided me with professional, personal, and practical assistance during the research and writing of *False Mystics*. I am indebted to Asunción Lavrin, who encouraged me to submit the manuscript to the University of Nebraska Press, to the press's anonymous readers for their extremely helpful advice on how the manuscript could be improved, to the editors there, who saw it through to completion, and particularly to the freelance copyeditor Jane Curran.

Innumerable scholars have helped me with the substance and presentation of this work at various stages. While initiating my research in Mexico City's archives, I benefited from discussions in Mexico with Dolores Enciso Rojas, Clara García Ayluardo, Manuel Ramos Medina, Antonio Rubial García, and María Cristina Sacristán. Many other historians of Spanish America's religious and social history—Silvia Marina Arrom, Jodi Bilinkoff, Felipe Fernández-Armesto, Allyson Poska, William Taylor, and particularly Nancy van Deusen—provided me with insight, suggestions, and encouragement while I wrote and revised the dissertation out of which this book emerged. I would also like to thank my dissertation adviser, Herbert Klein, and the other committee members, Electa Arenal, Jean Franco, Ben Vinson, and especially Pablo Piccato, for their input. Barbara Cutter, Jennifer Cooley, and Trudy Eden, my colleagues at the University of Northern Iowa, all helped me improve my writing during the manuscript's later stages.

A number of other friends and scholars played important roles in this book's development while I researched, wrote, and thought about the manuscript in Mexico. Coco Alcalá, Eduardo Douglas, and Ilona Katzew inspired me with their fascination with colonial artwork. I explored Mexico City, while enjoying provocative conversation (and good food) with Joan Bristol, Liz Castañeda, Alex Stern, and Gerardo Necoechea. I am thankful for the companionship of the other doctoral students at Columbia University, particularly Joshua Rosenthal, Andrea Ruiz-Esquide, and David Suisman, whose intelligence and friendship were important foundations for persevering in the study of the past. For many years, Sherrill Cheda, Julie Crawford, and Jennifer Harvie have influenced me on the importance of feminist thinking. My brother, Eric Jaffary, motivated me with his enjoyment of history and his creativity. Conversations and classes with several professors at Columbia—Deborah Levenson, Caroline Walker Bynum, Linda Green, Olivier de Montmollin, and Joshua Freeman—also helped shape my approach to the historical topics I treat here.

I would like to thank the staff of the National Archives of Mexico's *galería cuatro* for locating and copying hundreds of Inquisition tomes for me between 1996 and 2002. I gratefully acknowledge the financial support I received, allowing me to complete this project, from the Social Sciences and Humanities Research Council of Canada, Mexico's Secretary of External Relations, the John Carter Brown Library, the Huntington Library, Columbia University's Institute of Latin American and Iberian Studies, the U.S. government's Foreign Language Area Studies grants, and the University of Northern Iowa. I acknowledge with gratitude permission to reproduce portions of the following articles: "Virtue and Transgression: The Certification of Authentic Mysticism in the Mexican Inquisition," *Catholic Southwest* 10 (1999): 9–28; and "The Creation of Heterodoxy: 'Pseudo' Mystics' Visualizations of Catholic Doctrine in Colonial Mexico," *Studia Mystica* 24 (2003), 21–49.

I also wish to thank my parents, Karl and Ann Jaffary, to whom I dedicate this book. Their historical curiosity, support for intellectual pursuits, and love for the telling of a good tale were all important influences behind its writing. Finally, and most importantly, I thank my partner and colleague, Ed Osowski. I am profoundly grateful for the encouragement, intellectual engagement, and perceptive humor that he has extended to me on a daily basis over the past seven years while I worked on this book. It is a privilege to share my life and my work with such a fine person and such a fine historian.

False Mystics

Introduction

Ana Rodríguez de Castro y Aramburu
An Ilusa before the Mexican Inquisition

O n November 21, 1801, Ana Rodríguez de Castro y Aramburu appeared before the Mexican tribunal of the Spanish Inquisition to defend herself against allegations that she had engaged in unorthodox religious practices. Inquisitor Antonio Bergosa y Jordán asked Aramburu if she knew of anyone who feigned receiving divine revelations, visions, or favors from God, or who claimed to have experienced "the divine impression of wounds on the hands, feet, and side."[1] Aramburu replied that she had not, but declared that she had informed her confessors of some "interior affects she had felt in prayer respecting the love of God and the hatred of sin." Surrendering a letter from a former confessor that charged her with demonic possession, Aramburu explained that she desired to find "remedy for her soul" and said the Inquisition should punish her should it find her guilty of some crime.[2] She stressed, however, that she knew of no sin in herself.

Aramburu, a thirty-eight-year-old resident of Mexico City, stated that she "maintained herself by making cigars and by other female labors," including cooking and caring for the sick. She was married to Juan Ortiz, a tailor, but did not know of his whereabouts because they lived separately even though the *provisor* (a bishopric's chief ecclesiastical judge) had commanded them to "make married life together."[3] Aramburu called herself Spanish, but her racial identity was, in fact, more complex. Later in her trial, the court's secretary described her as "black" (*de color pardo*). Aramburu's kin ties to a family whose surname was Moctezuma suggests that she also had Indian ancestry.

Over the course of the next two years Bergosa and the tribunal's other officers interviewed numerous lay and clerical witnesses whose accounts of Aramburu's spirituality differed from her own. Many of them detailed the ecstatic fits, visions, prophecies, and bouts of demonic possession they had watched Aramburu experience. Some had seen her levitate, view souls in purgatory, and cure the sick. A number told of the supernatural illnesses that afflicted Aramburu, causing her to bleed profusely from various parts of her body. One of Aramburu's supporters, Ana María de la Colina, recounted how Aramburu had miraculously saved a woman from the repeated beatings of her abusive husband by rendering her invisible.[4]

Under interrogation, a few witnesses maintained their support for Aramburu, but others turned against her, alleging that she had feigned all her supernatural feats. Several hinted that she had used her own menstrual blood to fake stigmata. Others implied that she had only wanted to create the appearance of sanctity in order to collect alms from gullible admirers. Many observed that her behavior was inconsistent with the virtues of humility, obedience, chastity, and reclusion that true mystics necessarily practiced. One acquaintance testified that Aramburu was overly fond of alcohol and said he had heard her shouting and cursing in the streets at night. A former follower claimed that she had spied Aramburu doing with Ana María de la Colina "what a man can do in this manner with a woman and giving her kisses during the night." More scandalously, she declared that Aramburu had once told her that while holding the holy host in her mouth, she had "touched herself" and had then "put [the host] in her private parts, saying 'long live the devil and death to Jesus.'"[5]

By October of 1802 her inquisitors had amassed sufficient evidence to initiate Aramburu's prosecution. They ordered her seized and placed in the secret cells of the Inquisition for the remainder of her trial. She was apprehended three months later living in a town outside the capital with her husband and two other men. After another year's further investigation, the court reached its verdict and concluded that Aramburu was an ilusa, one deluded by the devil, and an *alumbrada*, a heretical "false" visionary who had feigned experiencing the divine spirit. In December 1803 the Holy Office ordered her to appear in an *auto de fe*, a public sentencing ceremony, and convicted Aramburu to six years' reclusion and service in a hospital and ten years' exile at a distance of twenty leagues from Mexico City.[6]

While awaiting her verdict in the dampness of the Inquisition's cells, Aramburu's health had declined. In February of 1803 Doctor Nicolás de Navas wrote the court that Aramaburu was suffering from an in-flammation in her uterus, perhaps caused by a venereal infection. The court dispatched a noted physician, Luis de Montaña, to investigate. Montaña recommended that Aramburu, whose symptoms included vomiting blood, be moved from the Inquisition prison to the San Andrés hospital. In 1809, a few months before the termination of her six-year confinement in San Andrés, Montaña advised the court that Aramburu's continued ill health required her immediate release. The court ignored his recommendation. Upon her release from San Andrés, Aramburu elected to live in Atlixco, a small town twenty leagues southeast of the capital.

The move did not prove auspicious. Aramburu wrote the Inquisition six times during the next two years with a variety of grievances and requests. Before her journey to Atlixco, the court complied with her first appeal for alms and sent her twenty-five pesos, but it ignored all her subsequent pleas. A year after arriving in Atlixco, Aramburu wrote her inquisitors again to inform them that she was on the brink of death. She pleaded for permission to return to Mexico City for health reasons and in order to conduct some personal business that required her verbal ratification. In a later letter she lamented her fate, asking "Why God wanted her to be prosecuted until her death?" The final document contained in her file is a letter composed in December of 1812 in which Aramburu complained of intense pain in her uterus and excessive discharge of blood from her vagina. She begged the court in desperation to send her "a little chili or beans" in order that she might avoid "falling dead in the streets."[7]

Ana Rodríguez de Castro y Aramburu was one of the last of the 102 women and men denounced to the Mexican Inquisition for being ilusos or alumbrados between the late sixteenth and early nineteenth centuries (see appendix 1 for a summary of these trials). The term *iluso* denoted people tricked by the devil into believing they had experienced "true" mysticism. Alumbrados were a group of mystics whose piety emphasized internal prayer and meditation. Tribunals of the Spanish Inquisition first prosecuted alumbrados as antinomian heretics in the sixteenth century. Aramburu's case shares many similarities with those of other false mystics investigated in colonial Mexico. (See table 1 for a summary of the changing labels of accusation over time.) Approximately half of the accused were female. Almost all of these women were either poor members of the laity or *beatas*, religious women who took the same vows as nuns but who did not live in cloistered seclusion, and whom the established religious orders

Table 1. Changing labels of accusations, 1593–1801

	Alumbrado	Iluso	Both	Molinista	Other[a]	Total
1593–1624	8	1	—	—	—	9
1625–1649	9	—	—	—	—	9
1650–1674	2	2	2	—	—	6
1675–1699	5	3	8	1	7	24
1700–1724	3	4	2	—	4	13
1725–1749	—	3	—	3	2	8
1750–1774	3	1	1	7	1	13
1775–1801	—	13	3	—	4	20
Total	30	27	16	11	18	102

Source: Archivo General de la Nación, Ramo Inquisición.

[a] Includes the terms *feigner of sanctity*, *embustero*, *estafadora*, and *hipócrita*, usually in combination with charges of alumbradismo or iluminismo.

subjected to little supervision. Most of the accused of both sexes were people of Spanish descent, but roughly 12 percent of the trials involved people of mixed Spanish, African, and indigenous ancestry. A few of the men investigated were poor members of the laity, either *beatos* or *ermitaños* (hermits). A greater proportion of the men, however, were friars or priests suspected because of the support they gave to visionary women.

These Mexican false mystic trials constitute a fascinating body of source materials that colorfully portray colonial Mexico's religious and social past. In this book I examine the history of Mexican ilusos and alumbrados from the perspective of the Inquisition and from that of the accused parties themselves, locating both within the social contexts from which they emerged. The Inquisition played a fundamental role in regulating orthodox Catholicism in colonial Mexico and, through this regulation, in creating deviant Catholics. I situate the tribunal of the Holy Office in the forefront of Mexican iluso and alumbrado history and argue that inquisitors founded their determination of false mysticism only partly on an examination of the religious practices of the accused.[8]

Some differences did exist between iluso and alumbrado spirituality and that of bona fide mystics. These false mystics incorporated concerns from their mundane lives into their mystical expressions much more frequently and with much less subtlety than did mystics whom the church endorsed. They also assumed different roles from orthodox mystics in their interactions with saints and with God. Furthermore, in some instances these "deviant" mystics also produced unconventional interpretations of the miracles and mysteries of Christian dogma. Officials of the Mexican Holy Office, however, did not base their assessments of mystical fraud solely on the scrutiny of such differences. They also evaluated the quality and character of those under investigation, suspecting, in particular, people of low social status who accrued circles of followers around themselves, people who exhibited too much self-pride and independence in their religious expressions, and those who contravened codes of behavior deemed appropriate for their sex.

Mexican inquisitors also maintained vigilance against Christian spiritual practices that they perceived Indian or African influences had tainted. In Spain the crime of alumbradismo occupied the position of the "fourth" heresy. Spanish tribunals considered alumbradismo the gravest menace to the maintenance of orthodox Catholicism after Islam, Judaism, and Protestantism. The Holy Office's concern with alumbrados on the early modern Iberian Peninsula partially resulted from its preoccupation with these more dominant heretical groups.[9] In the New World, concern with Judaism, Islam, and Protestantism exerted much less influence on the court's perspective of heretical false mysticism. In colonial Latin America the Inquisition was more concerned with maintaining the population's practice of orthodox Counter-Reformation Catholicism uncorrupted by Indian and African influences.[10] This was part of a broader ecclesiastical anxiety that the peninsular purity of spiritual individuals and religious institutions would become tainted and transfigured through their relocation to the New World.[11] The court's theological concern with safeguarding pure Iberian Christianity mirrored the state and elite society's preoccupation with maintaining New Spain's social and racial domination by *peninsulares*, Spaniards born on the Iberian Peninsula.

The court perceived as heterodox the ilusos' belief that they might serve as valid candidates for the receipt of God's mystical gifts. Conversely, the accused parties themselves saw nothing heretical about their assumption of these positions. Although the Inquisition designated them as "deviants," the women and men accused of being ilusos and alumbrados in colonial Mexico did not see themselves as spiritual rebels. When they engaged in mystical experiences, these people were not attempting to enact either symbolic or material challenges to the patriarchal and hierarchical institutions of colonial Mexico's church and state. Rather, they endeavored to experience true mysticism (or, at the very least, endeavored to convince others that they had done so). They reveal this goal in the degree to which their religious expressions incorporated the Catholic orthodoxy of the Counter-Reformation as defined by the Council of Trent and the Mexican church's Provincial Councils. Their religious expressions—spiritual writings, "paramystical" phenomena, reverence for sacred ceremonies, and piety involving the sacraments—also mirrored the spirituality of their most important role models: Saint Teresa of Avila and Saint Rose of Lima. They further enmeshed themselves in colonial social orthodoxy through their utilization of two of the most important corporatist systems functioning in the colonial world: familial networks and patron-client relations. Ilusos' and alumbrados' motivations for engaging in mysticism lay not in the desire to challenge the orthodox spirituality of their era or to overthrow the most powerful institutions of their society, but rather to secure spiritual and societal endorsement.[12]

Ilusos and Alumbrados in Colonial Mexico

Legal codes, church doctrine, and elite culture all worked to structure colonial Mexican society upon a rigid set of racial, economic, and gendered hierarchies. Initially only male peninsulares could occupy the most elevated positions in the colonial bureaucracy, ecclesiastical institutions, and commercial networks. However, between the late sixteenth and late eighteenth centuries, increasing numbers of *criollos*, people of Spanish descent born in the New World, gained access to these positions. Criollos' rising political and economic aspirations threatened both peninsulares and the Spanish crown. Beginning in the mid-seventeenth century, Spanish elites also grew wary of the demographic and economic expansion of the viceroyalty of New Spain's racially mixed population. In response, the crown—with peninisulares' support—adopted several measures to restrict access to power by criollos and *castas*, people of mixed racial ancestry.[13] The 1776 Real Pragmática, a decree the energetic Bourbon king Charles III issued, represented the culmination of the state's policy. The Pragmática attempted to legislate an end to marriages between people of differing economic and racial backgrounds by prohibiting individuals' ability to select spouses without parental approval.[14]

The institutional Catholic church and Christianity itself provided imperial Spain with both a practical administrative body and an ideological basis to facilitate the maintenance of these colonial hierarchies. The Catholic church was one of the wealthiest holders of real estate in colonial Latin America. Its officers in both the secular church and the regular orders also exercised considerable power in the political life of the colonies. Christianity had provided a moral justification for the sixteenth-century Spanish conquest of the Indies. Moreover, conformity to Catholic doctrine continued to constitute an important element of public honor for plebeians and elites alike throughout the colonial period.[15] People from all social standings displayed their religious piety by donating to Christian institutions, participating in Christian festivals, or joining—or securing a family member's admission to—a religious order or ecclesiastical body.[16]

Christianity was also an important source of contemporary beliefs about appropriate gender codes. The history of the religion's defense against the competing faiths of Old and New World Paganism, Judaism, Islam, and Protestantism influenced concepts of both idealized masculinity and femininity. In medieval and early modern Iberia, Christians proscribed Spanish women from having sexual contact with the Peninsula's Moorish and Jewish populations. Laymen's practice of constructing their masculine honor on the successful defense of female family members' chastity became particularly charged in this multi-ethnic context. Spaniards transferred this ancient insistence on female sexual purity to the Indies, where they created a new set of prohibitions against the co-mingling of Spanish Christians with Indians, Africans, and castas. In Spain *limpieza de sangre* (cleanliness of the blood) had denoted purity from the taint of Jewish lineage. In the New World the phrase described those who claimed they were unpolluted by Indian or African ancestry.[17]

Priests and friars also modeled their masculine identities on examples from the history of Christianity's defense against competing religious traditions and on the notion of the stoic physical suffering and sacrifice necessary for the religion's preservation. Images and texts celebrating the accomplishments of the founders of proselytizing religious orders and early Christian martyrs informed these men's religious imaginations. Colonial Christians adored images of Christ's physical torment during the Passion, the most frequently reproduced depiction of Christ in Spanish America.[18] The central achievement of Mexico's first canonized saint, Felipe de Jesús (dubbed Mexico's "patron" in the mid-seventeenth century), was his 1597 martyrdom in Nagasaki, Japan.

Both lay and religious women attempted to imitate the standard of femininity set by the Blessed Virgin Mary. Her widely reproduced image served as a constant reminder of the traits of female perfection: passivity, tenderness, forgiveness, and possession of the ability to act as a gentle intercessor for the benefit of lost souls. Beyond these qualities, Mary's most important legacy for women in the Ibero-American world was her embodiment of irreproachable chastity. Since the Spanish inhabitants of colonial Mexico believed that most women, left to their own devices, would fall short of the Marian model, they attempted to secure women's virtue by enclosing at least those who pertained to society's highest echelons within the walls of convents, secluded private quarters, and *recogimientos* (houses of spiritual reform for women).

Christianity and the institutions of the Catholic church played instrumental roles in the maintenance of colonial Mexico's economic, racial, and gendered hierarchies. One possible reason for Inquisitors' condemnation of Mexican ilusos and alumbrados, then, is that they saw these mystics as disrupters of these hierarchies. Many ilusos publicized ideas or engaged in activities that the Holy Office could have interpreted as either symbolic or concrete confrontations with the institutions of colonial society it supported. These mystics' most blatant challenge to ecclesiastical authority lay in their claim to having received their spiritual powers directly from God, a source whose authority superseded any mortal force imaginable. As Mary E. Giles has observed, in claiming to derive spiritual authority from sources independent of the male-dominated theological tradition, female alumbradas were the group who most consistently challenged ecclesiastical authority in both Spain and the New World.[19]

Mexican ilusos and alumbrados challenged the colony's social, intellectual, and spiritual hierarchies in other ways as well. Many of them were humble people who gained social power, either symbolically or practically, through their spirituality. The trial of one poor early-eighteenth-century *mestizo*, Ignacio de San Juan Salazar, contains transcriptions of a series of revelations he recorded in a spiritual journal. In one of these visions Salazar described how the Virgin Mary appeared to him and informed him "that I must go to Spain to help the King to die in peace," a duty Salazar proudly claimed he had performed. Several other witnesses testified that Salazar had told them that he and the pope frequently corresponded with one another. According to Salazar, the corrupt government of New Spain under the third Bourbon-appointed viceroy, the duque de Albuquerque (1702–11), greatly displeased the pope. As part of his campaign to reform the reign, His Holiness had appointed Salazar as the "censor" of the viceregal mail.[20]

A contemporary of Salazar's, mestiza Getrudis Rosa Ortiz, also informed the tribunal about many visions of Albuquerque's corrupt reign that she had seen. Ortiz was so strongly convinced of the authenticity of her visions that she appealed directly to the viceroy's wife, the duquesa de Albuquerque, to persuade her to steer New Spain back to a more righteous path. Ortiz's divine visions inspired her to create close spiritual bonds with several other women of the court, including the marquesa del Villar del Aguila and the marquesa's aunt, doña Juana Guerrero.[21] Other Mexican mystics claimed even greater positions of power for themselves. One eighteenth-century ilusa, Marta de la Encarnación, asserted that God had appeared to her in a vision and had anointed her with the lofty title of "Patroness of the Indies."[22]

Besides such instances in which poor people assumed positions of social power through their religious experiences, these mystics directly or indirectly challenged the church in other ways. In their spiritual proclamations, alumbrados Juan Bautista de Cárdenas, Ana de Zayas, Getrudis Rosa Ortiz, and many others frequently denounced the corruption of ecclesiastical personnel. Cárdenas, a hermit tried in the mid-seventeenth century, proclaimed publicly in the streets of Puebla that "the prior and the prelates are thieves" given to frequent illicit communication with women. Cárdenas also publicly addressed the Virgin Mary as "the Virgin of Thieves" and "the Virgin of Rats."[23] Juan Gómez, another midseventeenth-century hermit, alleged that the "friars of San Francisco do not keep the rule that they profess."[24] In one of Getrudis Rosa Ortiz's early-eighteenth-century visions, God warned her that he would destroy Mexico because of the impiety of its occupants, particularly its priests.[25]

Along with critiques of ecclesiastical corruption, many Mexican mystics also engaged in behavior that contravened orthodox gender roles and conventional morality. The court investigated many women because their religious practices breached contemporary notions of women's designated religious sphere. Although almost all the female ilusas experienced conventionally feminine "paramystical" experiences (visions, levitation, divine sickness, etc.), many of them also participated in practices reserved exclusively for male clerics.[26] They published their own ideas about church doctrine; they assumed the spiritual directorship of other laypeople; and they claimed the intellectual right to interpret the meaning of their own mystical experiences.

A number of accused women also violated entrenched gender codes in their secular lives. Refusing masculine protection of their sexual virtue, several ilusas chose to live separately from their husbands. Of those who remained with their husbands, a number imposed rules of chastity on their households, contesting accepted notions of conjugal obligations. Still others, in violation of conventional sexual morality, allegedly engaged in extramarital relations with either men or women or desecrated religious sites and symbols—altars, hosts, and crucifixes—with sexual acts. Eighteenth-century ilusas Josefa de Palacios and Ana de Aramburu, for example, were both charged with masturbating publicly during religious ceremonies.[27]

Male mystics violated orthodox gender codes in other ways. The majority of the men involved were priests or friars who renounced their own claim to spiritual privilege and proximity to God and supported their female spiritual prodigies' claims to such positions. Both court officials and members of the laity severely criticized male clerics who engaged in such acts. Priest José Bruñón de Vertiz's intensive support of the four alumbrada Romero sisters so outraged the court that although he had died in the cells of the Inquisition before the termination of his trial, in 1656 the court ordered that his bones be exhumed and burned in effigy.[28] One Spanish woman who testified against another priest implied she believed that he had forsaken his position of social privilege because of his support for such women. Rather than referring to this cleric by his professional title, she described him as a person "without learning" (*sin letras*).[29]

The peers of Eusebio Villarejo, another cleric who had unconditionally supported a female visionary, also perceived that this friar had engaged in a gendered inversion of power. One witness who testified in the case described Villarejo's peculiar behavior as originating in his womb (*utero matriz*).[30] In other instances those who appeared before the court described men participating in even more explicit inversions of gender roles. One witness in Ignacio de San Juan Salazar's eighteenth-century trial testified that after claiming paternity for an infant, Salazar "brought this child to his chest and fed her with the milk of his breasts as if he were a woman." Another witness told the court that she had heard that Salazar assisted women with difficult problems they encountered in their needlework.[31]

Both colonial Mexican inquisitors and twentieth-century academics have interpreted such episodes as acts of subversion against colonial society's rigid social hierarchies. Officers of the Mexican tribunal condemned mystics' actions and attitudes for a number of reasons, including their perception that this group threatened the existent social order. Court *calificadores* (theological evaluators) conveyed this attitude in their assessment of Ana de Aramburu's religious crimes. They opened their declaration by asserting that Aramburu's "laziness, lack of devotion, pride, haughtiness, and disobedience to her confessor" indicated her culpability in some religious crime. Later, they deduced that her vices of "arrogance, dishonesty, pride, drunkenness, [and] disobedience" all proved her guilt.[32] A central reason for the calificadores' condemnation of Aramburu lay in their perception that she had refused to accept her position in Mexico's social hierarchy. She "lazily" attempted to entice spiritual supporters to provide her with monetary aid in order to avoid taxing manual labor. She arrogantly presumed she could occupy a lofty position of equality with God and Christ. In addition, she refused to subject herself to the disciplined control of her confessors.

In his assessment of the religious experiences of ilusa Getrudis Rosa Ortiz, prosecutor Pedro Navarro de Isla indicated that Ortiz's claim to possessing interpretive power over her visions was the most damning aspect of her spirituality. He argued that Ortiz's confident assertion of knowledge about her visions' origins and meaning, despite the fact that these apparitions always came to her "very obliquely," demonstrated that she was likely a false mystic. Navarro pointed to Ortiz's statement that "it seemed to her that God gave her to understand that he wanted to punish Mexico and would begin with the clergy." If this were a real vision, Navarro argued, "It would not have been revealed to her with such uncertainty, letting her arbitrarily conjecture what it signified, without instructing her in a revelation." Navarro believed Getrudis Rosa Ortiz could not be a true mystic because she had grafted her own interpretations on to her visions. By doing so she had moved beyond the traditional experiential sphere of female affective spirituality and into the masculine domain of doctrine and analysis. Ortiz's claim that "God gave her to understand *that which she knew of on her own*" indicated that "these ideas are her own discourse, her own conjectures and imagination."[33]

Past and Present Approaches to Mexican Mystics
Examining the relationships of marginalized groups to institutionalized power has become a central activity in Latin American scholarship in the past three decades. Since the late 1960s many scholars have worked to displace an earlier depiction of the lower classes, women, and non-Spanish ethnic groups as unconscious victims of society's dominant forces, including institutions of the church and state as well as gender, class, and race ideologies. This new group of historians suggested instead

that such groups greeted encounters with political or intellectual oppression with a variety of creative strategies ranging from accommodation to resistance.[34]

Historians working in this new branch of social and cultural history often documented resistance by detailing narratives of individuals' everyday acts of symbolic power inversions. Traditional histories had examined resistance only as expressed in broad, public, and direct confrontations such as revolutions. These new approaches often focused on instances in which people contested their own marginalization indirectly and individually, such as in the rhetorical strategies contained in a nun's journal entry that documented women's resistance to patriarchy.[35] For such scholars, participation in even subtly defiant acts could have momentous implications because it implied that more dramatic social change could and should be initiated.[36] Despite its political and intellectual appeal, this new portrait of the relationships of disempowered groups to institutionalized authority is problematic.[37] The indiscriminate characterization of actions and beliefs of marginalized people as resistance strategies obscures an accurate understanding of what historical characters themselves thought they were doing when they exhibited certain attitudes to institutional power.[38]

Writers have employed the "resistance model" to illuminate the history of ilusos and alumbrados and other similar groups in colonial Mexico. Literary scholar Jean Franco rightly observes that a mystic's inquisitorial trial was "a drama or struggle over meaning waged between institutionalized male authority and informal and therefore illegitimate knowledge." I differ from Franco, however, in my interpretation of what ilusas' actions signified to these women themselves. Franco sees Ana de Aramburu as a resistor to institutional patriarchal authority and locates Aramburu's resistance primarily in the symbolic realm. She writes that many of Aramburu's actions—vomiting blood, simulating lactation, and rapture—involved the public performance of private events of female life: menstruation, motherhood, and orgasm. She observes that if Aramburu had used menstrual blood as charged—to fake the appearance of stigmata—"she symbolically used the very proof of women's inferiority to enhance her own status."[39] Franco also argues that one of the principal reasons why Aramburu threatened the Inquisition was that she "converted her own body into values that transformed the status of women, that turned the 'low' into the 'high.'"[40] Franco contends that elites would have been particularly disturbed by this subversion of the "high" (the patriarchal authority of the Catholic church) with the "low" (Aramburu's body and the femininity and poverty associated with it) in the context of the late eighteenth century, when the political ideology of the French Revolution had infiltrated Mexico.

Evidence garnered from the entire group of Mexican mystic cases calls for a reassessment of Franco's contention that Aramburu and other ilusas focused their religious practices exclusively on their bodies, "the only instrument they truly possessed."[41] In fact, many of these women produced copious written materials either through self-composition or by dictating them to their confessors.[42] They wrote prayers and theological treatises and recorded their visions. They dictated their lives to their confessors or publicized their prophecies through public speeches and written announcements.

The court certainly saw Aramburu and other ilusas as deviants who challenged institutional authority, but was this what mystics themselves were attempting to do? The focus of this interpretation on the symbolic connotations of mystics' actions presupposes that the mystics and the court shared a common initial perspective on the meanings of such entities as menstrual blood or motherhood. Ilusas would have had to apprehend institutional connotations of these entities in order to attempt their subversion. Contemporary evidence does not substantiate, however, that such commonality of perspective existed between the accused and their interrogators. It is not even clear that institutional authorities themselves could formulate a common view of such entities.[43]

Solange Alberro, a social historian who has worked extensively on the history of the Mexican Inquisition, provides a more materialist explanation of the motivating forces behind the religious expressions of another Mexican ilusa, Teresa Romero, a mid-seventeenth-century beata. Rather than attributing Romero's motivations for participating in "deviant" mysticism to a desire to symbolically contest ecclesiastical power, Alberro interprets Romero's engagement in mystical spirituality as an attempt to garner a respectable income for herself in the context of the mid-seventeenth-century economic depression. Teresa, she argues, "had difficulty securing the means to maintain honor."[44] She lacked the dowry necessary to contract a suitable marriage or enter the convent, and she was unprepared to accept social degradation, let alone the dishonor of prostitution. For Alberro (as for the inquisitorial court), the chief causes of Teresa's involvement in mysticism were financial and social: it provided a means for her to maintain herself honorably. Women who established a public reputation for themselves as mystics, particularly those who secured the patronage of powerful sponsors, certainly did reap material and social rewards in return for their gifts, and the inquisitorial court suspected their legitimacy because of this. Can we then conclude that securing such benefits was necessarily these mystics' primary objective? In this colonial society, material objects and financial sponsorship were intimately associated with orthodox spirituality. Why should we assume that Mexican mystics would have viewed their own situations differently?

Both Franco's and Alberro's interpretations of the forces motivating iluso and alumbrado engagement in mystical spirituality served as important starting points for me when I began to consider the meanings of these religious expressions. The longer I explored the inquisitorial documentation surrounding these cases, however, the clearer it became that neither explanation adequately addressed the possibility that genuine religious faith had motivated the women and men charged with these crimes. The more I read of their cases, the less it seemed possible that they had somehow succeeded in isolating themselves from the Christian beliefs that permeated their social context.

Catholic ritual, doctrine, and morality infused even the most mundane workings of everyday life in seventeenth- and eighteenth-century Mexico as, indeed, it continues to do in the present. Religious celebrations structured the passing of time in individuals' lives and in the annual public calendar. Colonial Mexicans believed the saints could—and did—intervene in the operation of their lives to rescue them from illness, poverty, drought, or other natural disasters. Catholic symbolism and architecture dominated New Spain's most important public meeting places, and Christian indoctrination served as the most significant formal education many residents of New Spain ever received. Given this historical context, how could ilusos simply have "used" Christian mysticism in order to serve their own political or economic ends? [45]

I argue, in the following chapters, that they could not. In the late sixteenth, seventeenth, and eighteenth centuries the officers of the Inquisition labeled these people *ilusos* and *alumbrados* and charged them with feigning the ecstatic fits, divine illnesses, and visions they experienced. By the close of the colonial era, both medical professionals and clerics began applying new labels to their behavior, describing many of the accused as either hysterics or epileptics. I believe, however, that these mystics are more aptly perceived as representatives of a wider segment of New Spanish society, rather than viewed as aberrations from colonial norms.

This body of false mystics roughly corresponds to the contours, in social and economic terms, of the demographic portrait of New Spain's major urban centers. [46] They also represent colonial society in the sense that many aspects of their piety resonated with widespread religious practices that the institutional church supported in the Counter-Reformation era. Particular aspects of their social or religious practices occasionally disturbed the court sufficiently for its officers to categorize them as heretics. The court itself rendered ilusos and alumbrados extraordinary, but they were also remarkable in another way.

Many of the accused revealed an uncommonly powerful faith in the validity of their own convictions and experiences. When called to explain her religious beliefs to the court, Ana de Aramburu, like many other such mystics, defended the legitimacy of her faith even in the face of an inquisitorial investigation. She did this in a context in which the humble admission of guilt and articulation of the desire for reconciliation to the church was the most expedient means of ensuring clemency. Intrigued by the possible sources of this uncommon confidence, I have set about tracing some of the influences on the formation of Mexican mystics' religious mentalities, including, in particular, how their own lived experiences shaped their spiritual development.

Methodological Considerations

Anyone using Inquisition documents to study popular religious experiences must question how records generated by a prosecuting body can be used to access the spiritual imaginations of those it investigated. The accused must have been uneasy (if not downright terrified) to appear in the formal setting of the court. Few would have had any previous contact with such powerful representatives of the Spanish church and state as its inquisitors. Many would have witnessed or heard of the punishments and humiliation that the Inquisition inflicted upon those it judged guilty in its public autos de fe. In the midst of this intimidating atmosphere the court's inquisitors obliged witnesses to recount in public intimate details about their spiritual practices and beliefs. How could the documentation produced in this context accurately reflect the experiences of the accused?

Such documentation may be legitimately used to study defendants' religious practices for a number of reasons. First, in addition to trial transcripts, many of these Inquisition files contain various types of documentation generated outside the context of the court proceedings. The files often include records of ilusos' visions or locutions, religious journals, prayers, correspondence, and spiritual biographies produced long before their investigations commenced.

Second, although the penal setting and symbolism of the tribunal must have created an atmosphere intimidating to witnesses, there are other ways in which the court's operation allotted them a remarkable degree of narrative control over the production of trial transcripts. Inquisitors permitted witnesses considerable liberty in their testimonies, allowing them as much time as required to recollect and recount their evidence. The court normally opened interrogations by asking the relatively open-ended question "Do you know of anyone who has said or done anything against the Catholic faith or the laws of the church?" If the witnesses did not, inquisitors might then lead them with more directed questioning to speak to the subject under investigation. Witnesses who continued to reply negatively were often dismissed. If they replied affirmatively, the court permitted them to continue speaking until they had exhausted all they knew. Often the testimony of both witnesses and the accused fill several folios of uninterrupted text.

The court recorded these witnesses' oral narratives, including the personalized nuances within them, in an exacting fashion. As Richard Boyer has observed, notaries took great pride in the faithfulness of their recordings of witnesses' statements. "To edit testimony," he writes, "would have been audacious, irresponsible, and irreverent. However banal the settings and details described by witnesses, theologians and judges needed to sift through all of it." [47] The court's procedure of ensuring that witnesses verified the exactness of all recorded testimony also assisted the production of accurate transcripts. Notaries routinely changed the tense of the speaker from first person to third and sometimes inserted formalized language and expressions into witnesses' statements, but for the most part the documentation they produced was very close to witnesses' actual spoken accounts.

Although it seems legitimate to use Inquisition records as a means of reconstructing the religious imaginations of those whom the court prosecuted, we do need to maintain an awareness of the role the tribunal played in generating religious deviancy. The Inquisition created the vocabulary of the alumbrado heresy, taught it to the public, who denounced practitioners in their communities, and catalogued its existence in trial proceedings. This point has particular relevance for the consideration of how statistical analyses of rates of denunciation, investigation, and conviction may be undertaken. Fluctuations in these numbers are much more likely to reveal shifting trends in the preoccupations of the investigators of religious crimes than transformations in popular spiritual practices themselves.[48]

When carefully used, however, the iluso and alumbrado trial documents permit us to reconstruct the sacred and secular imaginations of both elite and non-elite people in the colonial world. They depict the operation of spiritual and social hegemony in the intensely hierarchical setting of seventeenth- and eighteenth-century New Spain. We can use these documents to track the origins and diffusion of spiritual orthodoxy and deviancy and to delineate the boundaries various members of this society drew between convention and aberration.

For the purposes of this study I have suspended the evaluation of whether or not the accused really experienced "true" mysticism. I do not attempt to judge whether God actually selected these individuals to receive mystical experiences, whether they only believed that this was so, or whether they merely manipulated other people into believing in their mystical authenticity. These questions lie beyond a historian's purview and are better left to theological or psychological investigators. Instead of focusing here on the determination of whether these people really were authentic mystics, I ask how and why the accused and their contemporaries evaluated the legitimacy of mystical experiences. For this reason, as well as for expediency's sake, I have generally eliminated the use of the term *false* to modify *mystic* when referring to the Mexican ilusos and alumbrados unless referring to accusers' or prosecutors' perceptions of these visionaries. The terms *iluso* and *alumbrado* were only labels of accusation and prosecution; defendants never identified themselves by these or any such labels. Unless explicitly adopting the court's perspective, therefore, hereafter I refer to the accused only as *mystics*.

False Mystics adopts the following organization. Chapter 1 equips the reader with the historical background needed to understand the prosecution of mysticism by outlining the history of the Inquisition, the prosecution of alumbradismo in Iberia and the New World, and the development of religious orthodoxy in New Spain. Chapter 2 situates iluso and alumbrado piety in the social context of colonial Mexico and provides an overview of the central elements of their religious expressions. It describes the spiritual experiences of several of the key figures—Marta de la Encarnación, Getrudis Rosa Ortiz, Ignacio de San Juan Salazar, Pedro García de Arias, Ana de Zayas, and Antonia de Ochoa—whose stories are featured in later chapters.

In chapter 3 the discussion shifts to the rationale the Inquisition used to distinguish authentic from false mystics, examining both aspects of mystical spirituality and secular behavior that disturbed colonial ecclesiastics. Chapter 4 explores the meaning of iluso and alumbrado spirituality to its practitioners through the analysis of visions, the most predominant feature of their religiosity. Chapter 5 returns the discussion to the analysis of the particular ways in which the Holy Office perceived these mystics. It discusses how the court and other members of colonial society created distinctions between ilusos and alumbrados and other types of social deviants—the ill, insane, or demonically possessed—and considers the ways in which earlier spiritual concerns continued to inform the new discourse of the Enlightenment that began to circulate in Mexico at the close of the colonial era.

One

The Production of
Orthodoxy and Deviancy

Late-fifteenth- and early-sixteenth-century Spain produced and exported to Mexico both the court that prosecuted New World mystics and the heresy for which they were tried. Pope Sixtus IV granted royal jurisdiction to the Catholic monarchs, Ferdinand and Isabella, to establish the Tribunal del Santo Oficio, the modern Spanish Inquisition, in Castile in 1478. Unlike its medieval predecessor, which had fallen strictly within the papacy's jurisdiction, this new body was an agent of the monarchy. It became a hybrid institution, serving "both altar and crown, controlled by the religious state and the political church."[1] Ferdinand and Isabella founded the Holy Office during the era of Spain's political centralization, and its original objective was the imposition of religious uniformity on the newly consolidated state. It initially strived to purge Jewish and Islamic influences from the Iberian Peninsula, and by the early sixteenth century its scope had expanded to include the heresies of Protestantism and alumbradismo as well.

Four years after the establishment of the Castilian court, the monarchy founded tribunals in Seville, Córdoba, Valencia, and Zaragoza. The crown created additional courts in the late fifteenth, sixteenth, and early seventeenth centuries. At its peak, nineteen separate tribunals formed what is known as the "Spanish Inquisition," sixteen on the Iberian Peninsula and three in Spain's overseas colonies, in Lima (Peru), Cartagena (Colombia), and Mexico City. The Mexican court presided over a vast territory that included the whole of New Spain, New Galicia, Guatemala, and the Philippines. The Mexican tribunal was disbanded in 1819, in the midst of the Wars of Independence, while the Iberian institutions continued to operate until 1834.

Franciscan friars, the first Catholic missionaries in Mexico, administered the earliest courts of the Holy Office in the colony. Both the friars' Inquisition (1522–32) and the more regularized tribunal of the Mexican archbishop that followed it (1532–71) focused their investigations on the expurgation of Indian religious practices from the colony.[2] These bodies' overly zealous prosecution of indigenous people—most notably Archbishop Juan de Zumárraga's 1539 execution of don Carlos Ometochtzin, a Texcoco *cacique* (hereditary Indian governor)—occasioned the crown's decree that the Holy Office would no longer have jurisdiction over Indians after its formation as an independent tribunal in 1571. At this time Philip II established a separate court, the Provisorato del ordinario, or Office of the Provisor of Natives, to deal with Indians' religious transgressions. Although the regular Inquisition and the Provisorato were jurisdictionally separate bodies, some historians have recently argued that officials in the two courts had considerable administrative contact with one another.[3] Laura Lewis discovered numerous instances of Spaniards and castas who had received powders, herbs, instructions, and cures from Indians who charged money for their services. The Inquisition wished to "correct" those who "made use of witchcraft, a process which inevitably involved Indians."[4] Inquisitors working in the regular tribunal, then, remained aware of Indians' religious crimes throughout the colonial period, even though they were not technically responsible for prosecuting indigenous people.

The tribunals of the Inquisition established in the New World differed from their Iberian predecessors. On the Peninsula, the courts' original aim was to purge Spain of "falsely" converted Christians and alien heretical influences. Primarily, they targeted *conversos* (Jewish converts to Christianity), *moriscos* (Muslim converts), and *luteranos* (Lutherans). The Inquisition's purpose was to assist in the creation of an ethnically and spiritually unified nation of Christian citizens. In the colonies, however, the greatest potential source of spiritual heresy, indigenous idolatry, lay beyond the official bounds of the court's scrutiny. This difference would have profound repercussions for the prosecution of ilusos and alumbrados in the New World.

At the time Philip II founded the three overseas inquisitorial courts in the late sixteenth century, he faced a number of grave domestic and foreign political crises, including recent criollo revolts in both New Spain and Peru. Philip's control over his kingdom, empire, and right of *patronato real* all appeared uncertain. [5] In response, Philip's Junta General, his principal advisory body, proposed the creation of the colonial tribunals as part of a campaign to shore up the monarchy's diminishing power. [6] At the time of the Mexican Inquisition's establishment, its officers perceived an association between religious heresy, political dissension, and public disorder, and the court's anxiety over this association intensified in New Spain's multiracial environment. [7] In seventeenth- and eighteenth-century Mexico, challenges to imperial domination assumed the form of rising criollo nationalism, a growing mixed-race population, and the erosion of respectful obedience to royal and ecclesiastical agents and mandates.

The Mexican Inquisition was created in part to strengthen Spain's control of its New World territories. In the last decades of colonial rule officers of the Inquisition continued to express their ongoing concern with political matters through their censorship of republican ideas and prosecution of individuals, most notably radical criollo cleric Miguel Hidalgo y Costilla, suspected of revolutionary conspiracy against the crown. The court's political orientation does not imply, however, that its officers were unconcerned with matters of spirituality. The Inquisition was a religious tribunal, and its judges, highly educated in matters of theology, devoted themselves to policing violations of Catholic doctrine. Seventeenth- and eighteenth-century inquisitors did not separate sacred from secular concerns. They perceived crimes against the Catholic faith as crimes against the upholder of this faith, the Spanish monarchy. Spain had staked the legality of its rule over the Indies on its role as defender of Catholicism, and so any challenge to Catholicism was also a challenge to Spain's legitimate rule of this territory. The officers of the Mexican Inquisition acted simultaneously as agents of social stability for the Spanish church and crown. They were also, of course, bureaucrats eagerly pursuing their own career objectives, and their private interests occasionally clashed with those of the larger bodies they represented.

The Mexican Inquisition was a coercive body that attempted to maintain the practice of religious orthodoxy among New Spain's Christian population. It prosecuted people who broke God's laws or those of the church, who disrespected the sacraments, or who contravened the viceroyalty's Christian codes of morality. The Mexican tribunal prosecuted a smaller percentage of heresy cases than did its Iberian counterparts. This was likely in part because the Spanish crown restricted the passage of Judaizers, moriscos, and Lutherans to the Indies and in part because the overseas courts were founded after the termination of the major campaigns against these groups. [8] Rather than focusing on instances of heresy, most cases the Mexican court tried involved minor religious crimes (chiefly blasphemy), illicit sexual practices (bigamy and solicitation), and *hechicería* (spell making or witchcraft). [9] Such minor religious crimes were, in a sense, the quintessential forms of religious deviancy in the Counter-Reformation period. The Council of Trent (1545–63) defined this era's conception of Catholic orthodoxy. Trent's decrees outlined the laity's obligations to the clergy and called for their regular enactment of the sacraments and veneration of the saints. Most of the religious crimes investigated in the Spanish American tribunals involved the violation of one of these principles.

As an institution serving to regulate social and religious orthodoxy, the court did not act as an alien force imposed upon a resistant population. The Holy Office established and monitored the practice of orthodoxy, prosecuting those who transgressed its boundaries. However, as Richard Greenleaf asserts, the Inquisition "found ready support from the ruling elite and from the humble masses," who provided it with incriminating testimony and, most importantly, denunciations (see table 2). Greenleaf contends that the insularity, exclusivism, xenophobia, and racial attitudes that thrived among the population of colonial Mexico were the necessary fuel for the tribunal's successful operation. [10] Contemporary beliefs about appropriate gendered behavior also played a decisive role in determining those whom the colonial court both investigated and convicted.

The Mexican tribunal of the Spanish Inquisition, like all others, had an autonomous structure but was subject to regulation by the Consejo de la Suprema y General Inquisición (Supreme Council of the Holy Office). The Suprema set trial procedures and provided direction when Mexican officials required assistance. [11] The Mexican Inquisition was notoriously disorganized, at once understaffed, and overly bureaucratized. [12] The court itself was normally staffed by two inquisitors, a secretary, an *alguacil* (bailiff), a *fiscal* (prosecutor), *consultores* (theologians who formed a judgment counsel), and calificadores (secular clergy who acted as theological evaluators and censors). It was also assisted by other officers, such as *comisarios* (locally appointed judges who heard trials in places outside the colony's capital city), *familiares* (informants who reported on the populace's religious practices to the court), notaries, jailers, lawyers, and doctors.

Table 2. Status of denouncers, 1593–1801

	By clergy/court[a]	By a nun	By a layman	By a laywoman	Total
1593–1624	7	—	2	—	9
1625–1649	9	—	—	—	9
1650–1674	5	—	1	—	6
1675–1699	17	—	3	4	24
1700–1724	6	1	2	4	13
1725–1749	7	—	—	—	7
1750–1774	10	—	1	2	13
1775–1801	13	1	1	6	21
Total	74	2	10	16	102

Source: Archivo General de la Nación, Ramo Inquisición.

[a] Court—denotes officers such as familiares, who made denunciations, or cases in which a comisario or other Inquisition official initiated proceedings against a party implicated in a denunciation originally against another person.

A set of late-fifteenth-century regulations formalized by Spain's first inquisitor, fray Tomás de Torquemada, established both the court's structure and the procedures the Holy Office followed. An investigation normally opened when a member of the clergy, or less frequently a layperson, secretly denounced another's religious offenses to the court. Edicts of the Faith informed laypeople's denunciations. These documents, published at regular intervals in New Spain's population centers, catalogued the various heresies the Inquisition sought to prosecute. Edicts of the Faith, which provided the lay population with a vocabulary and telltale insignia by which to recognize religious deviancy, were at least partly responsible for creating deviancy itself.[13]

In some instances residents of New Spain attempted to use the Holy Office as a venue in which to pursue private vendettas by denouncing their enemies to the tribunal. Inquisitors, however, were aware of this tendency and occasionally dismissed cases that they judged denouncers had initiated for personal reasons. The Inquisition suspended María Ignacía's 1796 ilusa trial, for example, noting that "some species of jealousy" had prompted her acquaintance to denounce her.[14] Besides attempting to visit revenge upon their foes, residents of New Spain sometimes used the court to serve other nonreligious purposes. Merchant José de Villa Alta, for instance, played a key role in denouncing many of the clerical and lay supporters of late-seventeenth-century Franciscan beata alumbrada Antonia de Ochoa.[15] Then, ten years after the close of Ochoa's trial, Villa

Alta applied to the court for the position of familiar. [16] Villa Alta was a merchant with aspirations of upward mobility who apparently wished to elevate his position in society by becoming an officer of the Holy Inquisition.[17] Villa Alta may have denounced so many of his acquaintances in order to demonstrate to the court his aptitude for the work rather than because he had any particular concern with the orthodoxy of Ochoa's religious practices. In both of these cases denouncers could be seen as using the court to serve their own secular purposes. However, given the ideological preeminence of Catholic spirituality in New Spain's social climate, it is likely that both laypeople and clerics more often made denunciations in order to comply with the Inquisition's mandate of upholding the practice of Catholic orthodoxy in the viceroyalty.

After receiving a denunciation, the officers of the court conducted an initial investigation, interviewing the denouncer and at least two other witnesses. This initial phase of the trial could stretch out for several years and could even stretch out for over a decade. In cases involving accusations of heresy the inquisitors then submitted a summary of their initial investigations to the court's calificadores, who produced a judgment on the severity of the crimes. If the inquisitors decided to pursue a case (a *proceso*), they then called the defendant to appear before them. After surrendering his or her worldly goods to the court, the accused party remained incarcerated in the secret prison cells of the Holy Office for the duration of the trial. The tribunal continued interrogating witnesses for anywhere from a few days to several years.

Once having heard all testimony, the inquisitors read an accusation to the defendant, who could then reply to the charges, in some cases with the assistance of an attorney. If the fiscal suspected the defendant of withholding information, he could recommend the accused undergo torture, although the Inquisition infrequently resorted to this device in New Spain. [18] After the defendant had replied to the inquisitors' accusations, the court read this party an anonymous transcription of all the witnesses' testimonies, to which the accused again responded. The court's inquisitors and consultores considered all this material in formulating their final judgment.

The Inquisition attempted to reconcile convicted parties to the church by extracting their confessions and subjecting them to penitential acts in ceremonies of Reconciliation and autos de fe. In these fearsome rituals, penitents were paraded through the streets of Mexico, stripped from the waist up, carrying green candles or other insignia that designated them prisoners of the Holy Office, while their crimes were read aloud to taunting spectators. Viewers then gathered in a public square to witness the sentencing of the convicted. In some cases those found guilty of iluminismo and alumbadismo were whipped with up to two hundred lashes. Often, as in the case of Ana de Aramburu, they were sentenced to several years' confinement or service in a poorhouse, hospital, or recogimiento. If the court judged that the case had been only partially proven, it ordered prisoners to proclaim either an *abjuración de vehementi* or *abjuración de levi*, public oaths that attested to their penitence and desire for reconciliation with God. In the gravest cases of heresy the convicted were released to the secular arm for execution, normally burning at the stake, in an auto de fe.

In New Spain the regular Inquisition executed fewer than fifty people during the entire colonial period. Two of these were mid-seventeenth-century ilusos Pedro García de Arias and Juan Gómez. The court convicted García, a hermit and author of several theological tracts, for his unorthodox ideas and for his "heretical presumption" that God had inspired his knowledge of them. [19] Among the claims for which the Inquisition condemned García was his statement that "man was a slave, bought with the blood of Jesus Christ." He had also written that "when some repugnancy is natural and voluntary, it is not possible for a person to work against it without a command or fear of it." The court concluded that this belief was "*the heresy of the damned Lutheran inheritance* condemned by the Council of Trent" and sentenced García to burn at the stake in 1654. [20] One of the reasons for the court's harsh treatment of both García and Gómez, a Portuguese alumbrado condemned five years later, was that during their trials neither man renounced his ideas and submitted himself to the superior judgment of the Inquisition. Both García and Gómez retained their faith that God had inspired them directly with true religious knowledge.

Despite the "renaissance" in studies of the Spanish Inquisition since the 1970s, scholars have paid little attention to the history of the Holy Office in eighteenth-century Mexico. This may be due to the perception that the tribunal's activities diminished in importance during the Bourbon period. Historians often characterize the Spanish Inquisition as moving into decline after the 1620s, with the Mexican tribunal following suit three decades later after the staging of the last of the large autos de fe in 1649. To date, no one has published a comprehensive statistical analysis of the cases the Mexican court tried during the eighteenth and early nineteenth centuries.[21] The scarce existent information indicates, however, that the Mexican tribunal continued active operation in this later period. Over 850 of the total 1,553 volumes of Inquisition documents housed in the Archivo General de la Nación in Mexico City cover the period from 1700 to 1819.

The court certainly continued to prosecute ilusos and alumbrados at the same level of intensity in the second half of the eighteenth century as it had in earlier periods. Over half of the cases initiated and nearly 60 percent of the convictions against Mexican false mystics occurred in the eighteenth century (see table 3).[22] Both the numbers of cases prosecuted and the impressive length of some of the eighteenth-century trials indicate that the court's interest in the practice of false mysticism only intensified in this era.[23] The Inquisition obviously believed that ilusos and alumbrados posed grave threats to social and religious stability. It convicted those accused of false mysticism far more frequently than those denounced to the court for engaging in other types of religious crimes. During its operation, the Mexican tribunal conducted full investigations of only one-sixth of those denounced to it.[24] In the iluso and alumbrado cases, however, the court pursued procesos against over half of those denounced (56 of the 102 denounced cases were brought to trial). Richard Greenleaf found that the Mexican court convicted only 2 percent of those few cases it chose to pursue.[25] In the Mexican mystic trials, however, nearly 65 percent of the cases brought to trial (36 of the 56 cases) resulted in convictions. (An additional 12 cases would likely have ended in convictions, but the accused died in the court's secret cells before the court could pronounce its judgment.) The Inquisition's vigorous pursuit of these cases demonstrates the severity with which the court's officers viewed the social and spiritual implications of common people's claims to authoritative spiritual power.

The Historical Development of Alumbradismo and Iluminismo
Ferdinand and Isabella used Catholicism to consolidate Spain's political unity in the late fifteenth and early sixteenth centuries. Influenced by the ideas of Christian humanism that writers such as Desiderius Erasmus espoused, Isabella also encouraged the church's participation in a movement of religious reform in this period.[26] At the beginning of the sixteenth century the powerful cardinal Francisco Jiménez de Cisneros, Isabella's former confessor and inquisitor general beginning in 1507, endorsed this movement. He condoned the widespread publication of

Table 3. Dismissed and convicted cases, 1593–1801

	Clergy/nuns dismissed[a]	Clergy/nuns convicted	Beatos[b] dismissed	Beatos convicted	Laity dismissed	Laity convicted	Died	Total
1593–1624	3	2	1	1	1	1	—	9
1625–1649	—	—	—	2	2	—	5	9
1650–1674	—	1	—	4	—	—	1	6
1675–1699	7	—	5	1	7	3	1	24
1700–1724	2	—	2	3	3	1	2	13
1725–1749	2	2	1	—	2	—	1	8
1750–1774	6	—	2	1	2	—	2	13
1775–1801	3	7	1	3	1	4	1	20
Total	23	12	12	15	18	9	13	102

Source: Archivo General de la Nación, Ramo Inquisición.

[a] Includes cases in which the AGN records may be simply incomplete rather than definitely dismissed cases. See "Sentence" column in appendix 1 for further clarification.

[b] Includes ermitaños.

mystical writings by Diego de Estrella, Luis de Granada, Santo Tomás de Villanueva, and Francisco de Osuna that emphasized interior and meditative spirituality. Osuna, one of the most popular authors of the period, developed the theological concept of recogimiento in his *Tercer abecedario espiritual.* Literally translated as "withdrawal" or "retreat from the world," his concept of recogimiento described the meditative state whose attainment was necessary for those wishing to achieve spiritual union with God. Recogimiento required its practitioners to negate all consciousness of themselves and their surroundings and to meditate intensely on "nothing."[27]

These new spiritual practices attracted substantial bodies of lay and clerical practitioners in the first decades of the sixteenth century. By 1520 adherents had established houses of recogimiento across the entire Peninsula. The movement exerted a particular influence on members of the Franciscan order, including the twelve Franciscan missionaries who traveled to New Spain in 1522 to commence the proselytism of the territory's indigenous population.[28]

Just a few years later, however, ecclesiastical receptivity to the teachings of these mystical authors had dissipated. In large part this was due to the Catholic church's heightened anxiety about the spiritual and political challenges that the rise of Protestantism posed to its supremacy. Luther's teachings criticized the mediating role of the clergy in religious experiences and promoted the centrality of God's grace—as opposed to human action—in securing humanity's salvation. In response to such ideas the Catholic church began to censure all religious expressions that emphasized unmediated contemplation of God or promoted belief in the soul's passivity in mystical union.

The men and women whom the Spanish Inquisition prosecuted for alumbradismo in the sixteenth century were among the first casualties of the Catholic church's heightened suspicion of interior spirituality. Inquisitor General Fernando de Valdés's infamous 1559 publication of the *Index of Prohibited Books* most concretely expressed the intellectual "closing" that transformed Spain in the mid-sixteenth century.[29] Among other works, Valdés's *Index* banned fourteen editions of the Bible, nine of the New Testament, and a number of notable mystical and spiritual works including those of Erasmus. Valdés, as well as other Spanish inquisitors active in this period, expressed particular derision for the role women had played in humanistic spirituality. He proclaimed "the jewel which makes a woman prettiest is the padlock of silence on the doors of her lips for all conversation and particularly for the mysteries of holiness."[30]

Isabel de la Cruz, a Franciscan tertiary and descendent of a Jewish converso family, was the first person the Inquisition investigated for the crime of alumbradismo.[31] The 1519 denunciation of her activities to the Toledo tribunal coincided with the initial outcry in Spain against Lutheran beliefs that emphasized internal rather than ceremonial spirituality. Cruz was one of the many religious women whom the new spiritual writings of the early sixteenth century had profoundly influenced. Along with other members of her religious circle, Cruz had engaged in a spiritual practice called *dejamiento*, an extreme expression of recogimiento. Rather than encouraging mere isolation from worldly influences, dejamiento advocated complete abandonment of the will to God's power. Recogimiento involved the active seclusion of the mind in order to achieve union with God, whereas dejamiento called for the passive submission of the soul to God's will.[32]

Cruz had attracted a wide circle of followers from many ranks of society with her preaching and meditative instruction. One of her associates, Pedro Ruiz de Alcaraz, managed to obtain financial and social support for the group from the Mendozas, one of Toledo's wealthiest families. Several other clusters of alumbrados appeared in Toledo in the same period, many of them led by lay beatas who preached a doctrine of internal spirituality to groups of worshippers that included members of elite families. The conventicle (group) form of religious worship and the patronage of powerful benefactors are two of the only traits that New Spanish alumbradismo would later share with its Iberian precedents.

The Toledo court declared Cruz, Alcaraz, and their followers guilty of alumbradismo and punished them in an auto de fe in 1525 while simultaneously issuing an edict that catalogued their crimes. The 1525 edict, a compilation of forty-eight propositions formulated from testimony presented during their trials, became the basis for the court and the laity's subsequent knowledge of alumbrado religious practices.[33] Edicts issued in 1574, 1623, and 1668, as well as those sections of the General Edict of the Faith published in colonial Mexico, were all derived from this original document. The 1525 edict identified three principal features of alumbrado religious practice: endorsement of internalized religion promoting mental rather than vocal prayer; disdain for the ceremonial aspects of worship (for example, communion); and antinomianism, the notion that upon reaching a certain degree of spiritual union with God, the mystic was released from any possible sinful ramifications of bodily (and, in particular, sexual) practices. Subsequent edicts alerted their audiences to alumbrados' belief that ecstatic fits were demonstrations of God's grace and to this group's skepticism about the need to perform good works or practice the sacraments.

After the early-sixteenth-century investigations of alumbrados in Toledo, tribunals in Extremadura and Andalucía initiated the second and third waves of prosecution between 1570 and 1590. Contemporaneous to the earliest Mexican cases, the Sevillan court tried a fourth cluster between 1575 and 1623. Spanish courts examined few alumbrados after the mid-seventeenth century. On the Peninsula, as in Mexico, however, the Holy Office did investigate the related religious heresies of quietismo and molinismo in the late seventeenth and early eighteenth centuries. In the period between 1540 and 1700 the Spanish Inquisition prosecuted a total of roughly 150 people for false mysticism.[34]

Fear of the spread of Lutheranism played a definitive role in the Spanish Inquisition's prosecution of those it labeled *alumbrados*, but the court's anxiety was not limited to the threat of Protestantism alone. As Alistair Hamilton and others have argued, these mystics became the tribunal's victims because they were "caught between" its two more central contemporary preoccupations: the new heresy of Protestantism and the older heresy of crypto-Judaism.[35] Many of the initial practitioners of alumbradismo were from converso families, and many of their beliefs resembled those that Protestants endorsed.[36] Inquisitors wove the threads of their concern with these other heresies into their interrogations of alumbrados and into the edicts they issued against alumbradismo.

The eighth proposition of the Toledo Court's 1525 edict, for example, stated that alumbrados claimed "that confession is not of divine, but rather positive right. This proposition is Lutheran and is tainted with heresy."[37] In this document the court also described alumbrados' alleged disdain for Christ, a tendency that indicated possible Jewish influences on their beliefs.[38] The tribunal also voiced its suspicion of possible converso affinities among practitioners of alumbradismo in the last charge it leveled against Pedro Alcaraz. It stated: "'the said Pedro de Alcaraz and other people ate *adafina* cooked in the Jewish manner on the Sabbath as a Jewish ceremony and with the intention of observing Mosaic law.' To this Alcaraz replied that he had never eaten *adafina* (a form of stew) and did not even know what it was."[39]

The Protestant Reformation created an environment of heightened insecurity in the sixteenth- and seventeenth-century Catholic church. Ecclesiastical anxiety over the contagion of spiritual practices resembling Lutheranism prompted the Spanish Inquisition's prosecution of groups of mystics it labeled *alumbrados*. These preoccupations, rooted in the social context of the early modern Iberian Peninsula, directly shaped the initial trials of Mexican mystics. By the mid-seventeenth century, however, new social concerns tied to the particular racial and religious characteristics of New Spain became the chief determinants of a New World form of alumbradismo.

The Prosecution of Alumbrados in Mexico

In Mexico clerics and lay people denounced a total of 102 people for false mysticism between 1593 and 1801. Over one-third of these denunciations resulted in guilty convictions, 15 in the late sixteenth and seventeenth centuries and 21 in the eighteenth and early nineteenth centuries (see table 3 for a summary of rates of accusation and conviction).

The majority of the trials (76) transpired in central Mexico, most either in the capital itself (37) or in Puebla (18), the second-largest Spanish center in the viceroyalty. The court investigated a handful of mystics in several other urban centers of the colony, including in the cities of Querétaro (9), Oaxaca (4), Valladolid (2), Mérida (2), and Guadalajara (2). An additional 3 cases came from Manila in the Philippines.

The Holy Office tried the first cluster of Mexican mystics—four men and five women—between 1593 and 1604. Their cases most directly resemble those of the alumbrados investigated in Spain. In these early Mexican trials the preoccupations of the court officials were still rooted in the religious climate of sixteenth-century Iberia. Both the denouncers and nearly all the accused were peninsulares. Moreover, some of the defendants had drawn their spiritual influences from the same sources as those that had inspired Spanish alumbrados.[40]

On May 4, 1593, Dionisio Castro, a Dominican friar, denounced Juan Plata, a cleric in the convent of Santa Catalina de Siena in Puebla, for a number of ideas he had espoused that resembled those of Spanish alumbrados. According to Castro, Plata had discouraged his spiritual followers from praying vocally and had claimed that he did not need to do penance because he was "embraced and honored with the love of God" and formed part of the "choir of the seraphim."[41] Plata also possessed knowledge of the state of peoples' souls and, like many other members of this first cluster of Mexican mystics, had seen visions of Gregorio López, the mid-sixteenth-century ascetic hermit and botanist who became one of Mexico's candidates for beatification in the seventeenth century.[42] Plata, along with some of his followers, claimed that López had taught them in visions that a "New Jerusalem" would be formed in Mexico, and that they would people it eternally.[43] Along with these spiritual matters, Plata was also suspected of having had sexual relations with some of the nuns in the Santa Catalina convent and was accused of teaching these women that they did not sin when engaging in these acts as long as they never intended to sin.[44]

There are some similarities between the crimes for which the court suspected Plata and those of earlier Spanish alumbrados. More to the point, however, the man who denounced Plata had himself been immersed in the Spanish courts' prosecution of alumbradismo. Dionisio Castro was a protégé of another Dominican friar, Alonso de la Fuente, who had acted as the chief prosecutor of the alumbrados tried in Llerena, Extremadura in the 1570s.[45] Castro had witnessed the trials of the Llerena alumbrados and had preached against the evils of the heresy in Seville. Castro carried his knowledge of alumbradismo with him to New Spain, where he denounced the crime and, in doing so, re-created the heresy's existence on the western side of the Atlantic.

As well as investigating Plata's activities, the Inquisition opened cases against a number of his associates: the nun Agustina de Santa Clara, Plata's assistant, Alonso de Espinosa, and a laywoman, Catalina de Lidueña. The tribunal simultaneously opened cases against an acquaintance of Plata's, Juan Núñez de León, an official of the mint who lived in Mexico City. Núñez led a circle of spiritual devotees whom the court also examined. This group included Dominican beata Mariana de San Miguel, cleric Luis de Zárate, and Carmelite beata Ana de Guillamas.[46] The charges in all these cases resemble those leveled against Juan Plata. These mystics favored a religious practice promoting internal meditation and mystical ecstasy. For instance, one of the accused, Marina de San Miguel, testified that she had often seen visions of Christ "with her interior eyes."[47] The court condemned several members of this group, judging that they had disrespected the rituals of Catholicism, exaggerated their own virtue, and sinfully engaged in sexual improprieties.

The activities of these Mexican alumbrados resembled those of their Spanish counterparts, at least as detailed in the Inquisition's sixteenth-century edicts. These New World cases also resembled their European predecessors in terms of the court's perception that elements of crypto-Judaism and Lutheranism were intertwined in their mystical practices. Many of the defendants in this first cluster of Mexican trials claimed that Gregorio López had inspired them. In the first decades of the seventeenth century several powerful members of the colonial church began to promote López as a candidate for beatification, but at the time of these trials he remained shrouded in considerable spiritual suspicion. Before López's death in 1596 an envoy of the first Mexican chief inquisitor, Pedro Moya de Contreras, had investigated López, likely for the charge of crypto-Judaism.[48]

The perception of Mexican mystics' links to crypto-Judaism extended beyond defendants' associations with Gregorio López. In Juan Núñez's trial two of his cellmates testified that he knew much more about the Old Testament than the New, and that he failed to show sufficient devotion to the figures of either Jesus Christ or the Virgin Mary.[49] Núñez, so his accusers charged, had publicly decreed that "the Jews kept their God better than the Christians."[50] These witnesses also contended that Núñez was sympathetic to Protestantism, referring to him as a *gran luterano*. Further, they alleged that he had ridiculed the solemnity of autos de fe and had called both the inquisitor and the king "devils." These charges greatly disturbed the calificadores in Núñez's trial. Among other condemnations of his practices contained in their assessment of the "presumed crypto-Judaism of Juan Núñez," Jesuits Pedro de Hortigosa and Pedro de Morales wrote that he had exhibited tendencies "found in Jews to disbelieve that Christ our Lord is the promised Messiah." They further reasoned that his praise of the Jewish faith "has the sound and appearance of Judaism."[51]

The court perceived similar connections between alumbrados and crypto-Jews in the trial of Ana de Guillamas. Among the crimes for which the court accused Guillamas was her declaration that the devil had spoken to her while she was praying and said, "Poor Carvajal who was killed without guilt."[52] Carvajal was the surname of a group of Judaizers convicted in Mexico in the late sixteenth and mid-seventeenth centuries. Luis de Carvajal, the first family member prosecuted, was executed in 1597. The Holy Office convicted over one hundred Judaizers in Mexico, condemning several to burning at the stake in the largest auto de fe in the history of the Mexican Inquisition in 1649.[53]

Spanish precedents thus strongly shaped the initial prosecution of alumbrados in Mexico. Those who denounced and prosecuted these mystics had learned from the Spanish example how to detect and label this heresy. The text of Mexico's edicto general de la fe reflects the influence of the Spanish context on the Mexican production of alumbradismo. The Mexican Inquisition did not issue any edicts individually directed against the alumbrado heresy; warnings about their pernicious practices were instead incorporated into this General Edict. By the early seventeenth century the crime of alumbradismo appeared fourth in the General Edict's list of heresies, preceded only by those who followed the laws of Moses, Muhammad, or the sect of Martin Luther.

The description of alumbrados in the Mexican documents closely resembled those of the sixteenth-century Spanish edicts. In Mexico the General Edict warned the populace against those who believed that

> *mental prayer was the Divine Rule, and that vocal prayer mattered very little . . . that the servants of God did not have to work, or occupy themselves in corporal exercises. . . . That certain fervors, trembling, and fainting fits that they suffered were indications of the love of God, and through them it could be known that they were in grace and had in them the Holy Spirit. . . . That they only had to follow their interior movements and inspirations in order to do or stop doing any thing. . . . That some people had said, or affirmed, that having arrived at a certain point of perfection, they did not have to see images of saints, nor hear sermons, nor the word of God.*[54]

This edict provided the populace and the court with a set of indicators by which to recognize alumbrados in their midst. It preserved many of the identifying features of alumbradismo from the Iberian context but emphasized its manifestation in the heretics' physical ecstasies and fits. Such fits became the identifying insignia of the heresy in New Spain, while the earlier peninsular concentration on the question of internal versus vocal prayer receded into the background of the trials.

A fifty-year lull, during which time the court opened only one alumbrado case, followed the initial group of hearings in New Spain.[55] Then, starting in 1649 with the proceedings against the four beata Romero sisters, the Mexican Holy Office began anew to try cases of alumbradismo.[56] In the third quarter of the seventeenth century the tribunal also initiated suits against three male hermit alumbrados and three alumbrada *curanderas* (healers) who were sisters. The court also opened several isolated investigations in this period and then tried another cluster of defendants beginning in 1686 around the person of another criolla beata, Antonia de Ochoa. [57] During much of the eighteenth century, denunciations steadily trickled into the tribunal until 1774, when the court initiated another intensive period of prosecution, opening twenty-two cases in the subsequent twenty-five-year period.

The denunciations of false mystics made to the court starting in the 1650s differed in two significant ways from the earlier accusations. First, a member of the clergy had initiated the original denunciations of feigned mysticism in Mexico, and clerics almost exclusively continued to initiate the trials until the third quarter of the seventeenth century. Starting in this period, laywomen and laymen began playing a greater role in denouncing the crime to the court (see table 2). Second, the vocabulary used to describe false mysticism began to shift in the mid-seventeenth century. While almost all of the initial accusations were directed exclusively at alumbrados, beginning in the 1650s several of the accused were charged with being both alumbrados and ilusos (see table 1). The increase of the term *iluso*, one deluded by the devil, in conjunction with the correspondent decline of the use of *alumbrado*, a heretical "false" visionary, happened simultaneously with the rise of lay denunciations. Use of *alumbrado* may have required a greater degree of theological training than was available to laypeople.

By the third quarter of the century the court tried a significant percentage of people for being both ilusos and alumbrados and opened a growing number of cases against defendants labeled exclusively ilusos. In the eighteenth century most cases were directed solely at ilusos. However, the Inquisition also opened several cases against people accused of being alumbrados and molinistas. From the middle of the eighteenth century onward, inquisitors sometimes combined a whole set of terms in one charge, convicting María Cayetana Loria in 1792, for example, for being an "apostate, Molinist, alumbrada, Calvinist, quietist, and ilusa."[58]

The term *alumbrado*, defined by its own set of inquisitorial edicts, has a much clearer history than does the term *iluso*. Inquisitors and historians alike have often used *iluso* interchangeably with the term *illuminati*, the more favorably designated "enlightened ones." Claire Guilhem writes, in the context of Spanish trials, that *ilusa* referred to a woman who had been passively misled by the devil's illusions, whereas *iludente* designated someone who had actively misled others into believing her illusions. *Ilusas*, she states, always became *iludentes* when they made their illusions known.[59]

In the Mexican trials, however, the term *iludente* appeared infrequently, and the court's use of the term *iluso* did not indicate passivity. The Mexican Inquisition used *iluso* to connote many of the same things as *alumbrado*. Inquisitors frequently linked the two terms in accusations, qualifications, and sentences. In referring to early-eighteenth-century "iluso and alumbrado" Ignacio de San Juan Salazar, the court defined the terms to mean those "who believe that mental prayer is the most superior form of contemplation, and who engage in fits, visions, and miracles that make them appear superior and illustrious."[60] In the Mexican trials *iluso* most often referred to a person whom the church suspected of practicing a variety of feigned mysticism free of any formalized doctrine, originating either internally or in demonic *ilusiones* (delusions), or a person who had succeeded in deluding others into believing she or he was a "real" mystic.[61] In this sense the term is more closely allied with the labels *engañadora* (fraud or enchanter) and *embaucadora* (trickster or swindler), which inquisitors sometimes used interchangeably with *ilusa* in the Mexican cases.[62]

The shift in the vocabulary used to denote false Mexican mystics from *alumbrado* to *iluso* after the mid-seventeenth century indicates a transition in terms of the meaning and reasons for the prosecution of this group. The term *alumbrado* was linked more directly to the particular doctrines of the Iberian heresy as enumerated in the Spanish edicts. The court designated the earliest late-sixteenth-century Mexican mystics as *alumbrados* either because of the erroneous theological positions they supported or because of the indecent sexual acts in which they engaged. (The Spanish tribunal had previously associated such lasciviousness particularly with the Llerena alumbrados of the 1570s.) In the 1598 case against Ana de Guillamas, for example, the fiscal reported to the court that this beata had endorsed many alumbrada propositions. These included her statement that "the way of perfection did not consist in fasting and disciplines and other suffering, but rather only in loving God with a burning love." The calificadores in her case noted that Guillamas had heretically claimed that only love rather than mortification of the flesh was necessary for the union of her soul with God.[63]

If the term *alumbrado* referred to a heretic who promoted interior religion, the term *iluso* was used more broadly to denote someone who feigned mystical experiences. One 1715 ilusa trial opened when Isabel de Zavala, a prosperous criolla whose husband was a merchant, denounced "Catalina," a beata, to the court for false mysticism.[64] Zavala testified that

Catalina had told her that since she was a young girl she had experienced mystical raptures and seen visions of Saint Teresa and Saint Catherine of Siena. Zavala, however, doubted Catalina's mystical authenticity. She suspected the beata because she knew that Catalina was poor but did not act as a virtuous poor person should act. Catalina, she alleged, wanted to utilize her reputation of religious sanctity to turn a profit for herself.

Furthermore, she enjoyed activities more suitable to a woman of greater means. Zavala knew that Catalina had originally wished to enter a convent but had been unable to afford the requisite dowry. In order to earn some money to support herself, the beata circulated around several of Mexico City's churches, playing the guitar and singing. Zavala claimed Catalina had been thrown out of several churches for these *escándalos* (scandals), but Catalina told Zavala that God supported her despite some clerics' censuring of her actions. What most disturbed Zavala, however, was that she had seen Catalina drinking chocolate, eating well, and sleeping naked through the siesta. She closed her testimony with the indignant observation that she knew Catalina "did not sew or read for which she knew she was a *hipócrita* ilusa."[65]

As this trial illustrates, in the context of Mexico, the assessment of individuals' mystical authenticity had moved away from the concern with detecting particular dissident doctrines more typical of the Spanish trials. In the Mexican context, detection of false mysticism focused on a preoccupation with prosecuting individuals accused of attempting to impersonate others. The Inquisition's anxieties about alumbrados in sixteenth-century Spain ripened in an environment of hostility to the spiritual and social threats posed by Judaism and Protestantism. In New Spain, however, the courts'—and the public's—idea of an iluso developed in response to the particular tensions that characterized this different environment. Three sets of social tensions shaped this society: rising criollo nationalism, the growth of the mixed-race population, and the erosion of respectful obedience to the agents and dictates of the Spanish crown and the Catholic church. In this environment, the religious crime of *iluminismo*—the falsification of a mystical experience—was a reflection of elite society's fears that members of the colonial population possessed the ability to fake or "pass" for what they were not.

The Mexican Baroque and the Development of Criollismo

By the mid-seventeenth century, Mexican mystics were most frequently denounced for feigning supernatural episodes. The court tried them because they claimed to have experienced ecstatic fits and trances, supernatural illnesses, and visions of celestial figures. In addition, some had asserted that they could use religious objects—reliquaries, statues, or crucifixes—to work miracles. Their mystical episodes often occurred in the public settings of churches or in semipublic ceremonies in private homes in which the mystic's supporters had gathered. Many aspects of these religious activities, although denounced as heretical, in fact embodied central elements of orthodox Catholicism in the Counter-Reformation period.[66]

From the mid-sixteenth to the late eighteenth centuries, the Protestant Reformation directly shaped Catholic orthodoxy. Protestantism endorsed new forms of religious worship that sanctioned direct communication between Christians and God through prayer and contemplation of the Bible. Protestantism celebrated simplicity and downplayed the use of sacred images and ceremonial rites. In response, the Catholic church endorsed increasingly complex forms of religious worship. Catholicism called for the clergy to play a heightened role in regulating the laity's spirituality. It promoted the Christian sacraments and encouraged external demonstrations of piety, such as parades, pageants, and, most prominently, the cult of the Virgin Mary and the saints. Counter-Reformation Catholic orthodoxy exalted form over substance and encouraged the faithful to engage in pious acts and good works, rejecting the idea that grace alone was needed to ensure salvation.[67] Several historians have concluded that the particular nature of Catholic Reformation religious practice, in part because of its affinity with aspects of native spiritual traditions, made it much more effective than Protestantism in approaching the conversion of New World indigenous populations.[68]

The particular nature of Spanish imperialism helped define the contours of Counter-Reformation Catholicism in the New World. The legitimacy of the Spanish conquest and subsequent domination of Latin America depended upon Spain's declared mission to evangelize the barbarian indigenous populations of the region. Consequently, in New Spain and Peru, as opposed to in both French and British America, evangelization was conducted "principally as a state-backed enterprise." Missionaries initially used coercion and violence as proselytism tools, but by the late sixteenth century, following the Catholic church's revision of the nature of orthodoxy in the Council of Trent, they more often adopted the use of rite, sacrament, and symbolism as effective means of conversion.[69]

Spain's introduction of Catholic religious practices to its New World territories was one important component of its strategy to claim and subdue these regions and their inhabitants in order to re-create the Old World on the other side of the Atlantic. Spanish America, "a land of erstwhile idolatry . . . ripe for conversion, religious conquest, and, in some accounts, the readying of humankind for the Second Coming," presented Spain with a rich territory with which to demonstrate the righteousness of its Christian orthodoxy. The millenarian dreams of the Franciscans, the Utopian projects of the Jesuits, and the Carmelite establishment of female monasteries in the Teresan model were all manifestations of this effort.[70] As Jodi Bilinkoff observes, "the colonizers came brandishing swords, guns, and crosses, but also the battle cry of Santiago, statues of Our Lady, books on the lives of Catherine of Siena and Anthony of Padua. Thus the saints of the Old World were introduced to—and often imposed on—the New."[71]

In New Spain the institutional church declared its support for the tenets of Counter-Reformation orthodoxy in meetings of the archbishopric's ecclesiastical council in the late sixteenth century. In 1585 the third Mexican Provincial Council formally adopted the principles of the Council of Trent, mandated the regulations for saint worship in the viceroyalty, and pronounced a policy of flexibility regarding the possibility of miraculous happenings.[72] As the colony developed, such religious authorities as the celebrated seventeenth-century bishop of Puebla, Juan de Palafox, promoted these spiritual practices. Palafox especially encouraged popular participation in devotions to the Virgin Mary and the Infant Jesus. Palafox also fomented the construction of two of the greatest monuments to baroque architecture in Mexico: the basilica of Ocotlán in Tlaxcala and the nearby sanctuary of San Miguel de Milagros.[73] In the wake of the Reformation the institutional Catholic church called for the stricter regulation of mystical and supernatural experiences, but it had also founded its distinctive identity on the commemoration of such episodes, and so it continued to celebrate them. Mystical expressions proliferated in post-Tridentine Spain and its overseas colonies.[74]

The objective of Catholic mysticism is the achievement of a state of intensive spiritual bonding, literally referred to as *matrimonio espiritual* (spiritual marriage), between the mystic's soul and God. In order for this union to occur, the mystic must totally surrender her or his will to God. Progress along the journey toward mystical union is usually marked by the reception of a number of God's "gifts." As Caroline Walker Bynum writes, these physical displays, which include "trances, levitations, catatonic seizures, or other forms of bodily rigidity, miraculous elongation or enlargement of parts of the body, swellings of wet mucus in the throat . . . and ecstatic nosebleeds," have a historical association with women in the European tradition.[75] Saint Teresa of Avila, the most important figure of emulation for religious women in both Spain and its colonies in the seventeenth and eighteenth centuries, wrote extensively of her mystical experiences in defense of women's legitimate participation in this sphere of Christian worship. Even Teresa, however, underwent an inquisitorial investigation into the legitimacy of her experiences during her lifetime.

Besides its eager adoption of saint worship and acceptance of the possibility of supernatural phenomena, Mexico's enthusiastic implementation of Counter-Reformation orthodoxy is evident in the copious biographies of religious personnel published in the colonial period. Josefina Muriel documented close to one hundred nuns, beatas, and laywomen whose *vidas* (spiritual lives) or chronicles were published in New Spain between 1573 and 1803.[76] This plethora of hagiographical works highlighted their subjects' duplication of the miraculous sanctity and mystical expressions of such figures as Catherine of Siena and Teresa of Avila. These texts exerted a profound influence on the forms of religious practice in which a broad segment of the colonial Spanish population participated.[77] One such work, Francisco Pardo's biography of sor María de Jesús Tomelín (1579–1637), exemplifies the features of this religious orthodoxy, particularly as a model for female piety.[78] This Conceptionist nun was one of the nine figures whom the Mexican Church promoted for canonization during the colonial period.[79]

Augustina de Santa Teresa, another nun in María's order, had originally recorded María's story. Pardo rewrote Augustina's accounts for the published work in consultation with María's confessor, Miguel Godínez.[80] Pardo opens his work by outlining the history of the foundation of the convent of Limpia Concepción that María was destined to enter. He follows this with an account of María's life. The Virgin Mary had overseen María's portentous birth, and in her childhood and youth María had seen many visions of Christ and the Virgin Mary, who urged her to join the convent of Limpia Concepción. She also repeatedly wrestled with the devil, who attempted to entice her away from her spiritual path. As she matured, María adopted a harsh daily routine of physical discipline and rigorous spiritual meditation. She began to experience stigmata and could also foresee the future. On one occasion she used this gift to prevent a pirate attack on a Spanish fleet. María was recognized as so virtuous that her confessors permitted her to engage in lengthy sessions of mental prayer, a practice that when ill-used could lead to heresy.[81] María de Jesús Tomelín's spiritual biography, like those of many other celebrated female religious produced in this period, is replete with elements of orthodox Counter-Reformation religious practice. This orthodoxy endorsed ritualistic displays of religious devotion, exalted physical discipline, celebrated the occurrence of miraculous happenings, and praised the imitation and veneration of European saints' lives, providing all of these activities occurred within the tight bounds of clerical supervision.[82]

New Spain may have eagerly embraced Counter-Reformation Catholicism, but the social context of the colony also reshaped both the precise nature of Catholic orthodoxy and the culture of the baroque in this new setting. The term *baroque* is often used to denote the architectural, artistic, and musical aesthetic associated with Counter-Reformation Catholic orthodoxy. In the 1960s, however, Spanish historian José Antonio Maravall developed a broader set of implications for this term. Maravall insisted that the baroque should be understood neither in strictly aesthetic terms nor as the mere reflection of Counter-Reformation religious orthodoxy. For Maravall, the baroque denoted a seventeenth-century historical concept, consisting in the "response given by active groups within a society that had entered into a severe crisis in association with critical economic fluctuations." This "response," directed by the expanding absolutist monarchy and landed elites in a period of profound social crisis, "was the mobilization of an extensive social operation whose aim was to control those forces of dispersion that threatened to disrupt the traditional order." The Spanish baroque, then, referred to the monarchy's consolidation of power over the populace through both physical constraints (military force, institutions of social control) and psychological expedients (art, literature, and music) whose development the crown promoted in this era.[83]

The baroque, as it developed in colonial Mexico, was marked by several differences from its evolution in Spain. First, the baroque extended far later—to the last decades of the eighteenth century—than it did on the Peninsula.[84] Second, this era was conditioned by a slightly differing set of historical forces from those that defined Spain in the era of monarchical absolutism. In Spain the baroque was a manifestation of royal and elite attempts at social consolidation through a culture of order, hierarchy, and tradition. In the context of colonial Latin America, however, baroque culture was the means through which the criollo population struggled to assert its identity in terms of its domination over the other demographic groups who formed the colonies' demographic majority. It also reflected the criollos' attempt to assert their independence from the competing controlling force of imperial Spain. [85] Three of the traits commonly associated with the baroque—hierarchy, contrast, and the profusion of detail—are particularly evident in the development of the vocabulary of the casta system that categorized the population of colonial Latin America according to racial origin and status. [86]

The criollo, indigenous, and casta populations of New Spain also transformed the practice of Counter-Reformation Catholicism in the colony. The Roman church needed examples of saints and martyrs in the New World in order to demonstrate the success of its conversion efforts.[87] Inhabitants of the New World wished to satisfy their own agendas through the public acknowledgment of such figures. They tended to support greater numbers of local saintly figures than Spain (or Rome, for that matter) believed could qualify as veritable saints, and they endorsed spiritual objects and individuals (including many of those tried for false mysticism) whom the church deemed illegitimate. Criollos' veneration of New World religious figures and local miraculous sites illustrates their attempted articulation of a spiritual and political identity independent from Iberia. Such worship enabled the population of colonial Mexico to assert its fidelity to the religious orthodoxy that the Counter-Reformation Church promoted, while simultaneously establishing a New World foundation for its spiritual practices. [88] Rose of Lima, the first New World figure to receive canonization, and the Virgin of Guadalupe, the religious figure who eventually became most strongly identified with Mexico's national identity, were two of the principle objects of criollo devotion in seventeenth- and eighteenth-century Mexico. [89] A number of other figures, including the Virgin of Remedios and the Christ of Chalma, also served as popular symbols of public piety in the colonial period. Criollos' promotion of cults, as Antonio Rubial García has argued, reflected their desire to assert the religious authenticity of the territory they inhabited: "To show the presence of the divine on their earth became one of the central points of pride and security for the population of New Spain. The existence of portends and miracles made New Spain a place equal in comparison not only to old Europe but also to Jerusalem, cradle of the primitive apostolic church. In the prodigious, the laity located a key element for the formation of the collective conscience."[90]

The colonial church, operating within this climate of criollo support for locally produced miracles, found itself in a difficult position. In the wake of the Reformation the Catholic church had strictly controlled all religious expressions that de-emphasized the importance of the clergy and promoted individuals' unmediated relationships with God. The Catholic church, thus, was necessarily suspicious of anyone who claimed to have experienced mysticism. Nevertheless, the colonial clergy—particularly its regular branches—were also eager to exhibit the success of their evangelical efforts in the New World. They wished to demonstrate that they had brought the Christian God to the indigenous pagan population and had maintained spiritually orthodox practices among the Spanish, criollo, and casta populations. The clergy could make such claims to legitimacy by supporting the authenticity of local miraculous apparitions, relics, and other displays of God's presence in New World settings.[91]

The regular orders, who worked most closely with the indigenous population until the Bourbon reforms of the late eighteenth century, initially experienced some trepidation about Indian saint worship. As David Brading writes, these friars feared "the evident danger of confusion between pagan idols and Christian statues."[92] Several scholars, including Edward Osowski and Charlene Villaseñor Black, assert that Mexico's indigenous population did integrate either pre-Columbian spiritual beliefs or postcontact political strategies in defense of the autonomy of the Nahua elite into their practices of saint worship.[93] Members of the church expressed this tension in the ecclesiastical documentation they generated. The first and second Mexican Provincial Councils, held in 1555 and 1565, codified the viceroyalty's official Catholic doctrine. Their statutes acknowledged that miracles might occur in Mexico but cautioned the clergy to be vigilant in drawing distinctions between bona fide and erroneous supernatural phenomena. The first council warned its officers to guard against the many men and women who, "forgetting both the fear of God and their faith, and the confidence they must have of Divine Providence, use diviners, and witches, . . . and spells, and . . . take counsel with those who make such spells who are servants of the Devil."[94] Members of the church hierarchy thus conflated their anxieties over uncontrolled popular spirituality and saint worship with their fears of the possible influences of indigenous religious traditions on New Spain's non-indigenous population.

Conclusion

The Mexican Inquisition's investigation of the heresy of false mysticism in the seventeenth and eighteenth centuries was the by-product of the Spanish tribunals' earlier prosecution of interior religious practices in the wake of the Protestant Reformation. However, the social context of colonial Mexico defined how and why ilusos and alumbrados were tried in New Spain. When Spanish inquisitors began examining alumbrados in sixteenth-century Spain, they were preoccupied with contemporary investigations of two significant heretical threats: the emerging heresy of Lutheranism and the older tradition of crypto-Judaism. Anxiety about the presence of both these spiritual deviations from Catholic orthodoxy colored these initial investigations.

In the context of seventeenth- and eighteenth-century Mexico, the Inquisition's concerns, and those of the socially dominant peninsular and criollo populations, reflected the unique context of the colonial setting. The most prevalent competing religious system of concern to Catholic authorities in the New World was neither Judaism nor Protestantism, but rather indigenous paganism. The crown had moved prosecution of indigenous converts to Christianity beyond the Mexican Inquisition's official jurisdiction after 1571. The Inquisition's anxiety about Indians' idolatrous influences on the Spanish, criollo, and casta populations did not, however, simply disperse because of this administrative adjustment. Inquisitorial officers continued to fear the influences that indigenous and as well African spirituality might exert on the colony's body of practicing Christians. The church, moreover, striving to maintain its authority in regulating mystical spirituality, feared that indigenous people might abuse the colony's climate of popular support for prodigious phenomena in order to perpetuate their own religious practices under a cloak of legitimacy.

These tensions all contributed to the creation of a particularly Mexican concept of false mysticism. This creation was marked by the increasingly common usage of the term *iluso* to designate the religious crime of feigned mysticism over the term *alumbrado* starting in the second half of the seventeenth century. Whereas the Iberian Peninsula had produced the religious heresy of alumbradismo in response to the Protestant Reformation, the viceroyalty of New Spain generated a meaning for iluso that connoted an individual's fabrication of appearances and intention to pass—socially, racially, or spiritually—for what he or she was not. This New World connotation of false mysticism was partially forged in response to the evangelical nature of the Catholic church in the colonial context. It also reflected the social anxieties and racial attitudes of the peninsular and expanding criollo elite of New Spain. Given all these forces that influenced their formation, it is hardly surprising that the labels *iluso* and *alumbrado* least effectively communicate information about the very individuals they were generated to describe: Mexican mystics themselves. I now turn to a discussion of the actual religious experiences and spiritual practices of this collection of seventeenth-century women and men.

Two

Mystical Spirituality in the
Social Context of Colonial Mexico

I n the city of Puebla in the summer of 1717, the Mexican Inquisition
opened a hearing against Marta de la Encarnación, a *castiza* seamstress and spinner, whom the court later qualified as an "alumbrada,
hipócrita, and embustera."[1] During the next eight years the tribunal
repeatedly interrogated Marta, her confessor, Juan Manuel de Vega, and
dozens of other lay and clerical witnesses who had seen or participated
in Marta's controversial spiritual practices. In his first appearance before
the court Vega described the many diabolic episodes Marta had endured
in the five years he had known her. During these fits he had watched as
she painfully vomited a number of metal objects, including a reliquary
and a medal.[2]

Vega also described the intensive disciplines Marta regularly undertook. She fasted, deprived herself of sleep, and practiced severe mortification, wearing metal chains around her neck and waist to draw blood. As
was customary for confessors of prodigious people, Vega kept a journal
in which he recorded details about Marta's diabolic encounters, spiritual
disciplines, and visions. In his earliest appearances Vega appeared to admire his confessant's character, describing her as "humble and obedient."[3]
As her trial progressed, however, Vega's support for Marta waned.

Several witnesses provided the court with other details about Marta's
supernatural abilities. In her first appearance the defendant herself asserted that she had experienced repeated visions of God, the Virgin
Mary, Jesus Christ, and numerous saints. A number of her relatives and
acquaintances vividly described her ecstatic fits. They noted that although
Marta did not know Latin, she had spoken it during these raptures. They

spoke of her powers of levitation, of her spiritual travels to distant places, of her ability to release souls from purgatory, and to transfer the physical torment of those she could not release onto her own body. One witness informed the court that Marta also claimed she could alter the lives of sinners before they died. Marta had once told her that she had traveled "in spirit" to a sinful man she knew, "transformed as if she were a black woman [*negrita*] and told the man the story of his whole life and sins, warning him that he must amend his ways because if not, he would be condemned, and the said man did amend his ways."[4]

As well as collecting testimony about these spiritual matters, Marta's investigators devoted considerable attention to her sexual history. Francisco Javier Priego, a nephew of Vega's, was the third witness to appear in the case. Priego volunteered a story about how Marta had "seduced" him at the *hacienda* (large estate) where he lived and worked when his uncle brought her to visit.[5] The court assiduously pursued accounts of two other men, one Spanish and one *mulato* (a person of mixed African and Spanish descent), with whom Marta had also allegedly had sexual relations. The issue of Marta's sexual conduct was central to the Inquisition's condemnation of her religious activities. Her judges dismissed her claim that she possessed spiritual powers and argued that she had feigned both these and her episodes of demonic possession so that she would be "taken for saintly, securing popular applause, and veneration." They concluded that she had merely wished to appear virtuous so that she could "enter and exit houses, and pursue her lechery without losing any acquired credit."[6]

Marta de la Encarnación's history contains many parallels to those of other Mexican mystics. Like most of the women accused, Marta was a member of urban New Spain's "lower orders" who practiced her spirituality outside the bounds of convent life. (Of the 47 women accused of the crime, 24 were beatas and 17 were laywomen. Of the 6 nuns denounced, only one was convicted, while 11 of the beatas and 6 of the laywomen were found guilty. A further 5 women died before the completion of their cases.) The nature of Marta's religious expressions and the reasons why the Holy Office viewed her suspiciously were also elements common to a majority of other trials. Like many others, Marta de la Encarnación had surrounded herself with a substantial network of admirers and supporters to whom she performed her spiritual feats. Several clerics and roughly a dozen members of the laity—both poor and more prosperous criollos—confessed to consulting with Marta on spiritual matters or to witnessing her miraculous feats. The material support they gave her in return allowed Marta to spend more time exercising her mystical gifts. In the context of the racial and economic hierarchies of colonial Mexican society, the existence of these spiritual and material networks, which played such a central role in sustaining popular mysticism, greatly troubled the officers of the Mexican court.[7]

Plebeians and Elites in Colonial Mexico

Although they had experienced a massive demographic decline in the sixteenth century, Indians constituted the majority of New Spain's overall population throughout the colonial period. The preconquest indigenous population of roughly twenty-five million fell to just over one million by the first decade of the seventeenth century, but Indians still formed the majority of the viceroyalty's population even at this demographic low point.[8] Other types of demographic changes transformed New Spain between the late sixteenth and early nineteenth centuries. One of the most significant of these was the growth of the mixed-race population, particularly during the century after 1650.[9]

In 1646 New Spain was roughly 85 percent indigenous, 10 percent Spanish, and 5 percent casta.[10] Just one century later, in the midst of the dramatic demographic boom of the eighteenth century, New Spain's censuses recorded an even smaller Spanish population. Gonzalo Aguirre Beltrán calculated that by 1742 New Spain had a Spanish population of less than one-half of one percent and an Indian population of just under 63 percent. Meanwhile, he wrote that the casta sector had expanded to become 37 percent of the population. In the early 1790s the indigenous population continued to constitute the majority of the population in rural areas, but mixed-race groups formed an increasingly large proportion of New Spain's urban populations.[11] German scientist and traveler Alexander von Humboldt estimated New Spain to have a population that just exceeded 5.5 million by the early nineteenth century, half of whom were Indian and one fourth of whom were castas.[12]

During the colonial period New Spain's indigenous population re-mained largely rural, while peninsulares, criollos, and mixed-race people dominated its roughly twenty major urban centers. In the first decade of the nineteenth century. peninsulares and criollos constituted roughly half the inhabitants of the capital, a city of just under 140,000. Castas and Indians each comprised about a quarter of the inhabitants of Mexico City.[13] These urban proportions represented a near perfect inversion of the colony's overall figures. Cities, where the Inquisition pursued the majority of the iluso trials, were the most racially mixed spaces in the viceroyalty.[14]

The European-dominated urban centers of New Spain housed the most affluent sectors of the colonial population. A small elite, composed almost exclusively of Spaniards, lived in ostentatious luxury in Mexico's cities. At the close of the eighteenth century 16 percent of the population possessed three-quarters of the city's property.[15] The Mexico City census of 1811 classified only 4 percent of the residents it enumerated as *gente culta*, defined as those who could afford to employ more than four servants.[16] Agents of the state, members of the church's upper echelons, and individuals from a small number of merchant, farming, mining, and banking families made up this wealthy stratum of the colonial hierarchy. The viceregal court sat at the center of New Spain's elite society. Its members favored lavish public displays of their accumulated wealth that served to legitimize the power they wielded. The most flamboyant of these marked the inauguration of a new viceroy to the colony's seat of government.

Antonio de Robles, a chronicler of Mexico's history, recorded in his *Diario Curioso de México* the parade of significant events—autos de fe, religious celebrations, and natural disasters—that framed public life in late-seventeenth- and early-eighteenth-century Mexico City. In the last week of November 1702 Robles detailed the ceremonies marking the entrance of the thirty-fourth viceroy into New Spain. Fernández de la Cueva, duque de Albuquerque, was the third Bourbon-appointed viceroy to the colony. Albuquerque apparently deduced that the occasion called for especially grand celebrations. In his *Diario* Robles carefully documented the luxurious finery of the decor in the viceroy's public greeting rooms. He also observed that on the day following the initial ceremonies, Albuquerque called for bullfights to be staged in the Chapultepec woods.[17] Spanish elites, as Juan Pedro Viqueira Albán delineated in his study of popular culture in eighteenth-century Mexico, had a long tradition of using *corridas de toros* as public rituals that visually reinforced social hierarchy. During these spectacles, nobles on horseback fought bulls, symbolically reinforcing their right to dominate plebeians. Elite domination over the other estates, as Viqueira writes, "was justified in the festival as the former were the protectors of the latter." In the colonial context bullfights also illustrated the right of Spanish *conquistadores* to dominate indigenous people.[18]

Viceroys customarily marked their assumption of office with a bull-fight, but Albuquerque was particularly zealous in his invocation of this tradition. Five days after the initial ceremonies marking his inauguration, Albuquerque called for bullfights to again be held in Chapultepec. Early the following spring, the viceroy and his wife traveled to San Agustín de las Cuevas. Upon their return Albuquerque ordered three consecutive days of bullfighting. Three weeks after this round of celebrations, Robles wrote that Albuquerque had again spent the day attending *corridas de toros* in Chapultepec.[19]

Robles's careful notation of the sum spent on the feast celebrating Albuquerque's return from San Agustín may indicate his concern with the viceroy's lavish habits. Moreover, Robles's observation, on the occasion of the first *corrida* Albuquerque had staged, that "in the afternoon, there was a bullfight in Chapultepec, in full form, despite it being a religious holiday," suggests that Robles considered the timing of this secular celebration somewhat inappropriate.[20] Members of New Spain's plebeian classes criticized the viceroy's secular decadence more explicitly in a lengthy lewd poem they composed that satirized his rule.[21]

Ignacio de San Juan Salazar and Getrudis Rosa de Ortiz, two mesti-zos whom the Inquisition investigated for false mysticism in the early eighteenth century, also voiced pointed criticisms of the viceroy's impiety in their hearings. Salazar, as one witness testified, had declared that the pope had ordered him to inspect New Spain during Albuquerque's reign because of the viceroy's "offences to God."[22] Ortiz decried Albuquerque even more explicitly in her trial. She told the court of a vision she had seen of a pack of horrible demons that God later told her he had sent "to bring him the soul of Señor Albuquerque because he was very proud, very vain, of evil intention, and a great sinner." On a second occasion Ortiz saw the Virgin Mary crying because the colony's "Christians had rejected her, and had gone with the Archduke." In a third apparition Ortiz witnessed the viceroy's wife adorned with two beautiful roses behind her ears. As Ortiz watched, "the two roses became dirty . . . and in their place, her ears became covered with black cockroaches." A short while later God told Ortiz that the roses signified the "good words of the righteous, which were heard in conversations about God." The cockroaches, however, represented "the conversations of the rest of Mexico and of the people of the [viceregal] court who went to the palace and spoke with his Excellency about banal things."[23]

In its first decades of existence, peninsulares had exclusively dominated New Spain's viceregal court. By the late sixteenth century some criollos had managed to infiltrate the colony's upper strata.[24] By 1750 this sector also included small numbers of mixed-race and indigenous people.[25] This small but significant shift in the composition of the colony's elite occurred despite the Spanish crown's longstanding efforts to restrict Indians, Africans, and mixed-race people from engaging in economic and social mobility. Likely, many of the indigenous people who formed part of the mid-eighteenth-century urban elite were descendents of Mexico's original Indian nobility rather than commoner Indians who had managed to work their way up the social hierarchy.[26]

During the colonial period both *encomenderos* (holders of private rights to Indian labor and tribute) and the crown taxed commoner Indians in labor and in kind. These extractions, combined with the Indians' decimation through disease and loss of substantial tracts of agrarian land in central Mexico over the course of the seventeenth century, worked prohibitively against their accumulation of surplus capital. The crown further restricted commoner Indians' social status through a number of prohibitions on the activities and occupations they could pursue. Indians could not legally use firearms or swords, ride on horseback, enter into legal contracts, or purchase wine. The crown also forced free blacks and castas to pay tribute and barred members of either group from holding public office or joining artisans' guilds, although lighter-skinned castas who could "pass" for Spanish sometimes managed to circumvent these regulations.[27] This latter group's evasion of economic and judicial restrictions partially prompted the Spanish elite's increased vigilance of interracial mixing in the second half of the eighteenth century.[28]

Mixed-race people, Indians, and blacks only managed to "pass" for Spanish or otherwise circumvent impediments to social mobility in exceptional cases, however. Most members of these groups belonged to the "lower orders" of urban society. Petty merchants, skilled artisans, and tradespeople occupied the most affluent positions in this sector. But poor people who led much harder lives made up approximately 85 percent of the urban population of Mexico City at the close of the eighteenth century. They were the city's manual laborers, its unemployed, and the "ragged poor" who survived on what they could earn as domestic servants, seamstresses, cooks, and healers and by begging.[29] By the mid-eighteenth century, women, whose lives were often marked by homelessness and disease, formed the majority of this population.[30]

Roughly one-third of the viceroyalty's overall population, approximately 1.5 million people, suffered from indigence in the first decades of the eighteenth century. In January of 1705 a horrified duque de Albuquerque found time in between attending bullfights to report to King Philip V about the economic disorder of the colony: "I found idleness and crimes occasioned by it were very extensive in all the kingdom," he wrote. In a later report Albuquerque discussed "the innumerable number of people who populate this reign of various castas and undefined racial mixtures, who, in their multitude, maintain themselves at the expense of the natural richness of the country, without any application to work, which provokes in them their own laziness." As described by Albuquerque's successor, the duque de Linares, "the majority of the population of the city of Mexico is composed of miserable and poor people. Many live off alms, petty crime, and begging." And the late-eighteenth-century bishop-elect of Michoacán, Manuel Abad y Queipo, noted that by the century's close, out of 800,000 families living in New Spain, 550,000 suffered some degree of indigence.[31]

Many of the women and men accused of practicing false mysticism came from these poor sectors of colonial society. Several of them eventually testified that their miserable financial resources had partially prompted them to take up their work as visonaries. For example, one of the Romero siters, María de la Encarnación, told the court in September of 1649 that she had begun feigning sanctity to generate money "because she had had to do it in this way, or become a *mala mujer* [i.e., a prostitute]."[32] A remarkably high proportion—nearly 90 percent—of the accused were unmarried. (Out of the 102 accused mystics, just 5 laymen, 1 beato, 4 laywomen, and 2 beatas were married; there were also 2 widowers and 4 widows.) There was a high incidence of poverty among the unmarried people in the colonial era.[33] The Inquisition's inventories of its prisoners' possessions document the economic misery in which many of those accused of feigning mysticism lived. Prisoners of the Inquisition were expected to provide for all their basic necessities during their terms of confinement. When he was imprisoned in 1718, the items that beato iluso Baltasar Núñez de los Reyes brought with him included a sleeping mat, four shirts, three pairs of pants, and four pairs of stockings.[34] When Agustina Rangel, a mestiza who supported herself by providing spiritual and physical cures to her peers in Valladolid, entered the court's secret cells in February 1686, she carried with her a collection of more spiritually oriented items. Rangel's jailer noted that she had brought clothing, a cross, a small medal, and an icon of a saint.[35] Josefa Palacios brought a shawl, petticoats, a shirt, stockings, and a rosary. Unusually, she also had five *reales* and a number of little books.[36] When the alguacil entered Getrudis Rosa Ortiz's dwelling at the time of her imprisonment, he found nothing there worthy of itemizing, noting she owned only "some clothes ripped in scraps." Ortiz brought to her cell "a mattress, and the best clothing she had in the house . . . a small woven dress which she said was for the Christ child."[37]

Although the crown may have wished otherwise, impoverished mixed-race residents of New Spain, such as Ortiz and Rangel, lived and worked in situations of intimate daily contact with members of colonial society from higher social positions. In the sixteenth and early seventeenth centuries the Council of the Indies (the crown's advising body on imperial government) strove to implement legislation imposing the geographic and social separation of colonial society's various racial groups. These efforts failed. Various forms of physical, social, and geographical interracial mixing enlivened New Spain's urban spaces. In the grand houses of colonial city centers, where multistory dwellings housed African, Indian, and mixed-race servants on the lower- and upper-most floors and their wealthy Spanish employers in between, people of all racial backgrounds lived, quite literally, on top of one another.[38] In streets, markets, entertainment venues, and city squares, people of various classes and races came into daily contact with one another, albeit often with acknowledgment of the social hierarchies that separated them.[39]

New Spain's peninsular elite constructed the rationale of its economic domination of the other colonial ethnic groups on the notion of European racial and religious superiority. By the mid-seventeenth century, however, peninsulares began to grow alarmed at both the phenomenon of interracial mixing and the evidence of the increasing social and economic ascendancy of the criollo and casta populations. Elites became further disturbed by the awareness that some members of the colony's plebeian population were Spanish. The very existence of individuals who were both poor and white unnerved them, in Douglas Cope's words, because they "diminished the social distance between whites and castas."[40]

The Mexico City Poor House undertook directives in the late colonial and early republican periods that illustrate elite anxiety over the existence of a poor white population. In her recent study of the Poor House, Silvia Arrom discovered that at the close of the eighteenth century this institution directed a considerable amount of its limited resources toward the preservation of social status among the many poor Spaniards who became its long-term residents. "A hidden agenda of the reformed Poor House (probably present since the institution opened, though not as obvious)," writes Arrom, "was to strengthen the declining caste system by preventing the downward mobility of white paupers."[41] Poor Spaniards became even more problematic to the peninsular elite when they combined their impoverished whiteness with suspect religious practices, contraventions of contemporary gendered norms, or when their religious activities served as venues for interracial or interclass mixing in the colonies.

Patron-Client Networks and Mexican Mysticism

Many of the mystics investigated in colonial Mexico were charismatic lower-class women who surrounded themselves with circles of spiritual and material "clients" and "patrons" from a variety of social positions.[42] People from diverse racial and social backgrounds merged around a unifying set of religious experiences through their common connections to these charismatic religious figures.[43] Those who witnessed mystics' supernatural powers, consulted them on spiritual matters, and commissioned them to perform particular sacred tasks—such as retrieving souls from purgatory—became their clients. Clients often originated in the same social background as the mystics with whom they consulted, but the racial diversity of New Spain's urban centers was represented in mystics' clientele.[44]

Besides attracting clients, many ilusas also secured sponsorship from wealthier "patrons" who demonstrated their estimation of visionaries' spiritual abilities with various forms of long-term support.[45] A small number of Mexican mystics managed to secure patrons from the colony's highest economic echelons, including from the viceregal court.[46] The majority of mystics' long-term financial supporters, however, came from the middling ranks of colonial society. Most of these women's patrons were male; a number were craftsmen, merchants, or professionals. Their most consistent supporters, however, were the priests and friars who acted as their confessors.

For years before coming to the Inquisition's attention, for instance, early-eighteenth-century beata María Manuela Picazo received both spiritual and financial assistance from her confessor, a priest named Francisco Garibaldo. Ana de Aramburu's strongest supporters were also her confessors. One of them, fray Francisco de Jesús María y José, sometimes provided money and housing to Aramburu himself and sometimes arranged for others to support her. Fray Francisco testified that one such patron, don José Arrasola, had provided for Aramburu during the time in which she had lived in Toluca. When Arrasola died, fray Francisco persuaded an Indian family outside Mexico City to house Aramburu and then arranged for her to stay in the house of an affluent criolla, María de la Luz Rainaudo. During one of her periods of sickness Aramburu also lived for several months in doña Josefa Orcolaga's obra pía de Espinosa, a house of charity. Aramburu's other lay patrons included Juan D. Gutiérrez, a starcher (*almidonero*); Francisco Colina, a business and medical agent (*agente de negocios y de facultativos*); and don Antonio Zepeda, a doctor.[47]

The mid-seventeenth-century Romero sisters had great success in securing patrons and clients for themslves. One sister, María de la Encarnación, successfully mobilized a network of roughly thirty supporters. She first obtained the assistance of her godfather, scribe Diego Manuel de la Rocha, who permitted María and the rest of her immediate family to move into his home. Assisted by María's confessor, José Bruñón de Vertiz, Rocha then began inviting other family members and acquaintances to witness María's regularly experienced mystical episodes. Many of these supporters made financial contributions directly to María. One of the regular guests, Juan Maestre, an official of the Franciscan Third Order, testified that on the day after first meeting María he had sent ten pesos and a number of clothing and household items to the beata and her family because he had been so moved "at having seen them so poor and apparently virtuous." Further monetary donations and other items that María requested followed. They included some jars of a facial cleansing liquid (*agua de rostro*) and extract from the oil of "sweet almonds," which María claimed she needed to treat the wounds that her blood disciplines left on her body, but which Maestre later discovered she used to oil her hair.[48] As well as paying money to María directly, guests at the ceremonies sometimes contributed alms to one of the priests in attendance in payment for masses for beloved deceased relatives.

Knowledge of María's abilities continued spreading through her community, and she eventually managed to attact the attention of one of the most affluent landholders in central Mexico—the marqués del Valle de México—who ultimately arranged for María, her family, and her confessor all to take up residence on his estate.[49] Many other beata and lay ilusas received similar kinds of financial support in exchange for their performance of spiritual works.[50]

Confessors' material and spiritual support allowed these women to pursue their religious vocations. Those mystics with powerful clerical patrons who continued to support them in the face of inquisitorial suspicion sometimes escaped the court's harshest assessments.[51] The Inquisition declined to pursue an investigation against Isabel de la Encarnación, a seventeenth-century *poblana* nun rumored to be demonically possessed, partially because of her powerful clerical supporters.[52] Long before her exorcism, Isabel had gained the confidence of two of the most important theologians of her era: Miguel Godínez, author of *Practica de la theologia mystica*, and Luis Peña, who served as a calificador of the Holy Tribunal, among other ecclesiastical offices.

When confessors refused to renounce their support for mystics under examination, particularly if they were not men as prominent as Isabel de la Encarnación's confessors, the Inquisition might move to initiate proceedings against these spiritual patrons.[53] Some priests and friars— such as Juan Manuel de Vega, Marta de la Encarnación's confessor— renounced their support for female mystics near the outset of their trials. Others, however, remained steadfast in their backing of these women even in the face of the court's condemnation of their moral and theological credibility. Ángel Vázquez, the chief patron of late-eighteenth-century mulata ilusa María Cayetana Loria, for instance, maintained his outspoken faith in the validity of Cayetana's religious experiences long after her extensive accusation and death in the inquisitorial prison.

The tribunal deemed Vázquez guilty because of his involvement with Cayetana and sentenced him to six years' reclusion in the Colegio Apostólico de Misiones de San Fernando. There he suffered from bouts of grave physical and mental illness. A doctor who described Vázquez's state to the court in a letter written two months after the cleric's arrival at San Fernando, reported that the previous night, in an intense fury, Vázquez had ripped out the seven teeth that remained in his mouth. Elaborating in a second letter, the college director reported that a few days earlier Vázquez had left his cell completely naked and had roamed through the cloisters and dormitories, shouting that the end of the world was coming and mourning the death of his fond and absent "beata," María Cayetana Loria.[54] Vázquez's faith in Cayetana's spiritual virtue apparently withstood both the taxing inquisitorial investigation and his own debilitated condition.

Patrons and clients created relationships almost exclusively with female mystics in seventeenth- and eighteenth-century Mexico. After the cluster of trials pursued at the end of the sixteenth century in Mexico City and Puebla, when the tribunal investigated two principal male leaders, Juan Plata and Juan Núñez, few other trials featured male mystics surrounded by networks of predominantly female supporters and followers. (Two later exceptions were eighteenth-century beato Ignacio de San Juan Salazar and lay brother [*religioso lego*] Agustín Claudio.) Even the men whose religious practices most resemble those of female mystics—beatos and ermitaños—differed from female alumbrados in that they did not succeed in securing (or perhaps even attempt) such networks for themselves.

Although the few nuns investigated for false mysticism could not easily access lay sponsors for their practices, as laywomen were able to do, some nuns did have supporters within their convents. In 1746 the Holy Office opened an investigation of Josefa Clara de Jesús María, a novice in the convent of San Juan de la Penitencia in Mexico City. Another novice, suspicious of the episodes of demonic torture Josefa Clara claimed to regularly experience, denounced her to the tribunal. Several nuns who appeared at the trial stated that they had seen the bloody facial scratch marks that Josefa Clara maintained were signs of diabolic torture. One nun testified that in addition to the facial scratches she had seen the walls and tables of Josefa Clara's cell doused in blood.[55]

After two months of investigation, the comisario appointed to the case confidently reported to the tribunal that he had interviewed eighty-four nuns in the convent and that of these, only four had defended Josefa Clara. Another thirty-eight had never witnessed any display of extraordinary virtue in her, and five supplied him with damning testimony about a notably disobedient strain in her character.[56] In his submission to the court, however, he failed to acknowledge an outburst of a highly unusual nature that a group of the convent's nuns had precipitated in a show of support for Josefa Clara.

Two days into the hearing the notary recorded that just as madre María Francisca de Santa Ursula was concluding her testimony, thirty of the convent's nuns burst into the chambers in which he and the comisario were conducting their interviews. The nuns, he wrote, spoke "for a while, in voices that were somewhat raised." The comisario attempted to calm them, inducing them to speak in turn. The nuns explained that they objected to the manner in which the comisario had conducted the investigation. They criticized him for beginning by interrogating the convent's novices, rather than by questioning more senior nuns first, and for not allowing Josefa Clara to defend herself at the trial's outset. Believing the investigation unnecessary because Josefa Clara's vows of profession would clarify whether or not she was apt for the veil, the sisters concluded that if the comisario forced Josefa Clara to leave the convent, "they would follow her." The comisario, in an attempt to reestablish his jurisdiction over the case, informed the irate sisters that he had been authorized to suspend Josefa Clara from the convent during the investigation. The nuns continued to voice their support for the novice, affirming that in the context of the investigation "obedience had no place" in the convent. If the court expelled Josefa Clara, they asserted, it would prove only that "the Holy Spirit was not present here."[57] The comisario eventually reassured the nuns that he did not wish intrude on their jurisdiction but wished only to determine the nature of Josefa Clara's wounds. The thirty nuns, their ire somewhat allayed, filed out of the judicial chambers.

Anger over what must have appeared as an unjustified intrusion of an alien ecclesiastical body into their domain of spiritual power likely motivated the Santa Clara nuns to defend Josefa Clara. This investigation took place in the midst of the Bourbon monarchy's mid-eighteenth-century secularization campaign, which brought religious orders and allegedly decadent female monasteries under stricter state and ecclesiastical regulation.[58] Beyond expressing anger at the interference of outside administrators, however, the nuns' outburst also reflected their fierce loyalty to the novice Josefa Clara. Only their strong conviction that she was virtuous could have prompted them to take her defense in such a remarkable stance of opposition to the court of the Holy Office in acknowledged disobedience to their Mother Superior.

Gender Control in the Era of the Counter-Reformation

Bourbon administrators subjected Mexican nuns, such as those in the San Juan de la Penitencia convent, to increasing regulation in the second half of the eighteenth century, but curtailment of female religious orders had a much older history. The Counter-Reformation initiated an era of reduced female independence in both secular and sacred realms.[59] Beginning in the second decade of the sixteenth century, the Catholic church launched a campaign to curtail women's participation in religious devotion. Women had played important roles leading spiritual groups in the era of humanist Catholicism in the late fifteenth and early sixteenth centuries. During

Spain's mid-sixteenth-century "change of course," however, such women fell under increased scrutiny and suspicion.

The church viewed women, particularly those who possessed a measure of authority or autonomy, as the most potentially dangerous menace to Christian morality. As Mary Elizabeth Perry and Ann Cruz write, the church in this period "reinscribed misogyny by focusing on women's powers to lead men's souls to hell."[60] The church redoubled its efforts to control the female body and its sexual functions because it perceived unchaste women as a threat to the salvation of men's souls and the preservation of the social order. The Inquisition prosecuted female religious leaders. The Council of Trent subjected convents to heightened measures of seclusion and enclosure from the secular world and legislated female orders' administrative subjection to male orders.[61]

Within this context the mystical realm afforded women the largest measure of spiritual authority available to them. Women could not become priests and were therefore forbidden such male prerogatives as interpreting scripture, hearing confession, and performing the sacraments. The clause prohibiting women from even entering the choir of any church during the ceremony of the Eucharist, repeated at each of the four colonial meetings of the Mexican Provincial Council, illustrates the severity of women's mandated exclusion from the masculine realm of religious experience in New Spain.[62] Under these circumstances, assuming the role of the mystic—and thereby claiming direct access to God, the highest force of power imaginable in this context—was the most self-affirming and potentially subversive action in which women could engage. For this reason the church subjected women who claimed to be mystics to intensive scrutiny.

The percentage of women accused in the iluso and alumbrado trials is much higher than the percentage of women charged in Mexican Inquisition cases overall. In the years between 1571 and 1700, Solange Alberro found that women's percentage of the accused in all the cases brought before the court of the Holy Office fluctuated between 10 and 30 percent. Their low overall representation was due to the smaller proportion of females in the colony's Spanish population, the group the Inquisition was principally concerned with policing. The court also heard fewer denunciations against Spanish women than against Spanish men because women's restricted participation in public activities minimized the possibility for public scrutiny of their actions. Furthermore, in cases of such common crimes as bigamy, the court's perception of gendered sexuality meant that it laid responsibility for such crimes on men alone. The higher representation of women in the iluso and alumbrado trials was due, no doubt, to both their greater engagement in the practices associated with these crimes and to the church's increased vigilance against women who claimed to be mystics in the seventeenth and eighteenth centuries. Alberro found that women also represented greater numbers of the accused in cases of heresy, witchcraft, sorcery, and magic.[63]

The church inspected female mystics particularly in terms of their sexual virtue. Early modern Spaniards and Spanish Americans founded their concept of female virtue on women's success in defending their virginity or, if married, their chastity.[64] The church's suspicion of women's sexual virtue features prominently in many of the Mexican mystic trials, including that of Marta de la Encarnación. The church believed women's loss of virginity inevitably led them toward participation in a broad range of dangerous and socially disruptive behavior. As Perry writes in the context of Spain, "in the peculiar mathematics of Counter-Reformation moralists, the female who lost her chastity acquired in exchange a frightening license to break every other taboo."[65] In Spain's New World colonies sensitivity over female chastity escalated in the context of anxieties over interracial mixing. Only chaste females were secure reproducers of "clean blood" offspring.[66]

The Counter-Reformation Catholic church's vigorous promotion of the Cult of the Virgin Mary reinforced this exigency on female chastity in the colonial context. In the late sixteenth and seventeenth centuries Spain passionately endorsed Marian worship as a chief component of its campaign to uphold distinctively Catholic forms of religious worship. These efforts were tremendously successful in Mexico. The Virgin of Guadalupe became the most celebrated religious figure in New Spain in the century between 1650 and 1750.[67] Her perceived intervention on behalf of the capital's population during a devastating plague in 1736 cemented her popularity.[68] The Mexican populace's devotion to the Virgin Mary, however, extended far beyond participation in the cult of Guadalupe. Local cults dedicated to dozens of other Marian figures flourished among both indigenous and Spanish communities throughout New Spain.[69]

Spaniards and inhabitants of New Spain based their formation of both national and local identity in part on their devotion to Mary and to other virtuous female Christians in the early modern world. One seventeenth-century Spanish campaign attempted to replace Santiago with Saint Teresa as the country's patron saint.[70] In 1760 Pope Clement

XII declared the Virgin of Immaculate Conception (of whom Guadalupe was one incarnation) the Patroness of Spain and the Indies. [71] The rise of local criollo pride in the City of Kings was one of the most powerful forces behind the success of Dominican beata Rose of Lima's canonization campaign. [72] At the time of her 1671 canonization Rose was declared patron of both Lima and America. A number of powerful figures in Lima's criollo elite supported Rose's bid for canonization. As Ronald Morgan writes, the desire to display their triumph over the competing traditions of Protestantism and indigenous and African paganism fuelled their enthusiasm for Rose's cult. In the colonial context criollos "found it increasingly necessary to demonstrate the gulf that separated themselves both racially and culturally from Indians, blacks, and castas."[73]

Several institutions endorsed the Virgin of Immaculate Conception as patron of a variety of locales in colonial Latin America. Nevertheless, the very concept of her Immaculate Conception was also the subject of considerable theological debate in the seventeenth century. The doctrine of Mary's virginal motherhood had formed a central tenet of Christian theology since the religion's development, but the question of whether Mary herself was also conceived without the taint of original sin did not become part of church doctrine until 1854. Dominicans were the most outspoken opponents of the idea of Mary's Immaculate Conception in colonial Mexico. They followed Thomas Aquinas's lead in believing that not even Mary had managed to avoid the taint of original sin into which all of humanity was born. However, several other groups strongly supported the doctrine. The municipal council of Puebla adopted the figure of the Immaculate Conception as its spiritual patroness and urged its citizens during the commemoration of her feast day to never depart, "whether in public or private," from the "pious opinion which affirms that Our Lady the Virgin Mary was conceived without blemish of original sin." It instructed poblanos to teach this truth to their servants and children and "to introduce it to the soul of the faithful."[74]

The early-seventeenth-century archbishop of Mexico, Juan Pérez de la Serna, shared poblanos' admiration for the Virgin of Immaculate Conception and celebrated a mass in her honor in 1618. Mexico's viceroy, the marquis of Guadalcázar, doubted the orthodoxy of this initiative and asked the Inquisition to investigate. The two parties never ultimately resolved their dispute, but the archbishop drew support for his position from allies on Mexico City's municipal council. Debate over the question continued for the next several decades. In 1625 Philip IV issued a decree praising God for the protection that the figure of Immaculate Conception had provided to a Spanish fleet, led by the marquis of Cadereita, from Protestant Dutch privateers. A subsequent Mexican viceroy married the daughter of the marquis and, desirous of enhancing the legitimacy of his own rule, further promoted the cult of this miracle.[75]

The cult of female virginity, then, assumed multiple layers of significance in colonial Mexico. The church launched a variety of initiatives curtailing the independence of both lay and religious women in the Counter-Reformation era, and vigilance over women's sexual propriety was the first imperative of this movement. In the context of peninsulares' alarm at the growing strength of the criollo and mixed-race populations of the colony, defense of Spanish women's chastity became even more fraught. The church also vigorously promoted the worship of Virginal Marian figures as part of its initiative to establish new models of reformed Catholicism. Mexican institutions forged an association in this context between the figure of the Virgin of Immaculate Conception, criollo pride, and the legitimacy of Spanish rule in the Americas. In seventeenth- and eighteenth-century Mexico, the myriad implications of virginity forced officers of the Inquisition to engage in a heightened scrutiny of the practice of female chastity, particularly in cases of women who claimed they could communicate directly with God.

Iluso and Alumbrado Visions and Miracles

The Mexican Inquisition charged those whom it investigated for the crimes of iluminismo and alumbradismo with feigning a variety of supernatural feats. Tables 4 and 5 summarize the types of religious practices in which male and female ilusos and alumbrados engaged. Most of the women claimed they had experienced such paramystical phenomena as ecstasies, visions and locutions, bouts of diabolic possession, and stigmata. Many also averred that they could levitate, foretell the future, and travel in spirit to distant places. They often executed miraculous feats such as curing the sick or saving souls from purgatory by using relics, statues, or sacred images. Male mystics also saw visions, but far fewer experienced paramystical phenomena. More often the religious expressions concerned statements of a doctrinal or theological nature and support pledged to female mystics.

Mexican ilusos and alumbrados most frequently experienced the paramystical through visions. A number of the mystics prosecuted in the late sixteenth and early seventeenth centuries claimed to have seen

Table 4. Religious practices of female ilusas and alumbradas, 1593–1801

Type of practice	1593–1624	1625–1649	1650–1674	1675–1699	1700–1724	1725–1749	1750–1774	1775–1801	% condemned	Total
Visions	3	4	—	9	5	4	2	11	40	38
Demons	3	3	—	4	6	3	2	8	45	29
Miracles	1	2	—	5	7	1	3	7	42	26
Ecstatic fits	2	4	—	3	5	—	—	5	74	19
Doctrine	3	2	—	3	3	1	1	5	66	8
Disease	2	1	—	4	3	1	2	5	50	18
Sexual transgressions	3	2	—	—	2	1	1	3	58	12
Penitence	—	2	—	1	2	1	1	3	80	10
Levitation	1	1	—	1	1	—	—	2	100	6
Support	—	1	—	2	2	—	—	—	—	5
Total	18	22	—	32	36	12	12	49	avg. 55	181

Source: Archivo General de la Nación, Ramo Inquisición.
Note: The table records every type of religious practice engaged in by each individual. Condemnation percentages refer to condemned women whose religious experiences included such activities.

Table 5. Religious practices of male ilusos and alumbrados, 1593–1801

Type of practice	1593–1624	1625–1649	1650–1674	1675–1699	1700–1724	1725–1749	1750–1774	1775–1801	% condemned	Total
Doctrine	4	1	3	6	3	1	4	—	46	22
Visions	5	1	1	9	1	—	—	3	30	20
Support	—	2	1	5	1	2	3	6	52	20
Sexual transgressions	3	—	—	2	1	2	2	3	62	13
Demons	2	—	—	5	2	1	—	1	64	11
Miracles	2	1	1	3	2	—	—	1	80	10
Ecstatic fits	—	—	2	4	1	1	—	—	62	8
Penitence	—	—	—	2	1	—	—	—	33	3
Disease	1	—	—	—	—	—	—	—	100	1
Levitation	—	—	—	1	—	—	—	—	100	1
Total	17	5	8	37	12	7	9	14	avg. 63	109

Source: Archivo General de la Nación, Ramo Inquisición.

Note: The table records every type of religious practice engaged in by each individual. Condemnation percentages refer to condemned men whose religious experiences included such activities.

apocalyptic apparitions. They envisaged the "New Jerusalem," peopled by selected souls, which the revered hermit Gregorio López had foreseen would be established in Mexico. [76] Later Mexican visionaries, including eighteenth-century laywoman Marta de la Encarnación, also claimed to have experienced apocalyptic visions, although in subsequent decades ilusos saw the viceroyalty as the site of apocalyptic destruction, rather than God's haven from it. In these later apocalyptic apparitions visionaries often learned that their intervention had prevented God from visiting his ire upon the colony. [77]

Beginning in the 1640s, when the court opened its investigation of the four Romero sisters, a different type of vision became more prevalent. These beatas most often had visions in which they saw the state of the souls of people they knew and occasionally retrieved the souls of deceased people from purgatory. The trial transcript of one of the Romero sisters, María de la Encarnación, contains several detailed descriptions of how she executed such feats. For several months María performed weekly ecstatic fits in front of groups of her supporters. During these ceremonies roughly a dozen people gathered together in the home of one of her patrons. Kneeling, they commenced to recite the Pater Noster and Ave María in unison until María was led into the room and seated on a cushion in front of them. After a few minutes of quiet meditation, she fell into a trance and then levitated, remaining suspended in the air for several minutes. Her limbs became rigid as she stretched out her arms and let her head drop backward so that her body formed the shape of the cross. She was then set upon a bed at the side of the room, where she lay with her eyes open, murmuring in Latin and Spanish for several minutes. Her confessor, José Bruñón de Vertiz, then read her a list of names of people who had died, and María told her audience which souls had already risen to heaven. María often negotiated with angels for the release of those souls still in purgatory. [78] Many other ilusas performed similar feats, and some even asserted they knew the day on which their acquaintances would die. [79] One of María's sisters, Josefa de San Luis Beltrán, declared that she had single-handedly liberated eight hundred souls from purgatory in a single night, including those of Cardinal Richelieu and the Conde-Duque de Olivares. [80]

María de la Encarnación used her ability to communicate with the souls of the deceased to attract the support of her most important sponsors: Diego Manuel de la Rocha, Juan Maestre, and Urban Martínez. She cemented Rocha's admiration for her shortly after moving into his home when she saw a vision of Santa Juana de la Cruz while mourning the death of Rocha's recently deceased young son. Juan Maestre first encountered María soon after the death of his son when he learned from someone who had witnessed her spectacles: "that an honest woman had told him that the soul of fray Juan Maestre his son, a discalced monk of the order of San Francisco who had died . . . on October 29 had left purgatory the night before between ten and twelve and had been in purgatory for only three days." Maestre and his wife were overjoyed at this news and expressed their desire to meet María and her confessor. María met her third significant patron, Urban Martínez, after he learned that she had retrieved the soul of Luis de Carrillo, the governor of his estate, from purgatory.[81]

As well as securing supporters through her talents as an intervener in the supernatural world, María de la Encarnación also dazzled her audiences with an array of miraculous displays that provided tangible evidence of God's endorsement of her mystical abilities. She frequently experienced minor miracles in front of her supporters and impressed them with physical evidence of her ongoing intimate contact with angels, saints, and even God himself. Her repertoire of minor miracles included the ability to multiply coins and to receive "relics" from heaven in the form of hairs, clothes, and bits of the rosary that she then distributed among her sponsors.

Along with these powers Mexican mystics received many other types of supernatural signs including showing the marks of stigmata on their bodies.[82] Others possessed the ability to cure clients and patrons from their spiritual and bodily maladies. Seventeenth-century mestiza ilusa Agustina Rangel, for example, provided medical remedies to a number of people in her community. One witness testified that Rangel had cured a man by calling on the powers of a holy rose she held. Another told the court that Rangel had cured a woman with some "powders of the rose of Santa Rose." Rangel cured a third woman, suffering from an "ailment [achaque] the doctors could not cure," with her holy "rosa de Santa Rosa," a substance the court deduced was peyote, which Indians in Mexico had traditionally used for medicinal purposes but which the Inquisition banned.[83]

Mexican ilusos used a variety of supernatural objects to affect their cures. Getrudis Rosa Ortiz, the mestiza whom the viceroy's wife sponsored, possessed a statue of San Juan de la Penitencia that she used to cure people from physical ailments. Ortiz had also seen a vision of a holy child who had attributed her with the power to cure disease.[84] Beatriz de Jesús las Flores, a contemporary of Ortiz's from the town of Querétaro, had herself been cured from illness with a set of rosary beads blessed by the milk of the Virgin Mary and the blood of Jesus Christ. Other witnesses in Beatriz's trial testified that she had assisted others with her supernatural powers. One witness declared that Beatriz had once used her gift to save Querétaro from a serious drought.[85]

Ilusos could also use their supernatural powers to assist their supporters in domestic crises. Marta de la Encarnación once had a vision, for instance, in which she saw that a man was going to kill his wife. Marta then intervened and prevented the woman's death.[86] Getrudis Rosa Ortiz also described how she had used her supernatural abilities to assist women in similar ways. Ortiz said that from a young age she had often visited the houses of people in her community "where there was displeasure or quarrels, especially between spouses." The women who invited her into their homes wanted her to give their husbands something to "calm them down." Ortiz claimed she had a great deal of success encouraging these couples to make peace. She said that by talking to them and by "ordering their wives to give them chocolate and smother them with attention" she was able to soothe the nerves of even the angriest men.[87] Chocolate was another pre-Columbian substance that curanderas used in the colonial era to pacify their clients' errant male lovers.[88]

The consumption of food figured frequently in the mystical experiences of many other ilusos and alumbrados. Mystical experiences involving food became an established feature of female spirituality in the high Middle Ages. Eucharist miracles and the renunciation of eating served as extensions of that sphere of the mundane world—food preparation and distribution—that women most often controlled. Both ecstatic raptures of consumption and periods of self-enforced deprivation (holy feasts and holy fasts) were central elements of female mystical spirituality from the twelfth to the fourteenth centuries.[89] They included instances of women who sustained themselves by consuming only the Eucharist, women who tasted milk and honey when they drank from Christ's wounds, and women to whom the Eucharist magically appeared.

Some Mexican mystics' religious experiences echo these traditions of Eucharist miracles and divine fasts.[90] One early-eighteenth-century beata, María Manuela Picazo, for example, had a vision of Jesus Christ embracing her: "Christ put her mouth on his side wound and [she] tasted the blood that was there, and she put her mouth inside his wound and with her eyes did the same, and out of the wound came a fragrant scent like that which Saint Teresa had smelled."[91] María Lucía Celis, a mystic prosecuted at the end of the century, similarly experienced numerous visions involving nursing from both Christ's side wound and Mary's breasts.[92]

Mexican mystics, however, were often far less abstract in their experiences of consumption. Many of their trials contain descriptions of spiritual encounters in which God either provided them with mundane foodstuffs or else demanded such items from them. Marta de la Encarnación testified, for example, that on one occasion when she had been unable to prepare food for herself, a number of consumables including chocolate had supernaturally materialized before her.[93] One witness in the late-eighteenth-century trial of Josefa Palacios said he had heard both this beata and her sister attest that God regularly sent them plates of *arroz con leche* (rice pudding) or "some other dish."[94]

Ana de Colina, a devoted companion of ilusa Ana de Aramburu, testified that Aramburu told her that she had sometimes spent entire nights in conversation with God, learning and repeating his doctrine. Colina remarked that the doctrine Aramburu had learned "conformed to all she had heard preached and read in spiritual books," but not all of Aramburu's nighttime discourses conformed to traditional practice. At the close of one of these long fits, Colina told the court that God ordered Aramburu "to eat a little food and afterwards return to continue with the doctrine." Aramburu, Colina continued, then "violently" returned from her state of ecstasy "and asked for a little food, and having given her chocolate she drank it very quickly and then immediately returned to her state of privation and continued speaking."[95] Another witness who appeared in Aramburu's trial told the court that Aramburu had once "come by very tired after having seen the Holy Trinity, and had asked for a cigar." He had considered her request ridiculous, however, and "scorned it with laughter."[96] As well as enjoying cigars, Aramburu also had a fondness for *pulque*, an alcoholic drink of the Nahuas made from fermented maguey. Several other witnesses described how Aramburu was a talented healer, and one witness said she also used small dolls made out of cloth to cause illnesses.[97]

Josefa de San Luis Beltrán's participation in spiritually invoked feasting assumed another form. One witness to many of the fits of spiritual possession Josefa experienced described how the angel inhabiting her body requested that both food and tobacco be passed to him through her mouth. While in the "state of simplicity" Josefa assumed in such fits, he recounted, she directed him and his wife to put cigarettes in her mouth.[98] The angel who occupied the body of Josefa's sister, María de la Encarnación, also asked to be fed chocolate. María explained that the chocolate was necessary because "the spirit she had was thin and it was necessary to look after its nature and to give it comfort."[99] The doctor who denounced another late-seventeenth-century beata, Antonia de Ochoa, noticed that just before the bout of levitation and ecstasy that she performed in front of a group of spectators, Ochoa had been "sucking on a cigar."[100]

For the most part, experience of the paramystical (visions, miracles, supernatural gastronomic exchanges) was restricted to female mystics. Most of the men accused of false mysticism were investigated because of the support they had given to female mystics. Yet there were exceptions. Salvador Victoria, a hermit tried in 1659, asserted Gregorio López, God, and the Virgin Mary had inspired him with visions. He also possessed a miraculous statue that had helped him to escape imprisonment in Spain.[101] Another convicted hermit, Juan Bautista de Cárdenas, tried in 1673, also saw visions, experienced bouts of demonic tormenting, and possessed a set of sacred keys that had originally belonged to Abraham.[102] The court sentenced Juan de Luna, a layman who knew the future of his wife's soul and had received prophecies from San Juan de la Cruz, to eighteen months' reclusion and perpetual prohibition from reading spiritual books.[103]

The religious practices of eighteenth-century mestizo beato Ignacio de San Juan Salazar most resembled those of female mystics. The Inquisition had originally convicted Salazar in 1700 for charges of distributing false relics. In 1709 the court arraigned him again, this time for being an alumbrado and embustero.[104] Witnesses testified that Salazar experienced visions, ecstasies, and demonic torturing, read the state of others' souls and saved them from purgatory, and traveled in spirit to distant locations. The religious expressions of such men alarmed the officers of the Mexican tribunal. Normally they convicted men such as Salazar whose spirituality mimicked the pious expressions typical of female mystics.[105]

Passage into the Clerical Domain

The court was equally wary of humble male and particularly female mystics who entered into the privileged clerical domain of theological analysis. A number of Mexican mystics, including mid-seventeenth-century ermitaño Pedro García de Arias, wrote lengthy spiritual treatises. María de Jesús, a Spanish laywoman from Zacatecas, was denounced to the court in 1744 because of the more than twenty religious tracts discussing the seven seals in the book of St. John the Apocalypse that she had written.[106] Others, including lay beata Marta de la Encarnación, wrote spiritual accounts of their lives. Women in colonial Mexico were proscribed from producing such texts without strict supervision from their confessors.[107] María Cayetana Loria, an eighteenth-century mulata ilusa, composed a tract of her life that the court closely scrutinized for inconsistencies with revered women's religious writings.[108]

Ana de Zayas, a Spanish laywoman tried in the late seventeenth century, was one of the most prolific writers investigated for false mysticism in Mexico. The Inquisition determined that heterodox strains of illuminism, Jansenism, Lutheranism, and Pelagianism all influenced the many spiritual tracts she composed.[109] Zayas discussed such issues as the nature of virtue, the power of human will, and the force of predestination in her tracts. She asserted that she was so devoted to God that she would obey him in everything, even if he ordered her to sin.[110]

Among the various writings her inquisitors consulted in their judgment of Zayas were a sheaf of her poems, letters, and essays confiscated upon her arrest.[111] One poem, entitled "V," sets out Zayas's understanding of God's counsel for effective worship and meditation:

V

Keep vigil in profound silence
Battle like the valiant
You will fly, which is evident
Live without love of the world.
Keep vigil because if you are not spoken to
It is not the effect of insanity
Because my faith assures you
That you must defy the devil.
Keep vigil because your affection
is stripped bare, and you love me well
You do not have this to disdain
That the spirit is not flesh.[112]

Zayas's poem allows us to perceive some of the ways she understood her own religious faith and wished for others to understand it. It conveys the severity that was central to her piety and speaks of the trials she would undergo to uphold it. It also reveals the intimate bond she felt to God (he knows she "loves him well") despite the skepticism of her community. God counsels her to imitate the harsh asceticism of the monastic orders, divesting herself of worldly comfort and transporting herself beyond carnal temptation (or suspicion). These strict aspects of God's advice are at odds, however, with other features of his message. In contradiction to contemporary orthodoxy that held that women should practice their spirituality through secluded and regulated meditation, God instead tells Zayas to worship by battling "like the valiant" and flying, "which is evident."

He also provides her with even more controversial advice in the poem's closing lines when he observes that Zayas should not disdain the idea that "the spirit is not flesh." We would expect a God informed by Christian orthodoxy to command the devout that they should "disdain the flesh for not being spirit." The idea of the spirit's superiority to the body is central to Christian theology. Yet in Zayas's poem, God inverts this message. In these lines Zayas's God has rendered the body the more esteemed component of the flesh-spirit duality.

Her inquisitors were apprehensive of Zayas's theology for a number of reasons, but chief among them was her presumption that she had the sanctioned right to engage independently in its production. This perception was common to the court's view of numerous other mystics. Several ilusos, both male and female, were accused of having performed functions lawfully reserved only for members of the clergy. In three cases ilusos had allegedly acted as other people's spiritual directors, and in two of these instances witnesses asserted that members of the clergy condoned the mystics' assumption of these duties. One case involved an early-eighteenth-century investigation of a Spanish beato of the Third Order of San Francisco, Baltasar Núñez de los Reyes. The court charged Núñez with publicly declaring that he did not need a confessor since God had told him that he should assume his own spiritual direction. Several witnesses testified that Núñez had attempted to become the confessor for both a laywoman and a nun. The laywoman had resisted his attempts (in part, she explained, because Núñez had insisted that she share bodily as well as spiritual intimacies with him). The nun, Barbara Josefa de San Francisco, however, stated that Núñez had acted as her spiritual director for several months.[113]

María Josefa Rita de la Peña, a late-eighteenth-century Tolucan beata with a reputation for remarkable virtue, was accused of engaging in similar activities. In her posthumous trial the tribunal focused on investigating two of her previous confessors. After Peña's death these two men had orchestrated the distribution throughout Toluca of many of her personal possessions, instructing recipients to revere as relics these items, which included a pair of bloody slippers removed from the nun's corpse. One young laywoman who testified at the trial confessed that Peña had acted as her spiritual director for a year and a half. The witness described Peña as a very strict director, enforcing a daily regimen of three hours of prayer, mortification, fasting, and rigorous blood disciplines. At least four members of the clergy had condoned the arrangement.[114]

Conventional Mystical Piety

Although ilusos and alumbrados did engage in unorthodox religious practices, many of them, such as María Josefa, retained loyal groups of supporters around themselves, even in the face of inquisitorial investigations. Supporters may have been impressed with the miraculous displays many female mystics enacted, but they were also likely drawn to these women in part because their engagement in forms of conventional piety provided them with a halo of religious orthodoxy. Many of those accused of iluminismo and alumbradismo, for instance, followed taxing spiritual routines. When the Inquisition seized Franciscan *tercera* Antonia de Ochoa, it confiscated all the written materials found in her quarters including a number of daily spiritual schedules evidently designed by Ochoa's confessor. The most arduous of these dicated the following routine:

Morning

From four to five, prayer.
From five to five-thirty, tidy the bed and prepare the
    things of the house.
From five-thirty to seven, mass.
From seven to eight, breakfast and put the house in
    order.
From eight to eleven, handwork [*obra de manos*].
From eleven to twelve, prayer.
From twelve to two: read a chapter from Contemptu
    mundi; eat and sleep.

From two to three, clean and make the house ready.
From three to six, handwork.
From six to seven, rest.
From seven to eight, prayer.
From eight to nine-thirty, dine and tidy up from
    dinner, examine the conscience and go to bed.[115]

Many Mexican mystics devoted considerable energy to prayer and meditation. They most frequently modeled their meditative contemplation on the example provided by the writings of Saint Teresa of Avila. Antonia de Ochoa had drawn inspiration from a collection of spiritual exercises that she kept in her rooms, among them a popular contemporary prayer, often attributed to Teresa. This piece, which Ochoa had transcribed and signed, begins:

I will not be moved, my God, so that I may love you.
This is what you have promised me.
I will not be moved by hell so fearful
That I might in this movement offend you.[116]

Several other Mexican mystics also demonstrated the profound influence Teresa had exerted on their spiritual practices.[117] María Josefa Peña's Inquisition file contains a number of long excerpts from this Tolucan beata's spiritual writings. Peña's acknowledged imitation of Saint Teresa's composition *Las Moradas* in these passages reveals her desire to reproduce the spirituality of orthodox mysticism.[118] The forty-six "stations," a set of mystical visions Josefa de San Luis Beltrán had witnessed, fill an entire lengthy volume of Inquisitorial documentation. Josefa's visions also contain many parallels to recognized mystical convention. They deal with such topics as the nature of purgatory and hell, the difference between the path of grace and that of sin, the three grades of perfection, and the mercy of God.[119]

Other ilusas participated in similar expressions of conventional mysticism. A prayer that Ana de Aramburu recited and possibly composed resonates with references to accepted mystical conventions, including acknowledgment of God's overwhelming power, the use erotic language, and the idea of sacrifice. She begins:

You are the master of the world.
You are the master of my heart.
You are my sweet mate.
You are my Lord.

A later verse reads:

My Heart are you open?
My Will
So that there you will sacrifice
Soul, Life, Will, Love.[120]

A significant number of ilusas also attested to their familiarity with the vidas of several other important medieval and early modern mystics, including Catherine of Siena, Saint Brigida, and Saint John of the Cross.[121] These saints and many others, including Rose of Lima and Saint Ignatius Loyola, often appeared to them in visions.[122] Mexican mystics also spoke of having learned from the writings of seventeenth-century Franciscan nun María de Jesús de Agreda.[123] Although the court deemed these women and men heretical, they drew from a number of orthodox sources in the production of their religious expressions.

In their secular lives many ilusos and alumbrados attempted to re-create rules and other conditions of living similar to those that members of religious orders followed. A significant number of these mystics were members of the laity who had previously attempted to join convents or monasteries. These women and men had been unable to profess either because of religious orders' restrictions against admitting castas or because they had been unable to afford admission to such institutions. Early-eighteenth-century Spanish beata María Manuela Picazo, for instance, informed the court in one of her audiences that she had long dreamed of becoming a nun but had been unable to afford the convent's admission dowry.[124] This was also true of many of the male beato and ermitaño ilusos. Mid-seventeenth-century hermit Pedro García de Arias also testified that he had attempted to join the Carmelite order but had been unable to do so because he could not afford to pay for his upkeep within the monastery.[125] These women and men, denied access to the instiutions of religious orthodoxy, attempted to re-create the atmosphere of convents and monasteries in their own daily schedules, disciplines, and meditations.

Conclusion

Mexican mystics engaged in a variety of spiritual activities within the socially stratified atmosphere of colonial cities. In urban spaces that were home to both the lavish displays of the wealthy elite and the destitution of the majority of the Indian, mixed-race, and Spanish poor, Mexican ilusos and alumbrados practiced their particular variety of Catholic mysticism. Denied entrance to the colony's official establishments of religious devotion, they re-created the lives of nuns and friars for themselves in their own homes and those of their admirers. They fasted, prayed, confessed, and attended mass. They recorded their religious thoughts in spiritual journals or recounted their life stories to their confessors. Most frequently, they experienced different types of paramystical phenomena. They cured the sick, worked miracles, levitated, consumed supernatural food, felt the painful marks of stigmata on their bodies, and, most often, saw visions. Many of them integrated commentaries on their social contexts—observances of domestic violence, abhorrence of ill government, or judgments about the postmortem fate of acquaintances or of powerful people they had heard about—into their visions. Their capacity to provide immediate demonstrations of their connections to the supernatural world and to affect their supporters' futures likely promoted their popularity among the networks of spiritual patrons and clients that formed around them.

Mexican mysticism—or at least its prosecution—flourished in an era during which the Catholic church initiated increased curtailment of some forms of religious practice. A number of these mystics' spiritual expressions, perhaps generated in response to such restrictions, involved challenges to the notion of the clergy's exclusive right to engage in theological production. Many mystics drew inspiration from the example of Saint Teresa of Avila, the most successful defender of women's right to participate in mysticism in the early modern period. Despite the similarities in Mexican visionaries' religious expressions, those whom the court investigated did not constitute a discrete religious sect. These Mexican visionaries did not identify themselves as part of a distinctive group of worshippers unified through a set of theological principles or common spiritual acts. In fact, the only common identity linking members of this group to one another—and to their earlier Spanish predecessors—stemmed from the Mexican tribunal's application to them of the labels *iluso* and *alumbrado*.

Some of their beliefs and practices certainly contained elements of heterodoxy. Ana de Zayas's endorsement of private meditation in "profound silence" evidently sent a note of alarm through the minds of the theological qualifiers assessing her case. Zayas, Marta de la Encarnación, and numerous other ilusos' production of spiritual tracts induced great suspicion among the officers of the court. These women's use of New World substances such as peyote, chocolate, and tobacco were certainly not part of a canonical mystical tradition. Nevertheless, other elements of their spirituality were decidedly orthodox.

One of the central sets of beliefs for which the Holy Office had condemned Spanish alumbrados was their contempt for the sacraments, for public religious ceremonies, and for the ritualistic aspects of verbal prayer. There is little evidence that such contempt featured in the spirituality of these Mexican mystics. Rather, they embraced many aspects of Counter-Reformation orthodoxy. A number of them enthusiastically imitated the church's endorsement of formalized religious rites in the ceremonies they conducted for their supporters. Others incorporated the worship of holy icons and devotions centering on the Eucharist and the Passion into their private rites. They all founded some aspect of their sacred practices on the cult of the saints, an expression of piety that was central to Counter-Reformation orthodoxy, particularly in its New World context.

Mexican mystics engaged in a variety of other spiritual acts deemed orthodox in New Spain. They worshipped God with popular prayers, they practiced harsh physical disciplines, and they attempted to imitate the religious lives led by the saints they admired. Particular aspects of their spirituality led inquisitors, clerics, and some members of the laity to see them as heretics. However, the extensive networks of supporters these mystics attracted suggest that for many their religiosity, rather than representing "deviancy," actually reflected the spiritual aspirations of a much wider body of Christians living in the urban centers of New Spain. Although their supporters may have seen these mystics as embodiments of true religion, the Mexican Inquisition believed them to be spiritual deviants. Let us now turn to the examination of how the court drew such conclusions.

Three

The Evaluation of True and False Mysticism

I n the last week of April 1738 the Mexican tribunal received a flurry of letters from five clerics denouncing Agustín Claudio, a lay brother (*religioso lego*) of the order of San Hipólito Martír. [1] Two friars described how they had seen fray Agustín jump out of his chair during prayer, grimace, and contort his body strangely. A third reported that while in the midst of such a fit, Agustín had ripped apart a rosary and dashed a relic on the floor. A priest called before the court one week later testified that a Spanish woman had told him of the suspicious practices that Agustín engaged in with his daughters of confession. The Holy Office then interrogated two of these women, María Loba and Ana María de Castro. Loba informed the Inquisition that fray Agustín had told her and several other women he confessed that he had spent three days in hell wrestling demons until at last he had triumphed over the spirit of lust. Ever since, even though he might touch women intimately, "he did not feel any temptation of the flesh" but responded to such caresses only "as if he were a log." Fray Agustín told Castro that she might succumb to physical temptation with him without sinning because he had already defeated the devil. She had then lain with Agustín for nine nights, while he touched and kissed her, whispering that "this was how they had to practice vanquishing all temptation." Once when she asked him why he did not sin in committing these acts, "he raised his hand and slapped her in the face saying he would rather die than offend God." Before caressing her, he explained, he purified himself, exhorting to God about his horror of sin. Like many other Mexican mystics, fray Agustín also made prophecies and claimed he had the power to intervene on behalf of souls in purgatory. [2]

The Inquisition called several other witnesses to verify Loba and Castro's testimonies and then submitted a summary of their charges to four calificadores. These clerics produced a forty-page assessment of Agustín's controversial practices, painstakingly evaluating which components of his activities constituted heresy and which did not. They concluded that Agustín's claim that he could triumph over the devil's temptation demonstrated that he was a "hypocrite, iluso, and embustero." Yet they also argued that Agustín's belief that God could exempt him from sin, even in the midst of carnal acts, was "neither heretical nor erroneous," according to the dictates of Pope Innocent XI. Although his actions might be "false and reckless," consideration of various theologians forced them to conclude that Agustín's sexual activities did not constitute formal heresy. "Any ignorance," they observed, "even if it is affected ignorance, which causes error excuses the sin of formal heresy and the incursion of its accompanying ecclesiastical punishments, because it is not possible for a person to voluntarily contravene the church's authority who does not know that the church believes the opposite of him."[3] These clerics did find heresy in other elements of Agustín's case, however. They wrote that his call for daily mental prayer paralleled the errors of the false and scandalous alumbrados. They also considered heretical both his practice of sending his confessants to take communion without confessing after spending the night embracing him and his directive that they show greater obedience to him than to their own husbands.[4]

Four years after receiving this calificación, fray Agustín's inquisitors read him an accusation of 190 chapters. They charged him with supporting the sect of "alumbrados and molinistas, believing things full of illusion and hypocrisy . . . and introducing into women the most lewd and prejudicial doctrine in the filthiest ways." Agustín initially denied many of these charges, but he then fell into a mute stupor. After waiting six months for Agustín to respond rationally, inquisitors Pedro Navarro de Isla and Pedro Anselmo Sánchez de Tagle moved to induce Agustín to speak with the use of torture. Agustín remained dumb, however, until he found himself stripped and strapped to the torture bench. The pain was so exquisite that after the executioner had applied "one half turn" to this device, Agustín gripped onto the ropes binding him and broke his silence, shouting: "*God! I believe in God! I adore God, I ask that you give me an audience. I will speak, and before everything I say that I am a Christian.*"[5] Agustín's inquisitors continued interviewing witnesses for over two years after this gruesome session. Almost ten years after the tribunal received the first denunciations against Agustín, and before it had managed to formulate a final judgment of his activities, Agustín died, languishing in the cramped cells of the court's secret prison.

The Determination of Mystical Authenticity

The forty-page assessment that Agustín's calificadores produced hints at the complexity inquisitorial officials faced when judging the authenticity of mystical experiences. Many of the theological writings available for their consultation were inexplicit about the precise means of evaluating such occurrences. Moreover, both their divine origins and private transmission rendered mystical experiences unverifiable. As the following examples illustrate, the many similarities between descriptions of ilusos' and alumbrados' spiritual encounters and those of sanctioned religious figures further complicated these evaluations.

In his 1686 denunciation of Franciscan beata Antonia de Ochoa, doctor Antonio de Córdova described a rapture that he had seen Ochoa experience.[6] A number of Ochoa's followers had gathered at mealtime in the house of merchant José de Villa Alta, a supporter of Ochoa. Just as the servants put the first dish on the table, Ochoa, appearing "as if absent, or outside herself, let her head fall back and fixed her feet upon the ledge across from the table." A slave held her from behind, while Ochoa commenced sobbing, "as if demonstrating great pain in her heart."[7] The wife of another merchant who had also hosted Ochoa's mystical demonstrations testified that on one occasion she had given Ochoa some bread and wine as requested. Ochoa had then retreated into a corner and had begun "speaking with the bread and wine, and then on one side of her chest this witness noticed she had a red wound and that on the palms of her hands she had some little red or purple marks."[8]

Accounts of such episodes, which many other women convicted for false mysticism also experienced, do not differ markedly from those associated with bona fide mystics. In his 1676 biography of María de Jesús Tomelín, Francisco Pardo detailed the frequent ecstasies this noted mystic of the Pueblan convent of Limpia Concepción underwent during her adolescence. He wrote that on one occasion, while rapturously contemplating Jesus Christ's stigmata, María had felt "on the bottoms of her feet two wounds so penetrating that they passed from the upper parts of her insteps to the lower parts of her soles."[9]

As well as experiencing ecstatic fits and stigmata similar to those of revered nuns, ilusas had visions that often resembled those of their cloistered sisters. Carlos de Sigüenza y Góngora recorded, for example, a set of visions that the venerable madre Marina de la Cruz experienced in his late seventeenth-century chronicle of the Real Convento de Jesús María, *Parayso occidental*. He describes how, from a young age, María had repeatedly experienced bouts of demonic tormenting and visions of God, Christ, and the Virgin Mary. On one occasion, when she had retreated into her cell, "her spirit rose to the heavens, where she knelt before a beautiful throne of glory occupied by the Queen of both men and the angels, in whose arms could be seen, in the form of a beloved child, her precious Son." Madre Marina noted that the Queen was attended by "innumerable virgins dressed in the finery that is worn in the Empyreal."[10] María Cayetana Loria, a late-eighteenth-century mulata ilusa, described her experience of an almost identical vision, when she saw a finely attired woman, seated on an elaborate throne, attended upon by several angels and holding a precious child.[11]

Ilusos' accounts of diabolic encounters also closely paralleled "orthodox" descriptions. María Lucía Celis, a beata condemned in 1803, described in her testimony how Lucifer had repeatedly tormented her: "Grasping her by the hair, he whipped her, while pinning her shoulders against the wall, and he pulled her head from side to side with her hair beating her and shouting, 'I'm not letting you go, you lousy bitch, until I have ripped you to pieces.' And other demons continuously shouted oaths and said impure and dishonest things, at the same time as displaying their private parts."[12]

Similarly, in his *Vida admirable y penitente de la venerable sor Sebastiana Josepha*, José Eugenio Valdés recorded how the devil had ripped into the body of this revered eighteenth-century Mexican nun and torn out her intestines. Satan tortured sor Sebastiana day and night with horrible faces and then appeared to her in a vision "in unspeakable dishonesty, and sickening lewdness, moving her imagination with horrible suggestions and sending her burning messages of sensual fire."[13]

How could inquisitors, faced with accounts of defendants' paramystical experiences that so closely resembled orthodox descriptions, distinguish the "real" from the feigned? Nearly every denounced iluso and alumbrado claimed to have undergone some such paramystical experience. Yet it is difficult to detect differences in the nature of these encounters between the 35 percent of cases that ended in guilty convictions and the 52 percent that the court did not pursue or dismissed out of hand. (Defendants died in a further 13 percent of cases. See tables 3, 4, and 5.) Court officials must have struggled to separate truth from fiction and deceit when formulating their judgments. Nevertheless, in both the seventeenth and eighteenth centuries they did make such separations, convicting over one-third of the mystics who appeared before them of feigning their experiences. Given the complexity of the evaluations they made and the dramatic ramifications of their decisions, how did the court arrive at these judgments? Upon what foundation did it base its condemnation of these Mexican visionaries? Analysis of trial documents, contemporary spiritual guides, and vidas (spiritual biographies) of renowned religious figures reveals that inquisitors did not apply a uniform standard in their evaluations. Rather, they considered a web of interrelated factors when constructing their models of mystical authenticity and fraud.

Miguel Godínez was one of the most widely studied writers on mystical theology in seventeenth- and eighteenth-century Mexico. Calificadores frequently referred to his 1682 *Practica de la theologia mystica* in formulating their judgments of false mystics.[14] They also repeatedly cited Franciscan theologian Antonio Arbiol, known particularly for his *Desengaños mysticos a las almas detenidas, o engañadas en el camino de la perfeccion.*[15] A Carmelite friar, Francisco de Jesús María, produced a third tract that detailed how inquisitors might differentiate authentic from fraudulent mysticism.[16]

In some cases court officials evidently based their decisions on the two most explicit theological standards these authors articulated for determining mystical legitimacy: if an ecstasy, vision, or locution left a person's soul in a state of agitation or disobedience rather than in tranquility, the experience was likely either fake or inspired by the devil.[17] Second, true mystical experiences could not promote any idea that contradicted doctrine. As Miguel Godínez decreed, the church should beware of people whose revelations "contradict anything in scripture, the traditions, and uses of the church, [or] the moral doctrine of the church fathers."[18]

As the seventeenth- and eighteenth-century debate surrounding Mary's Immaculate Conception illustrates, however, theological doctrine was not immutable. Church leaders themselves sometimes disagreed over the content and boundaries of orthodox doctrine. Furthermore, ideas that might seem heterodox or foolish when voiced by one person could become orthodox or profound when expressed by someone of weightier spiritual and social credentials. Orthodoxy and heterodoxy in seventeenth- and eighteenth-century Mexico were not fixed and unambiguous categories, but rather concepts that worked constantly to define one another. And in this historical context (as in most), it mattered a great deal—in racial, economic, and gendered terms—who was attempting to construct these definitions.

Although the court convicted some ilusos and alumbrados who espoused blatantly heterodox ideas, it also considered other criteria when judging these mystics. Inquisitors closely scrutinized defendants in terms of their expressions of personal virtue. They also examined the social milieu in which visionaries practiced their religion, studying, in particular, the networks surrounding them. Various contemporary pressures, including shifting intellectual fashions, the court's prosecution of other heresies, and, most importantly, anxieties about interracial mixing and class transformations also profoundly influenced the court's assessment of mystical deception. In the evaluation of iluso and alumbrado mystical authenticity, context was all.

The Determination of Heresy

Inquisitors infrequently followed the theological directives of Miguel Godínez and other such writers that they should determine mystics' spiritual authenticity by evaluating the state in which a mystical experience had left a defendant's soul. More often, court officials appraised mystics' legitimacy by comparing ideas they promoted to orthodox dogma. The court deemed heretical, for instance, the statement by late-sixteenth-century beata Ana de Guillamas that "the way of perfection does not consist in fasting and disciplines and other pains, but rather only in the love of God." They classified as merely "reckless and presumptuous," however, her observation that two priests, including the provincial of her order, had not arrived at the way of perfection.[19]

Other ilusos posited controversial ideas about such doctrinal matters as the Trinity and the Virgin Birth. The court repeatedly questioned early-eighteenth-century layman Baltasar Núñez de los Reyes about his sacrilegious questioning of the Trinity and condemned late-sixteenth-century beata Mariana de San Miguel for her unorthodox revelation that there were five mothers of God, including separate ones for each component of the Holy Trinity.[20] The Inquisition also censured many of the revelatory ideas of late-eighteenth-century Augustinian beata María Guadalupe Rivera for contradicting doctrine. Guadalupe Rivera believed that God and human passions, rather than the devil, were the forces responsible for all the evils, wars, and temptations in the world.[21] The Inquisition also condemned many of the theological concepts that late-seventeenth-century laywoman Ana de Zayas supported in her writings. Among her many propositions, Zayas had declared that she would obey God in everything, including if he commanded her to sin. The court pronounced her ideas "heretical" and "tainted by Lutheranism."[22]

Mid-seventeenth-century hermit Pedro García de Arias publicized the most substantial body of unconventional theology from among this group of Mexican ilusos. García recorded his ideas in two spiritual tracts and numerous other writings that he submitted to the tribunal for inspection over the course of his lengthy trial. Many of his writings focused on the nature of free will and on the degree of humanity's participation in achieving grace, topics of heightened sensitivity for the Catholic church in the era of the Counter-Reformation. His calificadores and inquisitors decreed heretical nearly every idea he expressed.

According to García's inquisitors, the many heretical propositions he had supported included his notion that humans could resist the morally repugnant only out of fear. This assertion, they wrote, "denied the liberty of humanity's ability to resist temptation voluntarily . . . which is a heresy of the damned Lutheran inheritance condemned by the Council of Trent." They also classified his proposition that "man is a slave, bought with the blood of Christ, who does not act out of his own will, but rather that of the lord who bought him," as pertaining to the Lutheran and alumbrado heresies. [23] Although the court condemned García's ideas, other contemporaries apparently admired him. One priest who appeared in the concurrent iluso trial of Salvador Victoria testified that Victoria had told him he that "he and all the city had taken [García] for a virtuous man."[24]

Details such as this hint at the existence of a network of dissident Mexican visionaries, unified by an alternative Lutheran-influenced piety. The possibility that such a network existed certainly troubled the Inquisition. However, the scattered indications that defendants, in fact, did endorse a unifying group of alternative spiritual concepts are too rare to demonstrate the existence of a cohesive heretical sect in New Spain. In the majority of cases the religious expressions of the people the court labeled *ilusos* and *alumbrados* consisted in paramystical encounters devoid of substantial theological content, orthodox or otherwise. Inquisitors were often forced to look elsewhere for verification of the authenticity of these mystics' spirituality.

Trial records also indicate that inquisitors must have privileged other means of determining mystics' legitimacy because the court sometimes condemned visionaries who voiced orthodox ideas, while releasing others whose spirituality appears heterodox. Getrudis Rosa Ortiz, an ilusa tried in 1723, first appeared before the court after posting a letter around several of Mexico City's churches and convents that she asserted God had dictated to her. Ortiz had seen visions of great fireballs God had sent from the heavens to punish New Spain's irreverent inhabitants.[25]

The calificadores who evaluated Ortiz's prophecy did not object to her apocalyptic beliefs, but they did disapprove of a number of other aspects of her vision. They dismissed as ridiculous the kind of offensive behavior that God told Ortiz had provoked his wrath. Ortiz revealed that the citizens of New Spain had angered God by worshipping him while dressed inappropriately. Ortiz observed that men entered church unshaven and with long hair while women presented themselves to worship in "dishonest outfits." Moreover, their clothing made it impossible to "distinguish the men from the women." The court's fiscal, Pedro Navarro de Isla, found Ortiz's preoccupations with these matters of dress were "ridiculous and impertinent" and, as such, demonstrated that her visions could not possibly have originated with God.[26] He may have deemed trivial Ortiz's preoccupation with women and men's religious apparel, but less than a century later no less an authority than the archbishop of Mexico endorsed this very idea. In 1808 Archbishop Francisco Javier de Lizana y Beaumont published a decree critical of "the custom of women appearing with their chests and arms revealed" at religious services.[27] Endorsement of orthodoxy, therefore, did not guarantee mystics immunity from inquisitorial condemnation. The Inquisition sometimes convicted visionaries who espoused heterodox ideas, but this issue alone cannot explain the reasons for the court's condemnation of some Mexican mystics and dismissal of charges against others.

The Demographics of Sanctity

The church's efforts to control the conferral of mystical legitimacy intensified in the early modern period when faced with the threats of the competing systems of Protestantism in Europe and African and indigenous paganism in the New World. However, these initiatives had a much older history. The papacy began restricting the qualification of sanctity in the twelfth and thirteenth centuries in response to the Cathar and Waldensian heresies. These groups induced Pope Gregory IX (1227–41) to establish the first tribunal of the medieval Inquisition while at the same time decreeing that papal canonization was the only legitimate means of establishing a saint cult.[28] Pope Urban VIII (1623–45) called for even greater clerical control in determining sanctity. He issued decrees banning all public veneration (including book publication) of any reputed saint until beatified or canonized by the papacy, and he prohibited canonization until at least fifty years after a person's death. Later in the seventeenth century the Council of Trent augmented these standards, and in the eighteenth century Pope Benedict XIV's five-volume *De Servorum Dei beatificatione et Beatorum Canonizatione* further intensified these guidelines, demanding stricter proof of the occurrence of miracles.[29]

In the context of this development of church-regulated sanctity, a profile emerged of the type of religious figure most likely to receive Rome's approbation for canonization. Those people who were most likely to become saints in the early modern world were wealthy, well-born, white male members of important religious orders from powerful European countries.[30] Between 1622 and 1758 Rome canonized forty-one saints. Eighteen of these were Spanish. Most were members of the regular clergy (either mendicants or Jesuits). Priests, preachers, missionaries, or founders of religious orders were the most successful candidates, but one king, one queen, and a few nuns also received the honor. Rome canonized few Latin Americans in the early modern period. The exceptions were Dominican beata Rose of Lima and Dominican missionary Luis Beltrán, both canonized in 1671, and Franciscan missionary Francisco Solano and the archbishop of Lima, Toribio de Mogrovejo, both canonized in 1726.

The same demographic guidelines applied to those figures the colonial Mexican church most revered, despite its failure to secure their status as saints. Most of the hagiographies produced in New Spain recorded the lives of male religious figures.[31] The papacy did beatify a number of Latin Americans during the colonial period and canonized some of these in the modern era. Both Mexicans beatified in the colonial era were male members of regular orders: San Felipe de Jesús, a Franciscan martyred in Japan in 1597, was beatified in 1627 and later canonized in the nineteenth century; San Sebastián de Aparicio was beatified in 1790. The Mexican church also supported lengthy and expensive canonization campaigns for two male peninsulares, seventeenth-century poblano bishop Juan de Palafox y Mendoza and sixteenth-century hermit Gregorio López. Access to the status of the sanctified became increasingly strict as Mexico's colonial period progressed.[32] None of the visionaries whom the Mexican Inquisition tried for false mysticism, needless to say, fit the ecclesiastical profile of holiness in every respect. From the outset of their trials, therefore, the court would likely have viewed all their claims to sanctity with suspicion, but it distrusted some visionaries more than others.

Spiritual guides that court officials studied in formulating their evaluations of ilusos and alumbrados directed readers to exercise great caution in supporting any mystics other than those who came from the ranks of the elite male clergy. The authors of these guides wrote that women's emotional nature predisposed them to the receipt of mystical gifts, but they also argued that women's fickleness and deviousness, coupled with the fact that they did not have access to the same channels of worldly power as men, meant that women were likely to fake the experience of receiving these gifts. Antonio Arbiol, for example, reproduced in his tract a discussion he had engaged in with a learned woman on this topic. She claimed that most women who wished to trick the world by feigning sanctity were from "the lower orders" and said that very rarely did a noble woman of "good blood" fall into such hypocrisy. She asserted that everyone desired both comfort and estimation in the world. Men could secure these things through art, science, or sanctity. Women, like men, she observed, also vainly desired popular esteem. Women born rich and noble, "since they already possess established positions in the world, do not look for estimation with invention; but as regards poor, ordinary, and common women . . . in being taken for virtuous and saintly, they gain public praise and are given enough for the convenience of their lives. They are easily tricked in this way by the devil, and for this reason, there are so many more ilusas and embusteras who are common women than there are rich and noble ones."[33]

Miguel Godínez expressed similar views in his *Practica*. He wrote that although it was not alarming when men of good position within the church experienced mystical visions, claims to such experiences made by "melancholic beatas in ecstasy in churches, as well as by any young nuns of little understanding," should always be viewed with suspicion. He also warned his readers against claims to sanctity professed by "disheveled, idiot, popular hermits who are friends of stupidity, applause, praise, and gifts."[34]

Mexican inquisitors were predisposed, then, to suspect claims to mystical sanctity that poor people, especially poor women, made. Court officials frequently concluded that such people only claimed mystical sanctity in order to secure material goods or social advancement. The colonial church sanctioned widespread material investment in the spiritual realm.[35] Nevertheless, it expected visionaries to embrace Saint Teresa's refrain that mystics should disdain and separate themselves from the world.[36] As Antonio de Arbiol asserted in his treatise on mysticism, "saintly souls, illuminated with the Catholic faith, in whom the superior part of reason is already prevailing, are credible witnesses that all the delightful tastes and prosperity of the world are repulsive in comparison to the lightest consolation of heaven."[37] Such lack of concern with the material world, however, was much easier for wealthy people to make—including those living within ecclesiastical institutions—because they might pursue mystical contemplation without a care for their material survival.

The court's scrutiny of ilusos' attachment to the material domain assumed a variety of different formulations. Often inquisitors judged that mystics had feigned their religious experiences in order to cloak themselves in veils of virtue so that they might satisfy their base appetites for sex, food, money, or status. Evidence of seventeenth-century hermit Pedro García de Arias's enjoyment of good food and drink, for example, dismantled his credibility as an authentic mystic. Two witnesses who presented evidence against García stated that they had long suspected his authenticity because he "was very fat and very colored [red-faced] and he let people bring him cheese and worms for sustenance." A third testified that García had asked him to find him a more comfortable mattress for his bed.[38]

The court also condemned many ilusos for supporting themselves financially through their religious practices. Getrudis Rosa Ortiz, an early-eighteenth-century mestiza who eventually managed to secure the patronage of the duquesa de Albuquerque, had partially supported herself for years on the meager donations she collected from people who had faith in her mystical revelations. Some donors had given her two pesos per month, others enough money to purchase a daily *torta* (flour cake), and a third couple donated enough money for the weekly purchase of one pound of chocolate. A califidador evaluating Ortiz's case condemned her because he believed she had only wanted to appear like a saint, "selling herself" principally "to collect alms and pay her expenses."[39]

Inquisitors most often convicted poor men and women who were not part of the institutional church, such as Getrudis Rosa Ortiz, for feigning sanctity. Priests and friars, most of whom were supporters of female visionaries, constituted the largest group of men denounced to the Inquisition for iluminismo and alumbradismo. Thirty-seven out of the 55 men accused were members of the clergy. Of this group, 18 were members of the regular orders—the majority of them Franciscans or Carmelites—

and 19 were members of the secular clergy. The court convicted 13 of these clerics; 4 died during their trials (see table 3 for a summary of conviction statistics). Laymen, a number of whom were fairly wealthy, experienced lower rates of conviction than did clerics. One layman, Juan Núñez, was an official of the mint. Another was a surgeon, and a third was a merchant. Others, including a weaver and an ironworker, occupied humbler positions. Laymen accounted for 11 of the men accused, 2 of those convicted, and 1 who died. The court, however, convicted all but 1 of the 7 beatos and ermitaños accused of false mysticism who lived to the completion of their trials.[40] Very few nuns were investigated, and none were convicted for these crimes. Of the 6 nuns who were accused, 2 were Clarisas, 1 was a Jeronymite, 1 was a Dominican, and 1 was a Capuchine; the order of the remaining nun is unknown. The majority of women accused and convicted were beatas: 24 of the 47 women accused were beatas; of these, 12 were found guilty. The remaining 17 were laywomen. Many women in this latter group supported themselves by working as cooks, servants, seamstresses, and healers. A number of them, however, had adopted spiritual lives virtually identical to those of beatas, informally professing religious vows and living mainly off alms and patronage received in exchange for the performance of spiritual works. The court, however, convicted these laywomen less frequently than it did beatas: 17 laywomen were denounced, but only 5 were convicted.

Threats to Institutional Authority

The Mexican tribunal was most suspicious when beatas, beatos, and ermitaños made claims to mystical sanctity. Ecclesiastical authorities grew increasingly apprehensive of beatas in the early modern period because their liberty from clerical supervision rendered them "susceptible to heretical spiritual practices and sexually aberrant behavior."[41] They lived outside the supervision of the convent and beyond the institution of marriage. For the church it thus became imperative that these women uphold the Christian virtues even more rigorously than cloistered women, who were safely isolated from public scrutiny and earthly temptation. Beatas were also threatening because they had access to some of the same social advantages as nuns but were not controlled by the same mechanisms. Like nuns, many beatas obtained release from familial obligations through their religious devotion while at the same time securing a measure of education, a degree of financial independence, and a claim to spiritual legitimacy for themselves. Yet, beatas were not constrained by the same restrictions—forced reclusion, mandatory obedience, and legislated poverty—as nuns. In many ways, then, beatas, particularly independent ones, were surprisingly powerful women.

The majority of the Mexican ilusa beatas were "lone" beatas who did not live in communal homes and were not officially affiliated with any of the religious orders. Only two Mexican mystics were identified as members of the third order of San Francisco. Another two wore Franciscan habits, but it is not clear if they were official terceras (members of the third order). [42] Most of the Mexican ilusa beatas came from fairly humble socioeconomic backgrounds. Eight of them worked as seamstresses, either before or while pursuing their spiritual vocations, one had previously been a teacher, and another, late-eighteenth-century María Lucía Celis, was a former prostitute. [43] A number of them had been in financially desperate situations before becoming beatas.

The Catholic church increasingly curtailed these women's social and spiritual independence as part of its campaign of control over women's religious expressions in the Counter-Reformation era. Tridentine reforms placed *beaterios* (communities of beatas) under the regular clergy's direct authority. Subsequently, ecclesiastics attempted to exert greater control over the activities of lone beatas as opposed to those who lived in communal beaterios or who were members of the tertiary orders. One late-sixteenth-century tract written by a group of inquisitors in Seville warned against the religious women who were at that time venturing out into the streets of the city to join alumbrado sects: "These beatas, who profess obedience to particular individuals, must not, under any circumstances, be allowed to continue with these actions, because it is clear that this behavior is due to the intervention of the Alumbrados of these times. . . . With these practices they sequester daughters from the service and obedience they owe their parents, and the women from their husbands, and they carry them along behind them and do not allow them to do anything nor allow them to confess with others." [44]

Authors of seventeenth- and eighteenth-century spiritual tracts published in Spain and Mexico continued to criticize beatas for their pretense of leading spiritual lives in order to avoid performing the physical labor more suited to their natures. [45] One early-eighteenth-century priest who testified against beata Beatriz de Jesús las Flores in a Mexican alumbrada trial expressed his profession's ongoing skepticism of lone beatas. He informed the court that he had no particular evidence to declare against Beatriz except "for that which I have seen of these women who wear such exterior habits, I have never had a good concept of them, for the experiences I have had of them in working for forty years as a curate"[46]

Ecclesiastics in Mexico had attempted to ban beatas from wearing religious habits outside of convents as early as the late sixteenth century because such women "wandered all over the place with too much liberty."[47] Beatas, however, continued to defy this mandate throughout the colonial period. The institutional church intensified its campaign against lone beatas in the late eighteenth century, in conjunction with the Bourbon monarchy's increased efforts to control many forms of popular spectacle in public spaces. At its fourth meeting in 1771 the Mexican Provincial Council passed an injunction directed specifically against beatas' dubious claims to spiritual legitimacy. It stated that with the pretext of devotion, "many women called Beatas wear, without license, the habit of some official religious order or other, at their own arbitrary decision, and are found roaming about from church to church and from house to house . . ." The decree also noted that Rome had issued several ordinances condemning such beatas and concluded that, under pain of excommunication, such women were henceforth prohibited from maintaining their independence from the control of "a rule or constitution approved of by the Apostolic See."[48] The decree also ordered that all third sisters or members of *cofradías* (confraternities) must also cease wearing the habits of particular religious orders.

The late-eighteenth-century archbishop of Mexico, Alonso Núñez de Haro y Peralta, vigorously reinforced the Provincial Council's censure of beatas' public circulation. In an edict published in 1790 the archbishop decreed that, under pain of excommunication, "no woman of any estate, class, quality, or condition may dress herself in the habit of a beata." Núñez condemned beatas' habits for novel reasons. He feared that the "thick, coarse cloaks" that entirely covered these women's faces and bodies "have provided the opportunity for various criminals who have adopted this dress to commit diverse crimes and excesses, and hide themselves from the sight of judges and magistrates, in this way achieving impunity for their acts."[49] In this document the archbishop implicated beatas, figures whom the Inquisition had already linked explicitly to the mystical fraud of alumbradismo, to the social fraud of thievery. By the late eighteenth century, beatas had thus become associated with urban crime, deception, and trickery.[50]

The church and the court were wary of male beatos' spiritual and social practices for related reasons. Beatos and ermitaños were the group most consistently and most severely punished for feigning mysticism. They were also the poorest men convicted. Three of the male beatos tried for false mysticism wore Franciscan habits, but only one was a formally recognized tercero. Four of the nine were peninsulares, and many of them had traveled a great deal before adopting their spiritual lives. Many testified to having endured periods of financial hardship before embracing their religious vocations. One hermit, Pedro García de Arias, told the court that he had earned money several different ways before becoming a religious man, including by selling fruit in the streets of Spain and working as a farmhand on ranches in Mexico; Juan Gómez had also previously worked as a farm laborer. Salvador Victoria had been a carpenter, and in his sentence the court mandated that he travel to the Philippines and work as a carpenter, building structures for the church's missionary efforts there. Baltasar Núñez de los Reyes, a former mariner and barber, continued to cut hair in conjunction with living his spiritual life.

These men often expressed their piety by writing or proclaiming spiritual ideas they claimed God had sent them. The court disapproved of their public criticisms of members of the clergy and the discrepancies between some of their propositions and contemporary doctrine. As with female beatas, the church also feared these men because they lived beyond the control of the regular orders. The Mexican Provincial Council of 1585 had prohibited religious people from living isolated, solitary lives outside the orders' control, but the church did not effectively enforce this dictate.[51]

Inquisition officials also objected to these men because beatos and hermits disputed the naturalness of their occupation of debased positions within New Spain's social hierarchy. Beatos and hermits were, for the most part, poor and uneducated men who had nevertheless determined themselves worthy of making lofty theological pronouncements. In the opening lines of their accusation against seventeenth-century beato Juan Bautista de Cárdenas, for example, his inquisitors wrote that they condemned Cárdenas because he was an ignorant man who had attempted to speak of spiritual matters. They described him as "a complete idiot of a man, without any education whatsoever, not even of grammar," who dared to "interfere and speak about parts of scripture."[52]

Pedro García de Arias, the seventeenth-century ermitaño who penned *Desengaños del alma*, posited that God often chose to enlighten people "without education, like myself." He observed that the first apostles were "apparently the most rustic social outcasts." The two calificadores who evaluated García's mystical tract wrote that "its author is an idiot and presumptuous as is evident in his writing." They condemned him for engaging himself with "material that he does not understand is superior to his capacity and status."[53] The court produced similar condemnations in the cases of every beato and hermit tried.[54]

The rates of accusation and conviction for beatas and beatos reveal that these groups invoked the court's greatest suspicion in false mysticism trials. However, these statistics also show that individuals' status vis-à-vis the institutional church was not the only factor that determined how the court would assess mystical legitimacy. The tribunal dismissed several accusations against laywomen and beatas while condemning other mystics, such as fray Agustín Claudio, who held positions within the ecclesiastical hierarchy. Demographic factors, although tremendously important, do not fully account for the court's decisions about which cases to pursue and which to dismiss.

Sanctity and Feminine Virtue

In forming its appraisals of authentic and false mysticism, the Holy Office scrutinized not only the content and nature of spiritual experiences but also the attributes of the visionaries who claimed to have had them.[55] The church required that women who aspired to mystical sanctity conform to a particular model of feminine virtue. Contemporary theologians encouraged all religious women to practice obedience, humility, chastity, and reclusion. Miguel Godínez wrote that theologians should always suspect people who had "many revelations, visions, raptures, and other favors, without sufficient penitence, humility and obedience." Such people demonstrated more of a "deceiving spirit than a true one, because it does not pertain to God, but rather to the Devil, to build golden spires of visions without first constructing the solid foundation of the moral virtues."[56] Mystics' obedience to their confessors was particularly important because these clerics were the one channel through which the church could control visionaries' otherwise unmediated relationships to God. Humility was necessary because "true" union with God could only occur once mystics had negated their own identities, humbling themselves completely in order to unite with the divine spirit.

Court officials followed these directives when judging the authenticity of Mexican mystics. The calificadores in María Manuela Picazo's early-eighteenth-century trial wrote, for instance, that Picazo's disobedience to both her confessor and her husband demonstrated the falsity of her mysticism. They further suspected Picazo because of the "indecent, scandalous postures" she had assumed in her ecstatic fits. Furthermore, her inquisitors scorned Picazo's claim to having saved the soul of one of her acquaintances, Margarita Bella, from purgatory because Bella, as everyone knew, "was a woman of bad credit, sensuality, and scandals."[57] In Getrudis Rosa Ortíz's trial, calificador Domingo de Quiroga deduced that Ortiz's visions could not possibly have come from God because true visions should "cause the moral virtues of obedience, humility, and patience to appear in the soul, and to cast the opposite vices away from it."[58] Yet Ortiz had obstinately disobeyed her confessor on several occasions and had arrogantly assumed she could interpret her visions without his consultation.

Theologians wrote that virtuous women should devote themselves exclusively to simple physical labors, rather than troubling themselves with lofty spiritual matters. They cautioned against curious women who aspired to exercise their intellects. In his 1705 *Desengaños mysticos*, Antonio Arbiol asked, "Is there nobody to tell curious women that they sin mortally, wanting to know by divine revelation that which it is not important for them to know?" Arbiol argued that "any person of good judgment recognizes that women must be laborers. A woman through the work of her hands is good, and maintains her Christian modesty with less difficulty the busier she is; because the more she attends to her work, the less modesty she loses looking to other things."[59] The Inquisition consistently censured women who "looked to other things," venturing in their spiritual curiosity into the domain of clerical religious power. In assessing Ana de Zayas, a laywoman divinely inspired to write spiritual tracts, her calificadores wrote that Zayas's self-reliant assessment of her visions' origins showed she saw herself the equal of a priest.[60] Other women erred when they treated the spirits who inspired them with too much familiarity. Marta de la Encarnación's inquisitors remarked, for example, that she "amused herself with the Christ child as if he were any old child in the streets."[61]

Ana de Zayas's confessor attempted to curtail her heretical intrusion into the masculine religious sphere by dissuading her from writing or even from engaging in mental prayer. He advised her only to recite the rosary and counseled her to leave her house only to attend mass or other religious celebrations. In one of his court appearances he informed the tribunal that Zayas must learn to "apply herself only to the work of embroidery [*de la almohadilla*], to suffering, to obeying her husband, and to complying with all that was her Christian duty."[62]

The court condemned Ana de Zayas and other similar mystics because they stepped beyond the realm of spirituality that the church had designated the female domain. Women who gained social power through their accumulation of spiritual patrons and clients also drew the Inquisition's condemnation much more frequently than women who had not secured such entourages. Cases of beatas who lacked large numbers of followers ended in conviction three times and were dismissed eight times. The Inquisition also convicted ilusas whose literacy made them socially threatening. Although many of the accused came from relatively humble backgrounds, a remarkably high percentage of them were literate.[63] In the colonial period literacy was a privilege normally available only to members of the social and economic elite, the clergy, and female religious, such as sor María de Jesús de Agreda and Saint Teresa of Avila, as illustrated in figures 1 and 3. Reading and writing were deemed superfluous skills for poor women, whose education, if they had any at all, consisted in religious teachings and instruction in handicrafts and physical skills.

Not only was literacy an economic and social privilege in the Counter-Reformation era, but the church even viewed its acquisition as dangerous for non-elites. As Jacqueline Holler observes, "the rise of Lutheranism and the spread of *alumbrado* and illuminist sects in the first half of the sixteenth century suggested that there were worse threats than superstition. The literate laity came to be viewed with suspicion, their literacy correlated with heresy."[64]

Many Mexican mystics overcame these practical and ideological barriers to the "lower order's" acquisition of literacy.[65] In her spiritual biography one late-eighteenth-century mulata ilusa, María Cayetana Loria, articulated an explicit connection between her acquisition of literacy and her mystical gifts. Cayetana was born in Ixmiquilpán, a small town nearly three hundred kilometers north of Mexico City. Both her mother and father, a weaver and laborer, died when she was quite young, and various siblings raised her. As an adult she worked as a cook and domestic servant. At the start of her vida her confessor, Ángel Vázquez, recounted how Cayetana's illiteracy had impeded her desire to perfect her religious education. As a young adolescent Cayetana had been greatly distressed because "although her parents had put her in a house where she could learn [reading], she had never been able to learn even the first letters of the *cartilla* [Christian reader]."[66]

Cayetana, fervently desiring to read a spiritual book, pledged to the Virgin Mary that "if she conceded to allow her to learn to read, she would never read anything in her life except spiritual and devout books. The Virgin apparently listened to Cayetana's appeal, because shortly thereafter, she picked up a *calendario* (calendar of religious celebrations) and miraculously understood it. Cayetana happily practiced her new skill for several years, consuming innumerable spiritual books. Then, on one occasion, rather than a religious tract, she selected Cervantes's *Don Quixote*, a work the Inquisition had banned. To her consternation she found she was unable to comprehend the scandalous novel. Astonishingly, however, she could still decipher a book of Christian doctrine. Falling to her knees, Cayetana begged "God a thousand pardons for seeing that in this miracle she had broken the promise she had made, which up to the present day she has never broken again and has never read any book except devout and spiritual ones." [67] Cayetana's miracle appears designed to demonstrate how rare it would have been for a woman of her race and social position to become literate. Miracles are necessary when normal circumstances make it impossible for something to occur; without the Virgin Mary's supernatural intervention, Cayetana could never have learned to read.

Contemporary Anxieties, Shifting Influences
The Inquisition considered a variety of factors including the espousal of heretical ideas, status within the church, and adherence to appropriate gender codes in formulating its judgments of mystical authenticity and fraud. Yet these issues do not fully account for the temporal patterns that convictions of alumbrados and ilusos followed in seventeenth- and eighteenth-century Mexico. A fifty-year lull in which the court opened only one case followed the first cluster of trials held at the beginning of the seventeenth century. Starting in 1649, the Holy Office investigated false mystics at a steady pace for the remainder of the colonial era, although prosecutions intensified during the last two decades of both the seventeenth and eighteenth centuries. It is likely that the Catholic church's contemporaneous preoccupation with other types of religious crimes in the mid- and late seventeenth century accounts for the tribunal's intensified interest in false mysticism in this era. New Spain's shifting intellectual, political, and demographic climate at the close of the eighteenth century may explain this second period of heightened prosecution.

The court opened its mid-seventeenth-century false mysticism trials while it was engaged in the most vigorous campaign against crypto-Judaism of the colonial era. Suspicion that Mexican alumbrados also participated in such heretical practices colored the court's perception of both the late-sixteenth- and mid-seventeenth-century trials. Starting in the second half of the seventeenth century, however, the Inquisition more often created associations between Mexican mystics and the Lutheran heresy. In this period the Catholic church intensified its persecution of a wide variety of spiritual practices it identified as "quietist."[68] Quietists emphasized the idea of the soul's passivity in its union with God, rendering the divine will solely responsible for humanity's practice of virtue. Cornelius Jansen and Miguel de Molinos were two of the principle figures associated with quietist beliefs in both Spain and its colonies, and the papacy issued injunctions against the writings of both men in the mid-seventeenth century.[69] The increase in convictions against false mystics in Mexico in the same period was in part due to associations the court's officials created between alumbradismo, jansenismo, and molinismo.

Inquisitors and calificadores explicitly pointed to this association in their judgments. The first item of a 1694 accusation against Ana de Zayas stated, for example, that the court suspected Zayas because during an ecstatic fit she had learned through divine inspiration "that faith was the evident sign of predestination."[70] Her judges argued that this revelation demonstrated that she was guilty of the "heresies of Jansenism and Pelagianism."[71]

The Mexican court articulated its earliest explicit association between alumbradista and molinista practices in the 1713 trial against beato Baltasar Núñez de los Reyes. Among other acts, the Inquisition investigated Núñez for his declaration that God had told him that he required no priestly mediator and should confess directly to him. The tribunal accused Núñez of being an "iluso, alumbrado, presumed embustero, hypocrite, practitioner of the errors of Molinos, as well as suspected of Lutheranism."[72] Most of the subsequent charges linking alumbrados with molinistas occurred later in the century and involved denunciations of male clerics. Fifteen eighteenth-century cases of molinismo appeared before the court, ten of which involved joint accusations for false mysticism; nine of these were directed at clerics.

Both the new philosophies of the Enlightenment and the Bourbon monarchy's reforms of New Spain may account for the increase in charges against mystics in the last decades of the eighteenth century. Starting in midcentury, the Bourbons secularized the colony's ecclesiastical institutions, mandating in 1749 that all *doctrinas* (parishes), which up until then had been under the direction of the regular orders, would pass to the jurisdiction of the secular clergy. The Bourbon monarchy in this period also discouraged popular campaigns for the canonization of mystics and other revered individuals, viewing them as unnecessarily extravagant. For example, after he assumed the throne in 1759 Charles III withdrew the crown's support for Gregorio López's beatification campaign.[73]

The strengthened secular church promoted new forms of "rationalized" spirituality in the viceroyalty.[74] This transformation entailed a reorientation of religious practice away from excessive asceticism, the veneration of saints, and the celebration of festivals and toward a more subdued style of religious worship.[75] In this period the church particularly targeted the popular devotions of Indian and mestizo Christian groups.[76] In consequence of this reorientation the gulf widened between the spiritual practices Mexican mystics engaged in and those the institutional church defined as orthodox.

During the seventeenth century and the first half of the eighteenth century court officials frequently rejected the validity of iluso paramystical experiences because they believed that the devil, rather than God, had induced them. In the trials of Mariana de San Miguel, Agustina Rangel, and Antonia de Ochoa, for example, the court's qualifiers wrote that they judged the defendants guilty because they suspected the devil had possessed or made pacts with these women. The court did not dismiss outright the legitimacy of the kinds of supernatural phenomena such mystics experienced—ecstatic fits or bouts of levitation—but it believed that the devil rather than God had caused them.

After the mid-eighteenth century, however, the tribunal adopted an increasingly rationalist view of the source of defendants' guilt and was often hesitant to accept the legitimacy of supernatural displays as evidence of God's favor. In their qualification of late-eighteenth-century lay ilusa Ana de Aramburu, for instance, fray Cosmé Enríquez and fray Domingo Barreda wrote that they doubted that "the devil had any part" in causing the locutions and ecstasies Aramburu experienced. They concluded instead that nothing more than her "mundane spirit" had inspired her.[77] In his late-eighteenth-century assessment of María Cayetana Loria, calificador Matías de Navera wrote that he suspected that Cayetana's participation in heterodox practices had not been "caused by the devil, but rather by a natural inclination she had, born from her mother."[78]

Indians, Africans, and the Prosecution of False Mysticism

The court doubted María Cayetana Loria's mystical authenticity for a number of reasons. For one, as is further explored in the next chapter, her visions contained heretical depictions of the Virgin Mary. Her status as a female laywoman of questionable sexual virtue made her suspect as a legitimate mystic. Moreover, she experienced her visions in a period in which the church was discouraging popular religious practices involving supernatural experiences. María Cayetana's mulata identity played a decisive role in the Inquisition's classification of her as a false mystic. Contemporary social anxieties about race mixture, racial passing, and the influences Indians and Africans might exert on Christianity all contributed to the Mexican Inquisition's intolerance of iluso and alumbrado spirituality in the seventeenth and eighteenth centuries.

As a rule the colonial church was suspicious of the religious piety of all but peninsular or criollo Christians. Only a scattering of mestizos and even fewer Indians became priests or friars in the colonial era, and various segments of the ecclesiastical church objected to the construction of convents for Indian women in eighteenth-century New Spain. [79] In those exceptional cases when non-Spaniards became figures admired for their Christian devotion, it was often necessary for them to undergo symbolic racial transformations in order to receive endorsement from some branches of the institutional church. As Ronald Morgan's perceptive analysis of Catarina de San Juan, "La China Poblana," demonstrates, in order that this unusual character might become an acceptable object of saintly devotion, her contemporary biographer transformed her racial, religious, and social origins. [80]

Catarina, a woman born to noble parents in the Mogul empire of India, had been captured as a child by Portuguese slave traders, bestowed upon Jesuit missionaries in Manila, and purchased as a domestic servant by a merchant family in Puebla, Mexico. She became a popular figure of religious devotion in the seventeenth century. In detailing her origins in the three-volume biography he published shortly after her death, Jesuit Alonso Ramos transformed Catarina from a foreign, non-Christian slave into a noble, Christian white woman. Ramos conferred nobility on Catarina by theorizing that her grandfather might have been the great Mogul ruler Akbar (1556–1605), a pious Sunni Muslim. Ramos attempted to Christianize Catarina's birth by writing that her mother, when pregnant with Catarina, had seen visions of the Virgin Mary. Although her father may have been Muslim, Ramos underscored the parallels between Islam and Christianity by noting that in Catarina's early childhood her father prohibited idolatry at home, practiced monogamy, and did public penance. Later in her vida Ramos wrote that Catarina had seen visions of her parents' conversion to Christianity and of the baptism of great numbers of people in her homeland. Ramos also implied that La China Poblana had been born white. He wrote that she had begun her life as a girl "of rare beauty, her color more white than brownish, her hair more silvery than golden." As she aged, however, she became "more like a brown-skinned china than a white, fair-haired Mughal woman; more like a nut-brown Indian, that is, one of the darkest in all of the Occident, than like a white, beautiful Orientess from the region of Arabia Felix."[81]

Presumably, Ramos could not describe Catarina de San Juan as a white woman, two years after her death, to an audience of poblanas who knew her appearance well. Instead, he rendered her white, noble, and Christian by birth. Catarina de San Juan may have technically originated as a person who did not fit the colonial church's demographic profile of a likely candidate for mystical sanctity. However, Ramos's vida transformed her into a figure more compatible with this model.[82] The Inquisition's later banning of her adoration suggests, however, that some of the same forces that rendered suspect a number of those tried for iluminismo and alumbradismo also applied to its view of La China Poblana.[83]

The church particularly scrutinized all non-Spaniards who claimed to be mystics in colonial Mexico, but the majority of those who made such claims were white criollos. The church's racial anxieties directed at this population centered on its fear that African and indigenous religious practices might have influenced Christian mystics. Philip II had removed Mexico's indigenous population from the Holy Office's scope of inquiry in 1571. However, after this date inquisitors continued to monitor the influences that indigenous people, who formed the majority of New Spain's population throughout the colonial period, exerted on its other inhabitants.[84] The Iberian tribunals of the Spanish Inquisition, as Mary E. Giles writes, safeguarded Christianity from Islamic and Jewish influences, whereas their Mexican counterpart primarily "guarded against the blurring of boundaries between Catholicism and folk piety."[85] Given the demographic structure of New Spain, this folk piety necessarily entailed some indigenous and African elements.[86]

The Catholic church attempted to safeguard Indians and blacks from the poor example that less than exemplary Spanish Christians set for them. The calificadores in Getrudis Rosa Ortiz's trial wrote, for instance, that her religious practices were fearful in part because she might easily introduce her "errors and heresies among the vulgar mulatos and Indians because of their lack of reflection and prudency." [87] The church was also wary, however, of the potential impact such vulgar people might exert on New Spain's Christian inhabitants. The first meeting of the Mexican Provincial Council standardized the Christian doctrine the church attempted to enforce in New Spain for the next two centuries. In 1555 this body decreed that people who visited "sorcerers, spell makers, or diviners," three titles the church used to describe African and indigenous religious leaders, posed some of the gravest threats to the upholding of Christian orthodoxy in the colony.[88] The fear that Christians, particularly Spaniards, continued to frequent such figures endured into the last decades of the colonial era.[89] At the fourth meeting of the Council in 1771 a number of clerics articulated their fear that many Spaniards continued to frequent Indian religious and medical healers.[90] The Inquisition also prosecuted Spaniards for frequenting indigenous curanderos.

Mexican ilusos and alumbrados sometimes engaged in religious practices that resembled elements of both indigenous shamanism and African spirit possession.[91] The type of supernatural phenomena Mexican visionaries most frequently experienced after the mid-seventeenth century were visions of the state of others' souls, and the most frequent miracles they worked were the removal of these souls from purgatory. Many of them used substances, including tobacco, chocolate, and peyote to cure their clients of both physical and spiritual ailments. Some of the mystics, possessed by otherworldly spirits, also demanded to be fed chocolate, tobacco, or other foodstuffs.

The ability to remove souls from purgatory was a power that mystics within the European Christian tradition claimed. This ability, and many other practices in which ilusos and alumbrados engaged, however, were also common to African and indigenous curanderismo. Indian or African influences may account for the centrality in the Mexican alumbrado trials after 1650 of visions and miracles that focused on the state of others' souls. The Nahuas—the dominant indigenous group in central Mexico—held a belief in an animating force bearing some resemblance to the Christian idea of the soul, which they called *tonalli*.[92] Sometimes a person's tonalli could be "lost" because of injuries to the head, the site of its principal location. The tonalli might also be harmed through the force of divine wrath for impious, licentious, or arrogant behavior. Finally, the tonalli might leave the body of its own will if attracted to a more desirable place.

The tonalli could be restored to the body through the application of a variety of cures, but as Alfredo López Austin writes, they all served the central purpose of "bartering for the patient's 'shadow.'" In current medical practice in Mexico, which likely preserves many colonial roots, this "bargaining" is accomplished by tempting the tonalli back to the body with such substances as flowers, incense, or tobacco or by proposing to trade such items as chocolate, brandy, chili peppers, or red ribbons to the beings who had captured the tonalli. [93] It is possible that African beliefs influenced this Nahua belief in the colonial period. [94] Africans in Guinea, the Congo, and Angola also had a belief in a counterpart of the personality, called a "shadow," which abandoned the body at night and could be captured and harmed by a sorcerer. If the shadow was harmed while outside the body, a doctor was needed to restore it to the sick person. [95]

Mexican mystics, as described in chapter 2, intermittently incorporated chocolate, tobacco, and peyote in their enactment of spiritual cures and experiences of spiritual possession. Indigenous beliefs may have influenced iluso paramysticism in other ways. Several Mexican mystics experienced fits during which they vomited a variety of objects. The alumbrado trial of madre Paula Rosa de Jesús, for example, began when her confessor wrote to the court about the repeated fits this early-eighteenth-century nun had suffered during which she "spat through her mouth pegs, wire pendants, and nails." Another nun in the convent described similar episodes, saying that she had witnessed Paula Rosa having several fits in which she coughed up hair, large nails, and pins. [96] The Inquisition interpreted these episodes and similar ones in other alumbrado trials as diabolic fits or as the feigning of such fits. Yet these episodes also resemble the cures that indigenous curanderas sometimes used to address their clients' spiritual and physical maladies. [97] Further evidence of African and Indian influences on ilusos' religious practices is even more explicit. Ignacio de San Juan Salazar, an early-eighteenth-century mestizo beato, who was described as possessing the ability to "speak the language of the blacks," had cured several people in his community by using a rooster and a cat. [98] Both indigenous and African curanderos used animals and animal spirits as healing agents.

In some cases during their mystical episodes ilusos rendered the religious figures who inspired them Indian or African. Mid-seventeenth-century beata María de la Encarnación, for example, described seeing angels dressed in "clothes of Indians" in one of her fits. [99] In three of the trials (one of a castiza and two of mestizos) the accused described themselves as turning into black people in the midst of their mystical experiences.[100]

This evidence suggests that indigenous and African beliefs did exert some influence on the religious practices of some Mexican alumbrados, although the degree to which this occurred is less clear. It is undeniable, however, that the issue of African and indigenous influences on Christian mystics deeply troubled both officers of the Mexican Inquisition and a number of the residents of New Spain who testified before it. One of the witnesses who testified in the trial of mid-seventeenth-century beata Teresa Romero recounted how he had been "scandalized" to find that after she had experienced a mystical rapture in his house, "she got up and went to the kitchen, and was joking and laughing with the black men and women who were there and with a little mestizo [*mesticillo*] who she was in love with"[101] The court also condemned Teresa's "scandalous" practice of entering Indians' homes.[102]

In his tract on the determination of authentic mysticism, repro-duced within the pages of an eighteenth-century Inquisition tome, fray Francisco de Jesús María described another way in which the church linked indigenous idolatry to false mysticism. Fray Francisco wrote that inquisitors should understand as false any vision in which Christ, the Virgin, or an angel "appeared in the manner in which they are painted," because they should not appear as painted images since they were, in fact, of a "superior order." He argued that it was wrong for people to adore such visions because "it is not the same to adore the image of Christ as to adore the living Christ who actually appears, because one must not adore the image, but rather what it represents." Linking the practices of false mystics to errors associated with Indian spirituality, fray Francisco asserted that the worship of false images was characteristic of cases of "abominable idolatry."[103]

The trial of early-eighteenth-century Indian curandera María "*La Colorada*" further illustrates this phenomenon of the cross-identification of false mystics with indigenous paganism. Because she was an Indian, the court of the Provisorato del ordinario, rather than the regular Inquisition, tried María.[104] Two mestiza women, at the urging of an officer of the Provisorato, denounced María to the court in the spring of 1713. They, along with several other witnesses, including their Spanish employer, Francisca de Solis, testified about the various *hechizos* (spells) María had executed. They accused her of providing them with powders and herbs, including *pipilizintli* (which the Inquisition had banned), to execute love magic and cure diseases.[105] They also claimed that María had performed elaborate rites in which she invoked the saints in order to divine the location of lost objects. Adopting the labels to describe María's crimes that the inquisitorial tribunal had generated, the Provisorato convicted María for being an ilusa and embustera and charged her with making pacts with the devil. The inquisitorial court, meanwhile, launched an investigation into María's Spanish and mestiza clients.

The perception that African and indigenous practices exerted an influence on Christian mystics troubled the Inquisition. Elites were wary of the potential threats posed by the indigenous and black populations who provoked revolts in New Spain in 1611, 1665, and 1671.[106] Mestizos and Indians also played a central role in two urban riots in Mexico City in 1624 and 1692.[107] But rather than illustrating Spanish fears of riot and rebellion, the racial dimensions of the Inquisition's condemnation of false mysticism reflected broader social anxieties about race mixture and racial, religious, and social "passing" in New Spain. Missionaries had long feared Indians' ability to feign their adoption of Christianity. Sixteenth-century Franciscan fray Bernardino de Sahagún used the term *embustes* to describe the survival of indigenous customs among supposedly Christian Indians.[108] This is the same term the Inquisition used to identify the feigned mystical practices of Ana Rodríguez de Castro y Aramburu, whom it also labeled an *embustera* and *engañadora* (trickster and deceiver).

The court also applied the labels *embustera* and *engañadora* to many others tried for false mysticism. Starting in the last third of the seventeenth century, the court labeled ten defendants *embusteros* as well as feigners of mysticism. In the seventeenth and eighteenth centuries the Mexican tribunal most often used the label *embustero* to designate those who cured people with powders, bones, rocks, or other charms. Many of the people accused of these crimes were mulatos or mestizos (see appendix 2 for a summary of 30 eighteenth-century *embustero* cases surveyed). The Inquisition most often convicted embusteros whose religious practices had clearly influenced Christian Spaniards, or who had mixed elements of Christian practices with African or indigenous rites.[109] The court convicted one eighteenth-century embustero, for example, because he was a Spanish tailor who had used the remedies of his mulata slave to achieve romantic and gambling success.[110] A second of those convicted was a black slave who had invoked Christian saints in his cures.[111]

The court guarded against intermixing and passing that occurred in social status terms as well as racial and religious ones. In his tract fray Francisco de Jesús María condemned visionaries who attempted to assume higher positions in colonial society than those into which they had been born. He wrote of two cases in which mystics demonstrated their falsity in visions they had seen of themselves occupying prestigious positions in colonial society. Midway through his treatise, fray Francisco warned his audience against mystics who claimed to have had visions in which they "showed themselves to be very loved by God and stated that they would do very good and admirable works and that they did not need to pass by the broad path like the others did, but rather were to become bishops or reform the religious orders."[112]

Among such false claims he cited the example of Mexican alumbrada Agustina de Santa Clara, who had informed her confessor, Juan Plata, that he was destined to become the pope. Fray Francisco also discussed the case of a woman who had made a public announcement that her husband was fated to become the viceroy of New Spain. Fray Francisco declared that both these cases contained nothing but "lies and idiocies," because "rather than teaching us that a simple priest could be elevated to the dignity of the papacy or that a certain gentleman must be the viceroy of New Spain, God's spirit teaches us humility, mortification, loathing of the flesh, and suffering." [113] Fray Francisco's concerns, like those of the court officials who tried Mexican mystics, matured in a period that witnessed the growing expansion of New Spain's mixed-race population and a culture that grew increasingly anxious about racial mixing, passing, and social mobility. [114]

Conclusion

The Mexican tribunal of the Holy Office employed a complex set of criteria in order to assess mystical legitimacy. In some cases its officers based their evaluations on contraventions of orthodox doctrine that mystics espoused. In the context of the Counter-Reformation the court was particularly wary of ilusos who expressed doubts about elements of the Christian miracles and mysteries or who posited controversial ideas about human and divine will. The Inquisition, however, considered many other factors apart from the content of mystics' spirituality when assessing their authenticity. Some of the people labeled *ilusos* and *alumbrados* did espouse heretical ideas, but in many instances, their piety greatly resembled that of bona fide mystics whom the church endorsed. In seventeenth- and eighteenth-century Mexico the Holy Office often based its evaluations of spiritual fraud on the consideration of defendants' comportment according to standards of morality and social behavior deemed appropriate to their sex, economic status, and relationship to ecclesiastical institutions.

Late colonial Mexico's heightened anxieties about the rise of the criollo and mixed-race populations also influenced the court's—and the public's—concern with any figures who attempted to "pass" themselves off as something they were not. Furthermore, the Inquisition's suspicion of other "deviant" religious groups—crypto-Jews, Protestants, quietists, Indians, and Africans—also shaped the reasons for, and timing of, its prosecution of ilusos and alumbrados.

In many cases the Inquisition did not found its assessments of false mystics on the examination of the accused parties' spiritual experiences, but rather on the evaluation of those who claimed to have had them. The tribunal condemned beatas, beatos, and ermitaños who violated class and educational barriers. It convicted some women whose curiosity and confidence had prompted them to shun the feminized Christian virtues of obedience and others who had abandoned the feminized confines of experiential mysticism in their attempts to enter the masculine and clerical domain of theological doctrine. Frequently, those convicted of being ilusos and alumbrados failed to embody the Christian virtue of humility. They neglected to expurgate their own identities while simultaneously claiming to experience authentic mysticism. Their unequivocal assertions of spiritual self-worth point us toward an understanding of why inquisitorial authorities viewed these people with such trepidation. What other claims of validity might individuals aver who recognized their own spiritual worth in the eyes of God? The Inquisition sought to restore humility and obedience in these mystics and to negate the legitimacy of the claims to autonomous spiritual worthiness they themselves made.

Four

Orthodoxy and Heterodoxy in
the Visions of Ilusos and Alumbrados

"I saw Our Lord Jesus Christ crucified and suspended in the air very high and very distant from Mexico." So began a vision that Getrudis Rosa Ortiz, a poor mestiza laywoman, described for the judges of the Holy Office near the outset of her 1723 trial in Mexico City. "I could not distinguish what material the cross was made of, nor if the Lord was alive or dead. But I did see that a great flow of water that trickled in many drops was coming from the wound of his right side and falling on a great multitude of men and women who were on the ground under the cross with their mouths open, and who received in them these drops of water."[1]

As was the case for many of those investigated for false mysticism, apparitions constituted the most significant feature of Ortiz's religious expressions. Her trial is replete with intricate visual descriptions of the sacred scenes with which God filled her imagination. Her visions touched on a remarkably wide variety of subjects, portraying such momentous occasions as the most significant Christian mysteries as well as more localized revelations about the intimate lives of people in her Veracruz parish.

Ortiz started seeing imaginary representations of Christ in her childhood. When she was an adolescent, the image of Christ suspended on the cross above Mexico City appeared to her repeatedly. During the last period in which she witnessed the Crucifixion apparition, Ortiz perceived that "the drops of water that fell out of the side of the Lord were converted into fat pearls, and in this form those below received them in their mouths, like they had done with the water, and then I could better distinguish than before the people who received this gift, and I knew that there were men and women, and white faces and black ones among them."[2]

For a period of ten or twelve years after witnessing this apparition, Ortiz remained ignorant of its significance. Then one day God spoke to her while she prayed and told her that the vision she had seen of the water and the pearls signified the "conversion of these infidels." Later in her trial Ortiz described a similar vision to the court in which she perceived that her soul traveled in spirit to distant lands to accompany "Padre Marxil" on his missionary enterprises. She had assisted Marxil, she stated, in preaching "to many people, without knowing more than that they were many men and women, all mixed together, not knowing if they were blacks or whites." Another witness confirmed that Ortiz referred, in her vision, to Antonio Margil de Jesús, a Franciscan missionary who journeyed to Guatemala, Zacatecas, and Texas in the late seventeenth and early eighteenth centuries.[3] Seventeenth-century Spanish nun María de Jesús de Agreda had set an orthodox precedent of spiritual journeys undertaken to proselytize indigenous people who lived in these remote territories.[4]

Ortiz had begun her education in religious imagery early. She testified that one of her brothers-in-law who had helped raise her worked "adorning and setting up churches." She also claimed that since the age of four she had spent many hours each week meditating, confessing, and taking communion in a number of Mexico City's churches, including the cathedral, the parish church of Veracruz, and those of Santa Catarina and La Misericordia. Her religious imagination was steeped in the imagery of the religious paintings that covered the walls of these buildings. She would likely have contemplated these forms as she prayed, and they clearly influenced the ways she perceived her religious visions. She testified, for instance, that she had seen figures in one apparition of the Trinity "dressed in their costumes, as they are normally painted."[5] It is no surprise, then, that many of the iconographic elements that featured in Ortiz's vision of Christ are consistent with those contained in seventeenth- and eighteenth-century Mexican paintings of the crucifixion.

In her vision Ortiz specifically situated the cross over Mexico City, a common motif in the viceroyalty's sacred art that sought to demonstrate the Christian sanctity of New World locales.[6] In Cristóbal de Villalpando's *La Mística Ciudad de Dios*, for example, the figure of Mary associated with her Immaculate Conception floats above a walled city, denoted as the Mística Ciudad de Dios, the same title as sor María de Jesús de Agreda's celebrated biography of the Virgin Mary (see figure 1). Villalpando uses imagery to suggest in this piece that Spain's New World colonies were destined heirs of the Christian missionary enterprise. The "Mystical City" depicted in this work, rather than Jerusalem, is a city in Spain's overseas empire. Its architectural style is reminiscent of the Spanish Baroque, and the archangel Michael, symbolizing Christianity's triumph over the forces of diabolic paganism in New Spain, heralds Mary's Immaculate Conception over it.

Ortiz's fusing of two separate Christian sacraments—baptism and the Eucharist—in her vision also echoes contemporary artistic tableaux. One anonymous seventeenth-century work, *Bautizando los cuatro señores de Tlaxcala*, depicts Hernán Cortés assisting in the baptism of four Tlaxcalan caciques (hereditary Indian governors) instrumental in the conquest of Mexico. An image of Christ, suspended on the crucifix, hovers above.[7]

The sacred art of colonial Mexico seems to have partially fulfilled its creators' intent, then, of instructing viewers such as Ortiz on the orthodox visualization of significant elements of Christian dogma. However, several elements of Ortiz's vision also indicate that despite her immersion in instructional sacred art, she frequently diverted from convention in her own visualizations of religious episodes. In contemporary representations of the sacrament of baptism, including *Bautizando los cuatro señores de Tlaxcala* and Villalpando's *Bautizo de la Virgen*, now hanging in Mexico City's basilica of Guadalupe, the sacred baptismal water is always contained within a holy vessel held by a representative of the church. Ortiz's depiction of the baptismal/Eucharist substance flowing directly from Christ's side wound into the mouths of the "infidel" bypassed Tridentine orthodoxy's requirement of clerical mediation between human and divine contact. Her visualization parallels her own claim to having directly received God's spiritual teachings through her visions and thus suggests one reason for the image's disfavor among its clerical evaluators.

The second notable diversion from orthodoxy in Ortiz's Crucifixion apparition concerns the composition of the population she described awaiting conversion. Ortiz stated that the vision represented the conversion of "the infidel." Rather than linking this label to the indigenous population, its largest and most likely recipient in New Spain, however, Ortiz carefully specifies that in her vision both women and men, "blacks and whites," gathered below the cross to await baptism from the substances flowing from Christ's blessed wounds. Ortiz's observation that women as well as men formed the crowd that gathered below Christ is consistent with many contemporary paintings that dealt with this theme, including Miguel Cabrera's *Alegoría de la Preciosa Sangre* (Museo del Virreinato,

Figure 1. *La Mística Ciudad de Dios*, Cristóbal de Villalpando, Museo Regional de Guadalupe. Photo courtesy of Archivo Fotográfico Instituto de Investigaciones Estéticas, Universidad Nacional Autónoma de México (IIE-UNAM). Reproduction authorized by the Instituto Nacional de Antropología e Historia.

Tepozotlán, México), but her pointed inclusion of blacks in this group was unusual.

The religious art of colonial Mexico depicted blacks very infrequently. The figure of San Martín de Porres, a sixteenth-century Dominican mulato from Lima, did occasionally appear in colonial paintings and sculptures in New Spain, but Mexican devotion to this saint became widespread only after his nineteenth-century beatification. Blacks were commonly represented in eighteenth-century casta paintings, but such works normally accorded them very negative—and secular—connotations, linking them to racial degeneration, poverty, and violence.[8] As a rule, black figures appeared in only religious paintings representing the adoration of the magi, as representatives of the African continent, or else as secondary figures whose iconographic attributes suggest they were slaves.[9]

Ortiz's uncommon inclusion of blacks in this vision and many others may indicate her belief that blacks as well as whites required—and were worthy of—conversion from heterodoxy. Ortiz could not base such an assertion on models derived from the imagery of sacred art. Instead, her personal and social experiences must have influenced her formulation of this idea. Getrudis Rosa Ortiz was a poor woman who had survived on charity for much of her life. Like most of the non-elite population of urban Mexico, she lived, worked, and socialized with people from many different ethnic backgrounds—Indians, mestizos, mulatos, and Spaniards—who populated the viceroyalty's cities.

In the spring of 1723 Ortiz, who was illiterate, had begun dictating to her brother the messages God sent her. The two of them, assisted by a Spanish woman called Isabel Eusebia Mercado, then posted copies of these notices around several Mexico City churches and convents, including those of San Jerónimo, la Encarnación, and San José de la Gracia. A cleric, alerted to the posting of the notices, sent several copies to the Inquisition.[10] The documentation from the opening stages of Ortiz's trial, when her inquisitors were attempting to confirm her status and whereabouts, reveals the kinds of intimate relationships Ortiz had established in both her secular and sacred life with people of various ethnicities.

One of the witnesses interrogated at this stage of the trial, for example, was a mulato water porter, Domingo Antonio de Ribera. Ribera, who lived in Ortiz's neighborhood, knew Isabel Eusebia Mercado. It is likely that Ribera also knew, or knew of, Ortiz as well since they were neighbors. Yet when the court questioned him as to whether he had any knowledge of letters containing "threats and prophecies" that had been posted around the city, Ribera claimed total ignorance.[11] He may have been telling the truth. However, given the public notoriety of Ortiz's visions, it is more likely that Ribera, perhaps on friendly commercial or personal terms with Ortiz and Mercado, denied knowledge of the letters in order to protect one or both women from the Inquisition's inquiries.

There are some indications that Ortiz might have had African origins. She identified herself to the court as a mestiza, but other witnesses suggested she was a mulata. Isabel Eusebia Mercado described Ortiz as "a single woman, somewhat black," and one of Ortiz's former confessors classified her as "mestiza or mulata."[12] Ortiz, although instructed in the artwork that constituted the most important element of her religious education that blacks had little claim to Christian religious power, clearly believed in the legitimacy of her own visions. Surely she would not have subjected them to the public scrutiny of Mexico's ecclesiastical and political authorities had she not been fully confident of their authenticity. In contravention of conventional orthodoxy, Ortiz's Crucifixion vision, as well as other visions she experienced, expressed her faith that people of a variety of racial and social positions within the colony could, legitimately, rise to positions of great power within God's sacred sphere.

Getrudis Rosa Ortiz, like many other ilusos and alumbrados, drew heavily from the religious imagery of colonial Mexican art in the formulation of her visions. She wove orthodox iconography, styles, and scenes from this work into her visions, and they retained considerable fidelity to these influences. Yet she also incorporated ideas, episodes, and attitudes absent from the corpus of colonial artwork into her revelations. The examination of the modifications that Ortiz and other Mexican visionaries made to canonical religious art permits us one of the closest views of the sacred imaginations of non-elite people in colonial Mexico that we may ever be afforded.

Religious Art and the Formulation of Mystical Visions

Religious art played a vital role in the proselytizing efforts of the Counter-Reformation Catholic church. Visual representations served as some of the most important sources from which the illiterate—in Mexico and elsewhere—learned about religious concepts and biblical personages. The fundamental contribution of sacred art to the religious culture of orthodox Christianity in New Spain is no better illustrated than in the story of the Virgin of Guadalupe. Her most important miracle authenticating her appearance to Juan Diego in 1531 on the hill of Tepeyac that would later house her basilica was, after all, the creation of a miraculous painting.[13]

In the mid-sixteenth century the Council of Trent endorsed the use of sacred art to indoctrinate the populace, move the emotions of the devout, or inspire cults of devotion. The colonial Mexican church embraced this initiative but was wary of the possible idolatry, superstition, or irreverence sacred art might provoke if carelessly regulated.[14] Trent mandated that the ecclesiastical hierarchy should retain strict control over the production of religious images, and the Mexican Provincial Councils, wary of the sacrilege indigenous artists might introduce into such work, issued repeated directives endorsing this position. The colonial church was able to control artistic production because it was one of the few institutions with access to the financial resources necessary for artists' sponsorship. Before granting commissions to execute sacred images, the church required sculptors and painters in New Spain to undergo rigorous theological examinations to ensure the production of orthodox representations.[15] The Inquisition also fostered an environment that discouraged artists from departing from pictorial orthodoxy.[16]

The church viewed sacred art as an ideal medium for instructing the populace about saints' lives and complex theology. It was also well suited to the Tridentine mandate of promoting ceremonial forms of worship. As Elisa Vargaslugo writes, "religion and baroque art intimately related images with devotion and prayer, in the effort to produce visions and sensations of the supernatural world with the assistance of concrete forms."[17] Sacred art facilitated viewers' reception of religious ideas and provided them with a tangible means of imagining such abstract and incredible concepts as the Christian miracles and mysteries of the Trinity, transubstantiation, and the Incarnation. These miraculous episodes constituted some of the most frequently represented events in the paintings of the most celebrated Mexican artists of the viceregal era: Cristóbal de Villalpando (ca. 1649–1714), Juan Correa (1646–1716), Miguel Cabrera (1695–1768), and Juan Rodríguez Juárez (1675–1728).

Artistic renderings of these and other painters' representations of Christian doctrine shaped the visual imaginations of Mexican mystics.[18] Ilusos and alumbrados often provided the court with minutely detailed descriptions of the clothing, facial, and corporal features of the apparitions they saw, as well as of the settings in which they appeared. María Manuela Picazo, an early-eighteenth-century beata, graphically narrated the stylistic elements of her visions and even referred to the influences that particular paintings had exerted on them. On November 8, 1712, she testified that she had once seen a vision of the Virgin Mary, whose face was slightly pink, wearing a cloak of light blue and a dress of pale rose, as Picazo observed, "in the style worn by Our Lady of Guadalupe."[19] Picazo's description is consistent with Mexican artists' common depictions of Mary wearing sumptuous brocades and other rich textiles, along with extravagant jewelry.[20] In another vision Jesus Christ appeared to Picazo. She observed that he was a man "of good stature and thin with a cape of blue, with a dark and very generous skirt, and his interior clothing was red and the style in which he wore his cape was somewhat similar to the way in which he appears when in the [Church of the] Carmen he is shown with a ring."[21]

The stylistic elements of Mexican mystics' visions drew heavily from those characteristic of seventeenth- and eighteenth-century painting in New Spain, which was typified by the use of bold colors, sensual and natural tones, and abundant representation of Christian iconography.[22] Moreover, their visions, as with colonial artwork, most frequently depicted encounters with saints as well as the principle mysteries and miracles associated with Jesus Christ and the Virgin Mary.

Although orthodox influences affected their perception of these religious subjects, Mexican mystics' visions also contained elements that diverged significantly from convention. Many of these unconventional elements originated in their incorporation of elements from their everyday lived experiences into biblical and theological scenes. These embodiments of their lived experiences included reflections upon mystics' own social and economic positions, observations about human personality traits, and realistic portrayals of women's experiences of marriage, sexuality, and childbirth. Sometimes their visions also served as vehicles to express observations and criticisms about their own historical contexts or about Christian dogma.

Miracles and Mysteries of Christ and Mary
The Christian miracles and mysteries all involve instances in which supernatural forces render material objects divine. A sermon that one of colonial Mexico's most celebrated seventeenth-century clerics preached illuminates the Catholic Church's understanding of the significance of Christian miracles in the colonial era. Antonio Núñez de Miranda, rector of the Jesuit College of San Pedro and San Paulo in Puebla, calificador

of the Holy Office, and confessor to such celebrated individuals as sor Juana Inés de la Cruz, gave his address in January of 1678 to an audience that included the archbishop of Mexico and the viceroy of New Spain.[23] Núñez's sermon discussed a miracle that had recently transpired involving some biscuits (*panecitos*) baked to honor Saint Teresa. In the midst of their preparation Andrea de la Santísima Trinidad, a nun of the convent of Regina Coeli, accidentally placed the panecitos of Saint Teresa in a jug of water. They at once dissolved into tiny particles but then miraculously reformed themselves into their original shapes, with the image of the saint stamped upon them. The astonished nun tested the panecitos several times and found to her amazement that they proved themselves repeatedly capable of miraculous reintegration.

After describing the miracle, Núñez discussed how the church recognized its authenticity. He declared that neither science nor "elemental, celestial, nor human forces" could account for the consolidation of the biscuits' particles, and he observed that the phenomenon was so incredible that it even "appeared to have excelled the abilities of angels." Therefore, he concluded, only an exceptionally powerful force could have accomplished it. A satanic force could not be responsible because sor Andrea's reputation as a nun of recognized "virtue, sobriety, prudence, and sincerity" proved that only God could have caused the miracle.[24]

Núñez proceeded to link this event with other miraculous occurrences. He likened it to the reformulation of Christians' souls following from their participation in the sacrament of baptism when they vowed to imitate the example of Christ. He also compared it to the Virgin Mary's union "in her virginal entrails" of Christ's three substances—body, soul, and divinity—into the "bread of the Angels." He then discussed several other prominent biblical miracles: Christ's conversion of water to wine, the transubstantiation of bread and wine into the body and blood of Christ, the resurrections of both Christ and Lazarus, and the Incarnation of the Divine Verb.[25] All the miracles he included involved the transformation of natural into supernatural objects: bread, wine, and human flesh rendered into the divine body, blood, or eternal life itself.

As the catechism produced for the fourth meeting of the Mexican Provincial Council emphasized, Christ and Mary were the only figures in humanity's history to have simultaneously embodied both the human and the divine. Mary's synthesis of the carnal and the spiritual had occurred in the miracle to which Núñez twice referred: her conception of Christ. The Virgin, in her union with the Holy Spirit, as the catechism explained, "formed a human body, and in the same moment the Holy Spirit created a rational soul and united it to this body, composing of this soul and body together a true and perfect humanity." Perhaps anticipating the difficulty the laity might have had in comprehending such a fantastic event, the catechism briefly elaborated: "The sun penetrates a crystal without breaking it, and Christ exited his tomb without moving the stone. . . . If the sun can penetrate the crystal without breaking it, with what greater perfection did Christ penetrate the womb of the Virgin Mary without taint to her virginity." [26] This abstract explanation was the most explicit available to the colonial laity. Contemporary sources normally avoided altogether any discussion of the precise mechanics of the mysteries.

La Mística Ciudad de Dios, a biography that seventeenth-century Spanish nun María de Jesús de Agreda claimed the Virgin Mary had dictated to her, was one of the most widely circulated mystical tracts in colonial Mexico.[27] The Mexican Inquisition tried a number of mystics who declared their familiarity with Agreda's work.[28] Agreda's multivolume text purportedly treated every detail of the Virgin's life from her conception to her ascension. Several chapters are dedicated to a discussion of both Mary's Immaculate Conception and her miraculous union with the Holy Spirit, but no precise details regarding either event are contained in the text. In the only passage that even nears the discussion of this perplexing episode, Agreda writes that the Virgin Mary informed her that when the archangel Gabriel approached her, "the Mystery of the Incarnation was executed, and I conceived of the Verb or Term in my womb." Mary had then understood with "new light the Mystery—that the Divinity had humiliated himself to unite with human nature in the womb of a poor virgin, such as I."[29]

Some residents of New Spain may have taken greater satisfaction from their exposure to detailed artistic representations of this event than from such abstract textual explanations. The Annunciation, a scene that depicted the moment of the Incarnation, was an enormously popular subject for artists of the viceroyalty. One of Cristóbal de Villalpando's paintings of the scene, now housed in Mexico City's Museo Nacional de Arte, shows Mary, clothed in her traditional pink gown and blue cloak, interrupted in the act of reading by an angel bearing a white flower, presumably representing her preserved virginity. Mary gestures modestly to the angel, indicating that she has understood the word of God. A beam of light emanating from a dove hovering overhead simultaneously penetrates her.

Even such images, while magnificently representing Mary's virginal conception of Christ as described in the Gospel of Luke, may not have entirely satisfied the curiosity of colonial Christians who wished to gain full comprehension of this supernatural event. Believers, of course, were not meant to fully comprehend such happenings. Christianity's miracles and mysteries involve the accomplishment of the rationally impossible and can be accepted only through faith. Colonial artists could not even attempt, therefore, to represent these episodes in exact detail. The abstract portrayal of the Christian mysteries and miracles—Mary's Incarnation, Virgin Birth, and Ascension, Christ's transubstantiation and subsequent Eucharist miracles—allowed the Mexican populace to use their religious faith to complete the representation of these scenes. Leaving the door open to their faith, however, also meant leaving it open to their religious imaginations, as Mexican visionaries' innovations on orthodox renderings of Christian miracles reveal.

Visions of Christ and the Eucharist

Both colonial artists and Mexican mystics commonly pictured Christ in erotic terms. Within the Catholic church, professed nuns became the brides of Christ and celebrated ceremonial marriages to him. Although it was the devil who invited—or forced—religious women to engage in overtly sexual activities, Christ often appeared in their writings as a romantic paramour, and colonial artists often represented him in even more sexual terms.[30] The paintings, attributed to Miguel Cabrera, in an eighteenth-century *retablo* (altarpiece) devoted to Saint Rose of Lima in the Mexico City cathedral, illustrate both these tropes. In one image an enormous, dark-skinned, and seemingly naked devil pulls Rose toward his chest, attempting to engulf her in his muscular arms (see figure 2). Rose, pallid and placid in her Dominican habit, effortlessly pushes the beast away, foiling his lascivious ends. In a second painting in the series Rosa kneels beside Christ. He cradles her head in his hand and guides her lips to the wound on his side from which she lovingly drinks.

Ilusas and alumbradas often re-created such eroticized portraits of Christ in their visions. Ana de Aramburu, for instance, saw him in a vision as a young man, with handsome rose-colored skin, aquiline features, beautiful eyes, waist-length red hair, coral lips, and elegant feet and hands. Upon perceiving him she cried, "If all could know of the sweetness of our

Figure 2. *Las Tentaciones de Santa Rosa*, Miguel Cabrera, Catedral Metropolitana de México. Photo courtesy of Archivo Fotográfico IIE-UNAM.

love, they would not need to look for creatures. What a beautiful garden! I already see that I find you walking in your garden. Ah! Lord, but how they flower—your gifts and fruits."[31]

Although eroticism was a convention of baroque mystical visions, Mexican ilusas also incorporated a number of unconventional elements in their visualizations of Christ and the miracles associated with him. During her late-eighteenth-century investigation mestiza beata María Lucía Celis described many supernatural interactions she had had with Christ and the Virgin Mary in a spiritual diary she helped her confessor, Antonio Rodríguez, compose. In one entry Celis described how Christ and Mary had both appeared to her just as she was preparing to take communion. Approaching the altar where she knelt, they asked her, "Will you give us to suck?" She declared that she would "and gave them to suck, first to the Lord and then to the Lady." Having nourished the holy pair, Celis then begged them to nurse her, but "although she asked them, they did not want to give it to her."[32]

On another day, after having executed her daily disciplines, Celis saw a vision of her "dear husband" (Jesus Christ) and asked him for forgiveness of her sins. Christ and the Virgin Mary had then accompanied her to church for communion. Once in church, Celis had seen a vision of Christ on the crucifix, and he spoke to her, saying, "You see my daughter, my dove, what the sinners have done to me? Do you want to suck from this divine side?" Celis told him that she did but said, "*first that I* [Celis's confessor] *and her two little sisters should drink. And, in effect, this petition pleased the Lord a great deal and he gave all three of us to suck,* and then once she had drunk, she cried, 'I would like you to consent that the whole world could nurse from you.' And the Lord said . . .'I will give you this pleasure, if only everyone would love me, but look where they have put me with their sins.[33]

The Virgin Mary then materialized before Celis and laid Christ face-down in her lap. Celis's diary, mirroring the gruesome state in which colonial artists relished depicting Christ after the Passion, detailed Christ's wounds: "His back was so destroyed that his ribs had been peeled of flesh such that his entrails, heart, and intestine could be seen. The light of day could even be seen through his chest . . . he had been left from the whipping like a skeleton." This sight so moved Celis that she sobbed with such passion that Christ told her that the "balm of her tears, which had come from her heart," had entirely cured him.[34]

Later that day Celis went to the church of Santa Catalina and again saw a vision of Christ (dressed in a purple tunic and blue cape), and she invited him to lie in her lap and nurse from her. He refused, explaining, "'No, I am fine kneeling here. Give me your left breast to suck from,' and in effect, she gave it to him and for a long spell he gave her the same from his divine mouth."[35] Later, having nourished one another a second time, Christ led Celis to an altar where he showed her an image of his own crucifixion. Below the cross were gathered a group of lambs into whose open mouths fell drops of blood from each of Christ's wounds. Celis's perception of the flock of faithful lambs and her frequent sighting of Christ while she prepared to take communion were common elements of orthodox Eucharist visions.[36] The motifs of nourishing from the Virgin Mary's breast and from Christ's side wound also featured in iconographic traditions of mystical experiences dating back to the Middle Ages and commonly reproduced in colonial Mexico.[37]

Two elements of Celis's visions, however, are inconsistent with contemporary renderings of Eucharist miracles. First, her visions depict an uncommonly reciprocal element in her interactions with Christ and Mary. As was common to representations of Eucharist miracles, in her vision Christ and Mary nourish Celis, redeeming her with their blood and breast milk. Atypically, however, in Celis's vision they also beg for the opportunity to nurse from her breast as well. Rather than Celis alone receiving restoration from the blood of Christ's wounds, in her vision Celis's tears, which she sheds on Christ's broken body, restore him to life.

In Celis's vision she moved beyond the medieval tradition of Imitatio Christi (imitating Christ's suffering and deprivations) and actually became Christ in the sense that she became the source of restoration and healing. Perhaps this act articulated her faith that even she, a person marginalized from access to many sources of power in colonial Mexican society, could quite literally embody the most powerful Christian symbol. More concretely, in assuming the power to distribute her body's restorative fluids to Christ and to Mary, Celis mimicked a priest who distributed Christ's blood and body when executing the sacrament of the Eucharist.

Other Mexican mystics also perceived bodily reciprocity occurring between themselves and divinities. In one of her visions Ana de Aramburu claimed to have exchanged hearts with Jesus Christ. Such an exchange had a basis in one of Saint Teresa de Jesús's well-known ecstatic episodes that she described in *Libro de la vida*.[38] Nicolás Rodríguez Juárez's painting *Transverberación de Santa Teresa*, in which an angel penetrates Teresa's heart with a flaming sword, illustrated the episode.[39] The relevant passage in the *Libro* explains: "I saw an angel in human form appear at my left-hand side. He was not tall and was very handsome and his face was lit up as if he was one of the highest angels who are all fire. . . . It seemed to me that he left the sword in my heart for moments and my entrails were enraptured and when he took the sword out, it seemed as if my entrails were transported with it and I felt the most powerful love for God inside."[40] In a similar episode Teresa experienced another miracle in which she felt Saint Augustine writing directly on her heart. Juan Correa portrayed the scene, which helped to legitimize the orthodoxy of Teresa's visions and writings, in a painting in 1704 (see figure 3).

Figure 3. *San Agustín escribiendo en el corazón de Santa Teresa*, Cristóbal de Villalpando, Museo Regional del Virreinato. Photo courtesy of Archivo Fotográfico IIE-UNAM. Reproduction authorized by the Instituto Nacional de Antropología e Historia.

Aramburu's claim that she traded sensations with Christ did not end, however, with her allusion to the orthodox tradition of exchanging hearts with God. At one point in her trial one of her former supporters testified that Aramburu had revealed that she had experienced Christ's sufferings by feeling his wounds on her body. She also claimed that an image of the infant Jesus, who frequently appeared to her, felt her mundane suffering in his body. Aramburu had announced that "when she had congestion, so did the Child, and when her feet were swollen, so were the Child's." The experience of Christ's stigmata has a long history within orthodox mystical practice, but the idea that Christ, in turn, experienced humanity's pedestrian discomforts—swollen feet and congestion—does not. Aramburu's judges noted the heterodox tone of her mystical experiences. One of her confessors, in denouncing her piety, stated that Aramburu's experiences of the supernatural "do not correspond to the fire that a soul is supposed feel when consumed in the force of love experienced at the sight of a lover, and she talks with Him with too much familiarity."[41] Rather than imitating a conventional motif of passion and intensity wrought by God's penetration of her heart, Aramburu staked her claim to mystical authenticity on Jesus's experience of the pain of her own sore feet.

Aramburu's and Celis's apparitions both imply that they perceived a reciprocal relationship existed between humanity and God. Their visions reveal that they believed it was not only possible for humanity to access the divine through rites, mysticism, and bodily suffering, but also that divine beings—Christ and Mary—also participated in worldly, human life. They echoed the glorification of mundane experiences of the world Ana de Zayas had voiced in her late-seventeenth-century mystical poem dedicated to the letter V (discussed in chapter 2). All three women, through their religious expressions, elevated the value of humanity's worldly existence. Perhaps one of the reasons such perceptions of God disturbed the officers of the Inquisition was that they resembled some aspects of Nahuas' perceptions of the traits of divinities.[42]

María Lucía Celis diverged from tradition in her Eucharist visions in another way. She repeatedly described Christ's nature in these experiences in unflattering terms. In one of her visions Celis recounted how Christ and Mary, having taken refreshment at her breast, inexplicably refused to provide her with nourishment from their own bodies. On another occasion she portrayed Christ as a selfish and petulant savior who, on two occasions, pointed out to her that he resented the suffering humanity had subjected him to through its unthinking sinfulness. The Christ described in María Lucía Celis's visions (the Christ she believed herself capable of nourishing and incarnating) was not the selfless beatific Christ of conventional representations, patiently enduring the cross he was destined to bear. Celis described a bitter and irritable savior who unhappily acknowledged that humanity had taken him for granted. [43] Perhaps Celis found it hard to believe in—or identity with—a Christ who had born all the injustice and trials he faced with no more than a fleeting moment of doubt during his last moments on the cross.

One of Celis's acquaintances, beata María Rita Vargas, also depicted Christ in her visions in an atypical manner. In Spanish America representations of Christ in his infancy preponderated in orthodox religious art and sacred visions. Even when such sources depicted Christ in the first moments after birth, they represented him as serene, noble, and wise. Vargas's descriptions of her relationship with a series of infant Christ figures, however, little resemble the stoical baby Jesus of contemporary art. The child featured in Vargas's spiritual journal is often playful, occasionally mischievous or disobedient, and constantly jealous of her close relationship to her confessor. [44] Vargas, like Celis, Aramburu, Zayas, and many other Mexican mystics (and, again, like Nahuas) transformed conventional perceptions of Christ and attributed him with some of humanity's imperfections.

The Incarnation and Virgin Birth of Mary

Although Christ was frequently featured in the visions of Mexican alumbrados and ilusos, the most prominent figure who appeared to them was the Virgin Mary. [45] As in their Eucharist visions, Mexican mystics' perceptions of the Incarnation and Virgin Birth reflected many elements of conventional artistic representations but also diverged from these depictions in significant ways. Ilusos often incorporated their own experiences of sexuality, motherhood, and childbearing into their Marian visions and thus produced a variety of alternative representations of the Mother of Christ.

Getrudis Rosa Ortiz's visions of the Incarnation and Virgin Birth contained many such divergences. In her appearance before the Inquisition on April 28, 1723, Ortiz described one of her ecstatic fits during which she saw the Virgin Mary holding a child to her breast. Later, God relayed the vision's significance to Ortiz, telling her "that it was the Virgin Mary in the vision, and that she was her [Ortiz's] true Mother, who had looked after her ever since she was born, and that it had cost her a lot of work, and that her true father was her holy Son, who she was holding in her arms, and that she had been predestined to be a saint, and that for this reason, she would be loved and served for her entire life."[46]

Ortiz informed her inquisitors that the physical difficulties her natural mother had undergone in giving birth to her substantiated the revelation's declaration that the Virgin's participation in her birth had "cost her a lot of work." When Ortiz first emerged from her mother's uterus, those assisting in the birth believed her dead, but miraculously they succeeded in reviving her shortly thereafter. Ortiz's graphic description of the labor pains and difficulties of birth that her own mother endured—and symbolically the Virgin as well—was a subject studiously ignored in conventional depictions of the nativity.[47]

Ortiz's vision contains several other adjustments to orthodox representations of the Incarnation and Virgin Birth. First, the Virgin Mary revealed in this vision that Ortiz was her daughter. In Ortiz's vision the child of Mary, savior to the world, was a female mestiza born in Mexico. Second, Mary informed Ortiz of her celestial lineage while holding the infant Christ in her arms. This suggests that rather than replacing Christ, Ortiz saw herself destined to be his holy sibling. A Mary who mothered multiple children signifies more humanity and worldliness than does the conventional figure of Mary, virginal mother to Christ alone.

Other ilusas saw similar apparitions of Mary. María Cayetana Loria, a late-eighteenth-century mulata, told the court, for example, about a series of visions she had experienced of an exquisitely attired woman, whom two or three beautiful young girls attended. In one vision, when Cayetana saw the woman holding a baby boy, she asked her: "'Is this child your son?' And she responded, 'Yes my daughter, he is mine. He is the younger brother of the priest [a figure representing Jesus Christ whom Cayetana repeatedly saw.]'"[48] Cayetana's inquisitors classified as heretical her notion that the Virgin Mary could have borne more than one child. In their long list of accusations against Cayetana, they condemned the many errors her visions contained. At the forefront of these was Cayetana's challenge to the idea of Mary's perpetual virginity contained in her assertion that "after Jesus Christ, she had had other children."[49]

Besides implying that Mary had mothered more than one child, Getrudis Rosa Ortiz's vision of the Incarnation and Virgin Birth articulated other theologically controversial ideas. Ortiz learned from her apparition not only that Mary was Ortiz's true mother, but also that the infant Jesus Christ whom she held in her arms was Ortiz's father. Neither the awkward temporal logistics such a mating presented nor its incestuous element seem to have troubled Ortiz when she formulated her divine parentage in Christ and Mary.[50] Another remarkable element of Ortiz's vision concerns her reformulation of Mary's role in her miraculous conception. In Ortiz's vision Mary, rather than the Holy Spirit, was the active agent of conception. In this vision Christ conferred paternity to Ortiz, but Christ was only a passive child to whom Mary had already given birth.

A number of other Mexican mystics had similarly heterodox visions of the Incarnation. Agustina Rangel, a late-seventeenth-century mestiza ilusa, saw a series of such unconventional apparitions. Juana de Abalos, Rangel's mulata sister-in-law, provided one description of Rangel's unusual vision of this miracle to the court. She testified that Rangel had once told her about a vision she had seen after experiencing acute pains in her stomach. Rangel's sister, a curandera, had cured her with the assistance of an herb she referred to as *la rosa de Santa Rosa* (peyote). While she was healing, Rangel had witnessed an apparition in which

> the Blessed Virgin Mary had appeared to her and pressed on her with her hands and opened up her chest and saw everything in her belly from the inside out and saw that she was pregnant with a girl . . . and said that they would have to give her the name Rose, and said that she would have to die . . . in a very few days, and that having taken the rosa, Our Lady appeared for more than an hour on top of the said Agustina sweating, and that the Virgin said to her that she had to cure all the sick people and that her Majesty would tell her how.[51]

Another witness, Petrona Castro, a Spanish woman whose brother Rangel had also nursed, provided a similar account of this vision. She testified that Rangel had once told her that "judging herself to be pregnant with the baby of another man, not her husband, she had taken a drink so as to abort herself." After attempting abortion, Saint Rose had appeared to Rangel and addressed her in great anger, asking her why she suspected that "it was of another and not of your husband which you have in your belly." The saint then told her, "to look inside her own body and then Agustina could see everything inside herself and she saw that inside her own stomach that the girl she had was of her husband, and then Saint

Rose said you see how she is of your husband? She is also mine, and she must be called Rosa, and she will be born soon, but will live only for a short time because she is mine and I have only lent her to you."[52]

Rangel's vision deviated alarmingly from orthodoxy. In both testimonies, witnesses suggested that Rangel had been pregnant at the time she had seen the apparition. They described her anxiety over the child's paternity and told of her wish to abort the baby. In the midst of such speculation either the Virgin Mary or Saint Rose appeared to Rangel and announced that her child was a prodigious girl who would live only a short time before ascending to heaven. The first version of the episode linked Rangel's conception and loss of the child to Mary's endorsement of her work as a curandera.

As in Ortiz's vision of the Incarnation, in Rangel's apparition the supernatural child about to be born was female, and the active agent in her conception—the force responsible for conferring miraculous qualities upon her—was the child's mother. In Rangel's vision Saint Rose's revelation that the child was the product of her union with Rangel's husband both dispelled Rangel's anxiety over the child's paternity and effectively relieved Rangel of maternal responsibilities for the child.

A great many other ilusas also experienced alternative visions of miracles surrounding miraculous conceptions and births. Late-eighteenth-century Clarisa nun Ana María La Cal, for example, saw visions in which the Virgin Mary helped her procure an abortion. In the fall of 1788, when fray José Castro appeared before the Inquisition to denounce sor Ana María, he recalled how she had sometimes "executed lewd acts in front of others, speaking with the devil, as if she was sinning with him."[53] The convent's Mother Abbess swore that sor Ana María had told another nun that she was pregnant and that the child inside her stomach would be called Juan, and that "he was destined to be another Baptist and another Messiah that would save the whole world." Despite her impregnation with this miraculous progeny, however, sor Ana María, like Agustina Rangel, desired to abort her child. Fray Castro told the court that he had heard sor Ana María claim in public that "although I have been left pregnant, Holy Mary will save me," implying that the Virgin Mary would assist her in dealing with the problematic progeny from which this coupling had resulted.[54] He also declared that it was known throughout the convent that sor Ana María had procured an abortion. Several other witnesses confirmed his testimony.

The Sacred and the Secular

Why and how did women such as Getrudis Rosa Ortiz, Agustina Rangel, sor Ana María La Cal, and many others construct such alterations in their visions of one of the central mysteries of the Catholic faith, a scene that they repeatedly saw depicted in sacred art everywhere around them? [55] One quality shared by many of the women whom the court prosecuted for false mysticism was an uncommonly strong faith in the righteousness and validity of their own lives and experiences of the world. Sacred sources attempted to indoctrinate women with the idea that their worth could be measured by their ability to imitate the example of the Virgin Mary: they were to reproduce offspring while virtuously preserving their chastity, if not their virginity. Spanish Christian society taught disdain for women, particularly those of Spanish descent, who thwarted one or both of these prerequisites for female virtue.

In Latin America the stigma of illegitimacy dated back to the establishment of the colonies when Spaniards refused to recognize the inheritance rights of their offspring, who were often the product of extramarital unions with indigenous women. In its earliest usage in colonial Spanish America the term *mestizo* actually connoted "bastard."[56] As the colonies matured and as mestizaje increased, Spanish women in particular experienced the pressure of maintaining sexual virtue and diminishing the phenomenon of interracial mixing.

The documentation generated at the occasion of the late-eighteenth-century foundation of the clinic for *partos reservados* (confidential births), one branch of the Mexico City Poor House, illustrates contemporary attitudes toward women who had failed to maintain their virtue.[57] This institution, as its founders perceived, would address "the fear, shame, and desperation that seizes the hearts of fragile, fickle women after having blemished their own reputations and the honor of their marriages and families with their sexual excesses."[58] The proposed establishment would provide these women with a safe and discreet location in which to give birth to their unwanted children. Only Spanish women, whose family's honor most imperatively required preservation, could access its services.

Colonial society may have proclaimed the worthlessness, fragility, and fickleness of women who had tainted their sexual virtue, yet Mexican visionaries constantly absorbed contradictory information about real women's practices of virtue. Likely, they would have observed widespread engagement in adultery and would have been aware of the high rates of illegitimacy that characterized all levels of this devoutly Catholic colonial society.[59] No doubt they would have exchanged news with their peers and family members about upper-class women—their employers, patrons, and patients—who managed to preserve their reputations for chastity even while engaging in unsanctioned sexual activities. Many of them would have known of women who, for a variety of reasons, avoided becoming mothers through abortion.

The secrecy enshrouding abortion makes it difficult to trace with accuracy the frequency of the procedure in the colonial period. However, women throughout the Catholic world practiced abortion frequently enough to elicit a papal prohibition, reproduced in Mexico in 1684, of the procedure. Moreover, supporters backed the establishment of the partos reservados clinic in Mexico because they claimed Spanish women commonly procured abortions or practiced infanticide in order to avoid public disclosure of their unwanted children.[60] Ilusos and alumbrados also discussed abortions in their Inquisition trials. The parents of Marta de la Encarnación, an early-eighteenth-century beata ilusa whose sexual virtue the court suspected, apparently assisted their daughter in aborting a child. When Marta's father, Simón Avila, appeared before the court, he testified that on one occasion several years earlier he had noticed that his daughter's menstrual cycle had stopped. His wife confirmed the observation and added that she had noticed that their daughter's belly had started to rise. Avila mentioned the matter to his mother-in-law, who apparently took the appropriate measures, for one week later his wife informed him (either employing a euphemism or describing a most indirect method indeed) that "in only bleeding her ankle they had gotten rid of Marta's belly." One of Marta's acquaintances, Bartolmé Luis, also informed the court that the beata had admitted to him that she had had an abortion, perhaps referring to a separate instance from the episode her father had described. Luis testified that Marta had told him that a mulato, the son of a biscuit maker, had violated her virginity. Once realizing she was pregnant, and "when God was not watching, she took something to abort the child."[61]

Sometimes Mexican visionaries' religious activities were directly linked to abortions that they had received or performed. Juana de Abalos, one of the witnesses in Agustina Rangel's trial, testified that she had watched this curandera ilusa perform cures on various women. Rangel had once even attempted to cure the witness herself. Rangel began by administering some of the rosa de Santa Rosa to her in powdered form. She had then had begun revolving around Abalos, gesturing vigorously with her arms, but the cure did not appear to be taking effect, so Rangel approached her, shouting loudly, "while throwing herself against the ground with powerful and repeated blows, as one would use to kill a chicken. It shocked the declarant to see Agustina beating herself all over the room in this way with these great blows since she was pregnant at the time."[62]

Rangel then began to butt Abalos in the chest with her head until she fell down backward, at which point, Rangel, "grabbing her tightly by the clothes and with great violence, started hitting her belly (since that was what had been hurting her) with a closed fist." Although the first blows had hurt her a great deal, Abalos said she had not felt the subsequent ones at all. The curandera continued pressing Abalos's stomach with her head and made many gestures over her body, from the bottom to the top. On another occasion de Abalos testified that Rangel had given a similar cure to Inés de Bustos, a Spanish woman, first giving her the Rosa de Santa Rosa and then punching her repeatedly in the stomach.[63]

It would have been difficult for women who wished to emulate the examples of revered Christian mystics to avoid imbibing the Church's position on female sexual virtue, its prohibitions against both abortion and illegitimate births, and its reverence for the figure of a Virgin Mother, conceived Immaculately. The personal experiences of Mexican visionaries, many of whom considered themselves legitimate candidates for the receipt of God's mystical gifts, however, belied the possibility of embodying the Church's standard for female sexual virtue. Perhaps just as these Mexican visionaries had humanized the image of Christ in their visions of the Crucifixion and Eucharist, they also wished to render the image of the Virgin Mary more compatible with the knowledge they possessed of women's lives. Perhaps because they refused to discount the validity of their own experiences, they felt justified in modifying the impossible example the Virgin Mary had created for them, rendering her story more consistent with their own.

Jean Franco observes that ilusas Ana de Aramburu and Teresa de Jesús attempted to reformulate new categories for themselves within the limited possibilities that existed for women in colonial New Spain in part because of the model set for them by the Virgin Mary. "Both women," she writes, "transgressed the apparently natural categories of virgin or mother by claiming to be both."[64] Evidence from the stories of a number of these two women's contemporaries suggests that they also used their own lived experiences to reformulate the image of the Virgin Mary. Rather than accept the conventional model of the Virgin Mother, they created alternative icons. They saw a Virgin who had experienced difficult labor pains, a Mary who was mother to multiple children, and a Holy Mother who had attempted abortion before producing the savior.

They also grafted their knowledge of theology onto their understandings of their own lived experiences. Late-eighteenth-century criolla ilusa Barbara de Echagaray admitted during her trial to having had three abortions, one of which she had procured after her confessor had impregnated her. Echagaray incorporated the memory of these abortions into some of the sacred visions she experienced. She testified at one point that after her abortions she had seen visions of Christ surrounded by a group of shadows representing the children she might have had. On another occasion she denied willingly engaging in sexual relations with her confessor. She claimed she had only dreamed that she was fornicating with the devil and, upon waking, found to her surprise that she was having *comercio carnal* (carnal relations) with a priest, and that he was on the point of stabbing her with a dagger. In another appearance, rather than discussing abortions she had undergone to avoid unwanted births, Echagaray asserted that she had "given birth to devils," claiming to have mothered as many as fifteen such creatures.[65]

Two of the mid-seventeenth-century Romero sisters also recast their own understanding of pregnancy in terms of divine or diabolic encounters in order to disassociate themselves from the shame that would accompany such mundane events.[66] Over the course of her testimony Teresa Romero conjoined the memory of mundane and supernatural pregnancies. Teresa, pregnant when she entered the secret prison of the Holy Office in September of 1649, gave birth to a son in her cell later that month. She testified to the court that the father of her child was a certain young man (*mozo*), Nicolás Jiménez. But several years later, when the court published its sentence of Teresa, it referred to a vision of Teresa's in which a spirit appeared to her in a corn field in the figure of a blonde young man (*mozo rubio*) and tried to get her to sin with him. Teresa also admitted in her trial that she had been motivated to begin feigning her mystical raptures in order to regain the love that her father, Juan Romero Zapata, had lost for her because of her reputation for sexual promiscuity.[67]

Teresa's sister, Josefa de San Luis Beltrán, also incorporated her experiences of sexuality and its repercussions into her depictions of spiritual encounters. Josefa testified that several men had seduced her, but said she also had often been "afflicted by temptations of the flesh when the devil had tried to engage her in many deeds and offenses which she always managed to resist during the entire time her father had lived, but after he had died, being but a weak sinner, she let herself be vanquished."[68] Just as their experiences of sexuality, birth, and motherhood forced them to reshape conventional formulations of dogma, Mexican visionaries sometimes reinterpreted their own mundane transgressions of sexual morality in terms of supernatural experiences. This allowed them, in the face of contradictory evidence, to maintain their own embodiment of Christian virtue, either in their own eyes or in those of their supporters.

Mystical Visions of Race

Visual and literary depictions of Satan, who led colonial Mexican women such as Josefa de San Luis Beltrán and Barbara de Echagaray into sexual temptation, commonly attributed him with African or Indian ethnicity.[69] Mexican visionaries sometimes absorbed these tropes, describing in their own visions how "black" devils appeared to them and tempted them to sin.[70] Mexican ilusos and alumbrados, however, also experienced visions in which they attributed blackness with other qualities.

Getrudis Rosa Ortiz, the early-eighteenth-century mestiza viewer of the crucifixion vision with which this chapter opened, experienced several other visions that dealt explicitly with racial issues. She explained to the court at one point in her testimony that for a period of several years she had been unable to eat any food because of a series of visions she had seen. Just at the moment of consumption, she would suddenly perceive that whatever food was on her plate had been converted into clusters of wriggling ants, worms, and other insects. Needless to say, Ortiz would then lose all desire to eat.

The inability to consume food, described in Ortiz's trial as a type of a divinely induced fast, was not an unusual means for mystical women to demonstrate their sanctity and express their love of God. [71] The unusual aspect of Ortiz's experience, however, lay in the alterations that her own body underwent simultaneously with the changes that occurred to her food. For while the food on her plate turned into clumps of unappetizing bugs, Ortiz herself was also transformed into a black woman, a "conversion" that might have seemed feasible to her given her possible African ancestry. Ortiz stated that while she sat at the table, she watched the skin on her hands turn black, and although she could not see her face in a mirror, when she touched her hair, she felt that it had become curly "just like black woman's."[72]

Ortiz informed her confessor about this set of visions, and he told her that she was not black, and "that it appeared to him that what she had experienced was the temptation of the devil." A short while later, however, God sent a message to Ortiz explaining the experiences to her. God had told her, "my daughter, during all this time that you suffered in not eating because of those little bugs and became a black woman, I permitted it, that the devil should visit these harms upon you, for my greater honor and for the betterment of your soul."[73] With the help of divine—and demonic—intervention, Ortiz was transformed into a black woman. Her transformation was associated with physical suffering because she was unable to consume food while she was black, but her status as a black person was ultimately redemptive. God revealed that he had allowed her to become black for his own glory and in order to assist her on her journey to religious purification.

Ortiz's vision may have served as a vehicle that allowed her to criticize the status—and treatment—of blacks in her historical context. In her vision blackness carried with it the negative connotations of suffering and punishment, but the meaning of these attributes is complicated. In *Holy Feast and Holy Fast* Caroline Walker Bynum astutely challenges previous interpretations of medieval religious women's engagement in extreme penitence as evidence of their assumption of a misogynist and dualist perception of female carnality.[74] Bynum argues that their asceticism and practice of Imitatio Christi illustrate the positive understanding women could have of their own bodies and the powers associated with them. Such women, she demonstrates, did not understand their bodies only as the sin-filled components of their lower natures, but as the means through which they could follow Christ's divine example. Getrudis Rosa Ortiz similarly implies in her vision that her transformation into a black woman was a necessary step in the eventual salvation of her soul.

Ortiz experienced a number of other visions in which she expressed criticisms of colonial Mexico's racial hierarchy or suggested alternative perceptions of blackness. Several days into her trial's proceedings Ortiz testified that on one occasion, when journeying to the church of Santa Catalina to pray, she had seen an apparition of

> *a dead horse, which many dogs were ripping at with great rage, and having arrived at the church the vision continued while she was in prayer, and when she went to take communion, the Lord said to her in the accustomed way already referred to that*

> the dead horse was the soul of a mulata slave owned by doña Mariana Terán, a widow, now dead, in whose house she had entered with familiarity, and that doña Mariana had already punished the said mulata and had sent her to a workshop with prisoners, to punish her more, and that the slave was saying many oaths, but had not yet reneged on God although she was very close to doing so, and to becoming desperate, and hanging herself, and that if she died, the devils would take her away and treat her like the dogs treated the horse.[75]

The intensity of the punishment this mulata's mistress was inflicting greatly disturbed Ortiz. The vision so horrified her that she attempted to convince doña Mariana to end the abuse. She refused, and Ortiz continued to experience the vision. Ortiz's confessor eventually advised her to tell another priest, don Hipólito de Acosta, about the vision. Ortiz traveled to Acosta's church of La Misericordia and described the apparition to him while in confession. Acosta, accepting the veracity of Ortiz's vision, instructed Terán to release the mulata, which, reluctantly, she had done.

Conclusion

The visions of Getrudis Rosa Ortiz and those of many of other Mexican ilusos and alumbrados transcended conventional mystical experiences. Many of the accused believed themselves to be bona fide mystics, and all of them wished their communities and the clerical authorities they encountered to see them as proponents of spiritual orthodoxy. Perhaps for these reasons, their visions did conform, in some respects, to seventeenth- and eighteenth-century artistic representations of the miracles of the Eucharist, Incarnation, and Virgin Birth with which they were intimately familiar. Their visions, however, also contained many elements that deviated widely from orthodox norms.

In her religious experiences, Ortiz pictured blacks as potential Christians, virtuous redemptors, and people mistreated by other members of colonial society. Contemporary sacred sources did not assign them any of these roles. Ortiz drew from the knowledge she had acquired in her daily interactions with blacks and people of a variety of other ethnicities in order to modify their virtual exclusion from institutionally generated representations of Christian virtue. In at least one instance she was also able to use the mystical legitimacy that many powerful members of colonial society accorded her to address the abusive treatment to which blacks in colonial Mexican society were often subjected.

Other Mexican visionaries drew on their experiences of family life, motherhood, and sexuality to modify institutional representations of Jesus Christ and the Virgin Mary and used their experiences to question the church's teachings about the most important miracles and mysteries of the Christian faith. They incorporated their own experiences into these canonical stories and refashioned both elements of orthodox doctrine and attributes associated with the central figures of the Catholic faith.

Mexican visionaries were people who claimed to have experienced the highest levels of God's divine affections, but there were also people who lived within the corporality of colonial Mexican cities. Many of them were poor women who daily observed—or experienced—the concrete expressions of New Spain's racial, economic, and gendered social hierarchies. They were also women who worked, sustained friendships, and—sometimes outside the sanctity of marriage—had sexual relations and gave birth to children. The "deviant" elements contained in their visions reflected such experiences, all of which conventional representations of important religious events and figures omitted. In their visions ilusos and alumbrados reconciled the inconsistencies they perceived between the canonical norms they had learned and the divergent social, economic, and political experiences they had endured in their own lives.

Five

The Classification
of Female Disorders

C lerical, lay, and medical witnesses who testified in Josefa Palacios's late-eighteenth-century ilusa trial all had great difficulty
comprehending and classifying the disturbing fits they watched
her experience. A Franciscan friar from the town of Pachuca originally
denounced Palacios along with her confessor, Eusebio Villarejo, in a
letter to the Inquisition dated July 4, 1788. Fray José Zubía y Martínez
suspected that the devil had "possessed or obsessed" Palacios, a criolla
beata identified elsewhere as "the child of distinguished parents, who
maintained herself by labor and charity."[1]

During her trial several witnesses testified that the devil frequently
possessed Palacios, shouting sacrilege through her voice and filling her
body with violent power. Palacios herself confessed to the court that one
time, when she was about to receive the Eucharist, she had screamed out
"that she shat on the Holy Communion." A priest who often accompanied
Villarejo on his regular exorcisms of Palacios described the furious fits
that frequently racked her body. During these spells she hurled herself
against the floor, levitated, wrenched her clothing, and wounded herself
so severely that he dismissed the Inquisition's suggestion that she might
have feigned the episodes, affirming instead they must have originated in
"a natural sickness or from the devil." Palacios's denouncer feared that
she had entrapped Villarejo in her web of "pernicious illusion."[2] Other
clerics described Villarejo as "infested with the contagion" of demonic
possession.[3]

One of his colleagues described Villarejo, a priest of "good reputation
and customs," as *"iluso, crazy, or maniacal."*[4] Others witnesses asserted

that Palacios was also a virtuous Christian. Padre Francisco Matías Puerta described Palacios as a virginal maiden who comported herself "like an angel." However, in her first appearance before the tribunal in April of 1791, Palacios confessed that she had not always managed to practice the virtuous Christian life she fervently desired. Since becoming a woman, she stated, she had frequently suffered from "temptations of the flesh" but had always managed to resist them. In a later appearance her judges informed her that they had evidence that she had "engaged in the carnal act with the devil . . . who had infused her entire body, procuring her to impure movements and sins." Palacios confessed that the court's evidence was true and declared that she experienced these sins of impurity while prostrate and praying. She testified that "while kneeling in prayer, she felt, a cold wind that blew on her private parts." The wind moved her to wicked imagination, but she resisted such impure thoughts until one day she felt as if a bird had flown out from behind her and was "encircling her private parts." She was brought by this movement to orgasm (*a la polución*).[5]

The Holy Office continued to pursue the investigation of Palacios and Villarejo over the ensuing six years as court officials wrestled with various witnesses' differing explanations of both parties' alarming behavior. The trial's third witness, one fray Matías de los Dolores, introduced a new explanation for Palacios's fits. He asserted that a medical practitioner (*enfermero*) in the college had concluded that "everything [in her behavior] was caused by a hysterical accident [*accidente histérico*]" and had treated her with a few spoonfuls of wine and a cup of broth. Fray Matías concluded his testimony by asserting that "inside as well as outside the college, people take the beata for hysterical; all of her accidents and fits—for which she has been believed to be an ilusa or madwoman [*energúmena*]—have originated in this state."[6]

Another important figure in Palacios's trial, Pachuca's comisario, curate Mariano Iturria, who also judged that Palacios was likely suffering from hysteria. He based his assessment on his observation of her physical symptoms as well as on his familiarity with medical literature. In his judgment Iturria wrote that Palacios suffered from "maniacal melancholy of a distinct origin and principle, that is to say hysteria . . . which is known by the symptoms of sadness, sighs, crying fits, unpredictable laughing fits, gloomy dreams, immoderate vigils, and speaking and working furiously." Other witnesses did not know what to make of Palacios's fits and were unsure whether to classify her as hysterical, possessed, or a feigner of mystical experiences.[7]

Although presented with so many differing explanations of her perplexing behavior, Palacios's calificadores and inquisitors eventually settled on a decisive classification of her. Their judgment of Palacios's engagement in sexually inappropriate behavior was central to their assessment of her mystical fraud. The charge that Palacios had betrayed her parents' attempt to ensure her adoption of a suitable station in life, instead allowing "sensuality" and "other temptations of the flesh" to dominate her while she feigned a life of spirituality, headed the court's forty-one-chapter accusation against Palacios. On February 1, 1794, the tribunal convicted her of being a "false visionary and ilusa and iludente, hypocrite and feigner of sanctity and a molinista."[8] Her inquisitors ordered her to proclaim an abjuración de levi, exiled her from Mexico City, Madrid, and Pachuca for ten years, and commanded that she spend the first two of these in a recogimiento in Puebla.

The Holy Office and the Classification of Experience

As Josefa Palacios's trial illustrates, lay, clerical, and medical witnesses could and did perceive experiences that defendants claimed were mystical raptures in a variety of other ways. The competing explanations for her behavior that ran through Palacios's trial were common to those of many other Mexican mystics, particularly in the eighteenth century, as tables 6, 7, and 8 illustrate. In over one-third of the total iluso and alumbrado trials, witnesses suggested alternative rationales for defendants' behavior. Such differing explanations—insanity, diabolic possession or obsession, or illness—were especially common in the trials of female mystics.

Witnesses most often claimed that either insanity or diabolism accounted for defendants' behavior. In twenty-one of the thirty-one "alternative explanation" trials witnesses described defendants as having had contact with the devil. They identified defendants as mentally ill in twenty-two cases. Various labels of defendants' mental illnesses span the entire period under study. The terms *loca* (insane) or *locura* (insanity) were most frequently used and designated men more often than women (seven times for men versus four times for women). The term *melancolía*, an infirmity associated with an imbalance of the humors, was also applied with fair regularity, almost exclusively to female defendants (five of six Mexican mystics described as "melancholic" were female). A few instances occurred in which witnesses described the accused as

Table 6. Identification of illness in ilusos and alumbrados, 1598–1799

	Year	Illness	Case	Identified by	Other labels	Result
1	1598	Enferma, sangrante	Mariana de San Miguel	Laywoman	Insanity, demonism	Convicted
2	1687	Mal de corazón	María de San José	Merchant, doctor	—	Dismissed
3	1700	Epilepsia	Juan Luis Torres	Doctor, priest	Insanity, demonism	Dismissed
4	1717	Epilepsia	María de la Encarnación	Doctor	Insanity, demonism	Convicted
5	1747	Enferma	Sor Josefa Clara	Doctors	Insanity, demonism	Dismissed
6	1785	Epilepsia	Barbara de Echagaray	Layperson, lawyer	Insanity, demonism	Convicted
7	1788	Epilepsia	Sor Ana María la Cal	Doctor	Insanity, demonism	Dismissed
8	1799	Sangrante	Ana de Aramburu	Laypeople, doctor	Insanity, demonism	Convicted

Source: Archivo General de la Nación, Ramo Inquisición.

Table 7. Identification of insanity in ilusos and alumbrados, 1598–1799

	Year	Type of Insanity	Case	Identifier	Other labels	Result
1	1598	Melancolía	Mariana de San Miguel	Calificadores	Illness, demonism	Convicted
2	1598	Loco	Luis de Zárate	Doctor, inquisitors	—	Dismissed
3	1659	Delirio	Salvador Victoria	Layperson	—	Convicted
4	1684	Demencia/loco	Manuel Fernández	Priest	—	Dismissed
5	1694	Loca	Ana de Zayas	Inquisitors, priest	Diabolism	Convicted
6	1696	Loco	Antonio Moncada	Priest	—	Dismissed
7	1699	Falta de juicio	Juan Fernández	Priest	—	Dismissed
8	1699	Loco	Juan de Luna	Alcaides	—	Dismissed
9	1700	Loco	Juan Luis Torres	Calificadores	Insanity, demonism	Dismissed
10	1709	Loco/simple	Ignacio S. J. Salazar	Beata	—	Died
11	1717	Loca/melancolía	Paula Rosa de Jesús	Nuns	Demonism	Dismissed
12	1717	Demente/loca/melancolía	Marta de la Encarnación	Priests	Demonism	Convicted
13	1747	Melancolía	Josefa Clara	Nuns	Illness, demonism	Dismissed
14	1778	Locura/melancolía	Ángel Vázquez	Priests	—	Convicted
15	1785	Melancolía/histeria	Barbara de Echagaray	Laypeople, priests	Illness, demonism	Convicted
16	1788	Histeria/manía	Josefa Palacios	Doctors	Demonism	Convicted
17	1788	Hipocondría/delirio	Eusebio Villarejo	Priests	—	Convicted
18	1788	Loca/histeria	Ana María La Cal	Priest, doctors	Illness, demonism	Dismissed
19	1794	Histeria	María Lucía Celis	Priest	Demonism	Convicted
20	1794	Histeria	María Rita Vargas	Priest	Demonism	Convicted
21	1796	Histeria	María Ignacia	Priest	Demonism	Dismissed
22	1799	Histeria	Ana de Aramburu	Priest	Illness, diabolism	Convicted

Source: Archivo General de la Nación, Ramo Inquisición.

Table 8. Identification of demonism in ilusos and alumbrados, 1598–1799

	Year	Type of demonism	Case	Identifier	Other labels	Result
1	1598	Revelations	Ana de Guillamas	Layperson	Illness	Convicted
2	1673	Possession, fits	Juan Bautista de Cárdenas	Layperson	—	Convicted
3	1694	Revelations	Ana de Zayas	Priest	Insanity	Convicted
4	1694	Tormenting, disease	Tomasa Gonzáles	Layperson	—	Dismissed
5	1700	Obsession, fits	Juan Luis Torres	Priests, doctor	Insanity	Dismissed
6	1700	Tormenting	Ignacio de S. J. Salazar	Laypeople	Insanity	Died
7	1717	Tormenting	Paula Rosa de Jesús	Nun, priest	Insanity	Dismissed
8	1717	Tormenting	Marta de la Encarnación	Priests, doctor, laypeople	Illness, insanity	Convicted
9	1723	Revelations, torture	Getrudis Rosa Ortiz	Calificadores	—	Died
10	1723	Tormenting	María Felipa Viruete	Priest	—	Dismissed
11	1738	Possession	Agustín Claudio	Priest	—	Died
12	1746	Tormenting	"una mulatilla"	Priest	—	Dismissed
13	1748	Tormenting	Josefa Clara	Nuns	Illness, insanity	Convicted
14	1778	Tormenting	María Cayetana Loria	Priest	—	Convicted
15	1788	Sex, tormenting	Barbara de Echagaray	Priests, laypeople	Illness, insanity	Convicted
16	1788	Obsession, possession	Josefa Palacios	Priests	—	Convicted
17	1794	Tormenting	Ana María La Cal	Priest	Illness, insanity	Convicted
18	1794	Tormenting	María Lucía Celis	Priest	Insanity	Convicted
19	1794	Tormenting	María Rita Vargas	Priest	Insanity	Convicted
20	1796	Tormenting	María Ignacia	Priest	Insanity	Dismissed
21	1799	Possession	Ana de Aramburu	Priest, layperson	Illness, insanity	Convicted

Source: Archivo General de la Nación, Ramo Inquisición.

"demented," "delirious," "lacking judgment," or suffering from "lesions on their brains." However, the third most often used term for mental illness, and a label reserved exclusively for women, was *hysterical*. With two exceptions, every ilusa or alumbrada described as suffering from a mental illness after 1785 (six times by clerics and once by a doctor) was designated *hysterical*. Church officials, rather than members of the laity or medical personnel, were the group who most frequently used labels of insanity to describe defendants' behavior. Medical professionals made such associations in only three of the twenty-four cases studied.[9]

As well as perceiving mental illness in ilusos and alumbrados, laypeople, clerics, and doctors all described Mexican mystics—women much more frequently than men—as suffering from demonic possession, obsession, or tormenting. Eighteen female and four male defendants were described as experiencing demonic interactions. Descriptions of diabolic episodes increased dramatically in the eighteenth century and, as in the case of the classification of insanity, were especially high after 1775. Clerics or nuns provided such descriptions about three times as frequently as did laypeople. Only two doctors described defendants as diabolic, the latest one in 1717.

Besides attesting to defendants' mental illnesses and diabolic episodes, witnesses occasionally referred to various types of disease in order to account for the perplexing behavior of the accused. Witnesses described the accused as ill in nine trials and, once again, described women as suffering from physical illnesses in eight of these cases, perhaps reflecting the historical association between women's physical illness and mystical ecstasies. A range of different kinds of people made such identifications in the trials, including laypeople, nuns, and priests, but doctors were the most frequent providers of this evidence, beginning at the close of the seventeenth century. Epilepsy was the most frequently identified disease in the iluso and alumbrado trials, with four defendants in the nine trials described as epileptic. The other cases involved unspecified "illness" and bleeding. Epilepsy began to appear in the inquisition trials only after the turn of the eighteenth century, the era during which discussions of this disease began to circulate in New Spain's medical literature.[10]

Various individuals and groups within colonial society competed with the court's inquisitors for the power of assigning judgment to defendants' behavior, but the officers of the Holy Tribunal possessed the ultimate authority of assigning a definitive label to the accused. The inquisitors' final classification of defendants according to one or other of these categories had distinctive repercussions. The court viewed those classified as ill, insane, or demonically "obsessed" as essentially innocent and in those cases might dismiss the charges against them. In María Anastasia Lozano's 1790 ilusa trial one witness who testified against Lozano stated that while it was widely known that she had claimed to have had revelations in which God informed her that she was one of his most favored creatures, the witness believed that Lozano was a faker and a hypocrite. The witness hastened to add that no excuse existed for Lozano's behavior because it was widely known that she was "neither crazy nor demented."[11] If the court had considered Lozano insane, its officers could have overlooked the heretical tinge of her behavior and dismissed her case. Barbara de Echagaray's late-eighteenth-century trial contains a similar illustration. In his response to the court's long accusation against her, Echagaray's defense lawyer twice appealed to the court's inquisitors that they should dismiss his client's case since she had clearly been out of her senses, suffering from *furor uterino* (i.e., hysteria) when she had engaged in activities and propounded beliefs that the court found so disturbing.[12]

In terms of interactions with the devil, diabolic "possession" and "obsession," terms that witnesses frequently used in these trials, carried with them entirely distinctive ramifications. Demonic "obsession" connoted an afflicted individual's extreme virtue, whereas "possession," a term that was often employed in conjunction with convictions of false mysticism, generally heralded condemnation by the court for grievous sins.[13] Pedro Salmerón's late-seventeenth-century biography of his confessant, Isabel de la Encarnación, the exalted mystical nun of Puebla's Carmelite convent, provides a helpful definition of the distinction between these two types of demonic encounters. Isabel had experienced mystical raptures and seemingly miraculous illnesses during her lifetime, and some of her contemporaries viewed her as a woman of extraordinary virtue. Others, however, suspected that these paramystical signs indicated the presence of a diabolic, rather than divine, spirit in the nun.

Isabel's confessor arranged for the exorcism of her spirit in order to determine the type of demonic presence she had experienced, since the devil was known to torment two types of people. The "possessed," Salmerón wrote, had the devil "inside their bodies because of grave sins that they have committed." The obsessed, on the other hand, were tortured "outside of their bodies, causing grave martyrdoms and tormenting of the soul, and these are souls of great purity and sanctity, as were Saints Job and

Antonio."[14] In demonic obsession, Salmerón continued, the devil did not actually penetrate the body but instead tortured the soul, understanding, and will of afflicted people.[15] Isabel de la Encarnación's behavior during her spiritual examination led her exorcisers to conclude that she had been obsessed rather than possessed by the devil. She was therefore redeemed from all suspicion of sin and instead was honored by the other members of her convent as a virtuous soul.

Fits of demonic obsession and torturing by the devil were some of the most common paramystical phenomena that Mexican mystics experienced, suggesting that demonic "obsession" was widely understood to denote individual virtue, sanctity, and divine favor. About half of those accused claimed to have had demonic interactions. Fernando Cervantes, in his treatment of the image of the devil in the New World, explains that demonic interactions were commonly understood in the early modern period to entail an indispensable means to salvation. Cervantes argues that by the height of the baroque period, the Catholic church came to view diabolic obsession as an almost crucial element in the journey toward union with God because of the purgative and cleansing elements associated with it. As he explains, God used diabolic contact "to 'purge' a favorite soul in preparation for the mystical union." In this era, he continues, "all diabolical instigations to blaspheme, to renounce God, to commit 'impure acts' or even to despair of divine mercy could be seen as ideal means to combat self-love, especially when the individual soul was humbled to the degree of thinking that it might even have committed those horrors voluntarily."[16] In the Mexican iluso and alumbrado trials, the devil featured most prominently in encounters in which the afflicted demonstrated their virtue through resistance to the carnal temptation Satan represented.

Laypeople, clerics, and medical professionals often perceived the origins, physical evidence of, and, in cases of disease and demonism, remedies for the various states of illness, insanity, diabolism, and mysticism as interrelated and indistinctive. Both ordinary and learned people perceived the existence of a high degree of permeability between the various states of mystical rapture, demonic possession and obsession, bouts of insanity, and physical illness. Various witnesses who observed the accused experience the same phenomena—most often spastic fits or ecstatic swoons—concluded that these revealed defendants' embodiment of different states, or else showed that they had simultaneously embodied more than one of them.

In the repeated investigations, spanning from 1785 to 1799, of the criolla Barbara de Echagaray several witnesses offered conflicting explanations of the same phenomena to the court. Several of those who testified described observing the fits, raptures, and bouts of intensive bleeding that Echagaray had claimed were manifestations of God's love for her. A comisario dispatched to Jalapa to assess the case reported to his superiors in October of 1792 that many of Echagaray's peers judged that the devil was tormenting her. A priest who described bouts of illness that had seized Echagaray agreed. He declared that many of his colleagues believed that demonic possession had caused the episodes of vomiting blood, convulsions, and trembling that Echagaray had experienced. Another priest, don Alonso José García, who also wrote the court, recounted that Echagaray's acquaintances held several differing opinions about the root of her malady. García wrote that he "had sometimes thought she was, possessed, and at other times thought it was the sickness of hysteria; many thought it came from some of her scruples, and others thought she was faking. Balboa [a curate] and other priests thought she was possessed by the devil."[17]

Other lay and clerical witnesses expressed different opinions regarding the nature of Echagaray's affliction, terming it variously "melancholic" and "epileptic." Ignacio Ruiz, a doctor who treated Echagaray when she resided in Puebla, explained her behavior by intertwining several other witnesses' descriptions with references to humoral theory. Ruiz testified that Echagaray was a person of "sanguine and choleric temperament, who had suffered from powerful uterine hemorrhaging." He noted that he had examined her on several occasions when she had been "entirely delirious," a state produced "as much from the loss of blood as from the epileptic afflictions which she has suffered."[18]

During the seventeenth and, especially, the eighteenth centuries many witnesses attempted to persuade the court that it should classify defendants as insane, ill, or diabolically obsessed rather than as false mystics. The officers of the Inquisition, however, most often ignored these other assessments. In over half of the cases (eighteen of thirty-one cases) in which witnesses presented alternative explanations to account for defendants' unorthodox actions and beliefs, the court dismissed these assessments and convicted the accused for false mysticism. In only a handful of the cases in which the court dismissed charges against mystics (or declined to pursue investigations beyond the initial denunciation and interviews) did inquisitors reveal that their acceptance of the alternative explanations of illness or insanity had secured these adjournments.

As in the Inquisition's determination of the distinction between true and false mysticism, its officers did not base their assessments of defendants' illness, insanity, or diabolic obsession primarily on the analysis of the actual experiences the accused had endured. Rather than assessing these experiences themselves, the tribunal's judges based their decisions to classify individuals' experiences in the "innocent" categories of illness or obsession or the "guilty" categories of possession or mystical fraud on assessments of the moral conduct and social position of the people involved. Specifically the court based its decisions on assessments of the degree of obedience, humility, and passivity the accused had exhibited, as well as on defendants' record of conforming to contemporary standards of sexual virtue and to social behavior appropriate to their rank and race.

The Court's Determination of Illness, Insanity, or Demonism
Those few occasions upon which inquisitors dismissed trials because they agreed with witnesses' assessments of defendants' illness, insanity, or demonic obsession further illustrate the court's reasoning in formulating such evaluations. Juan Luis Torres's iluso hearing was the only instance in which inquisitors explicitly dismissed an iluso trial because they judged the defendant to be ill rather than feigning mysticism. Torres was a surgeon practicing medicine in late-seventeenth-century Mexico City. A layman had first denounced him to the court in 1700 for publishing ideas "against the faith." Torres had allegedly stated that no priest existed in all of the kingdom of Spain competent enough to be his spiritual director. He had also avowed that a prophetic spirit had spoken to him on several occasions. Finally, he had publicly asserted that legions of demons constantly tortured him. Periodically, over the next seventeen years, several of Torres's patients appeared before the court, confirming his denouncer's accusations and testifying that Torres had also been known to refer to the Holy Roman Catholic church as a *puta puerca* (whoring pig).[19]

When called to testify, Torres acknowledged that he had claimed to have visions of the Virgin Mary and Jesus Christ and appealed for the church to be merciful in judging his erroneous assertions. A court qualifier who assessed the case in 1718, wrote that he did not believe Torres was suffering from any fault of judgment, as the inquisitors had speculated, but instead thought that the surgeon had been "obsessed" by a type of epilepsy that caused him to act as if he were "beside himself," making him appear demonized.[20] Torres's inquisitors dismissed the case on the grounds that his physical affliction had rendered him innocent of any heretical elements in his behavior.

There seem to be two main reasons for the court's acceptance of the label of epileptic in Juan Luis Torres's case. First, Torres was male and, as a surgeon, occupied an elevated social position in comparison to the bulk of those both denounced and convicted of false mysticism. Second, in his first appearance before the tribunal Torres admitted the error of his ways, begged for forgiveness, and atoned for his errors. Torres therefore posed no threat to the court. These two factors induced the court to label him an "epileptic" and dismiss his case, even though some of the activities he had engaged in were identical to those of people whom the court convicted.

In addition to Torres's acquittal, the Inquisition dismissed three of the other eight instances in which witnesses described defendants as physically ill at some point in their trials, but inquisitors did not indicate, in any of these other cases, that assessments of the accused parties' ill health had secured their exoneration.[21] In several other trials court officials ignored possible medical interpretations of defendants' exhibited symptoms, rejecting illness (and therefore innocence) as an explanation for their behavior. The early-eighteenth-century ilusa trial of Marta de la Encarnación, for instance, contains many detailed submissions by medical experts certifying that this beata suffered from several illnesses, including gonorrhea.[22] Admission of the presence of this disease in the beata could have explained some of the symptoms that she had experienced, including emissions of blood and violent moods. Her inquisitors, in formulating their sentence against Marta, however, ignored the explanative powers of doctors' testimony and settled instead upon a characterization of her as a feigner of mystical sanctity.

In other cases inquisitors rejected contemporary medical beliefs that could have explained defendants' experience of bleeding bouts from various parts of their bodies. Fray Agustín Farfán proffered a medical explanation for such fits in his 1592 *Tractado breve de medicina*, one of the best-known medical treatises published in New Spain and a work Mexican physicians continued to consult throughout the colonial period. Farfán explained women's propensity to bleed from various parts of their bodies in the following way: "All evacuations of blood (besides the regular bleeding of women that happens every month) do not pertain to the supernatural because almost always when blood comes out of other parts of them, it is because of some indisposition of the body. Sometimes nature shoots it out of the nostrils, and it also comes out of the head and through other parts of the body."[23]

The idea that menstrual blood, if somehow retained, could flow from parts of a woman's body besides her vagina continued to carry legitimacy in the late colonial period. John Tate Lanning, in his research on medical education in the Spanish Empire, found that Dutch physician Hermann Boerhaave (1668–1738) was among the most important influences on the colonial medical profession by the late eighteenth century.[24] In his tract titled *Of the Diseases of Women and Children*, Boerhaave discussed the important influence that detention of the menses had on women's overall health. Like Farfán, Boerhaave stated that if detained, menstrual blood "has been seen by Physicians to force its way through at the Eyes, Ears, Nostrils, Gums, Salivary Glands, those of the Gullet, Intestines, Bladder, Breasts, the Skin, through particular Wounds and Ulcers."[25]

The inquisitors of the Mexican tribunal could have perceived infirmities from which a number of Mexican mystics, including Ana de Aramburu and Marta de la Encarnación, suffered in strictly medico-physiological terms. In both of these trials, however, inquisitors ignored the possibility that bleeding from various body parts might indicate medical conditions and interpreted them instead as evidence that the accused had faked the receipt of mystical gifts. These women had demonstrated their guilt to the court in their exertions of will in defiance of God and the church. The tribunal judged, therefore, that their bloody emissions were signs of mystical fraud rather than of divine blessing or physical illness.

The Inquisition was marginally more sympathetic to explanations of insanity that witnesses offered to account for defendants' behavior. The court dismissed—or chose not to pursue—nine of the twenty-two cases in which a person accused of iluminismo or alumbradismo was also identified as suffering from some kind of mental disorder. However, the tribunal only explicitly linked their dismissals with judgments of defendants' insanity in two of these cases, those of Luis de Zárate and sor Ana María La Cal. Luis de Zárate, a peninsular cleric and resident of Cholula, was a member of the first cluster of alumbrados tried in the late sixteenth and early seventeenth centuries. Zárate was denounced for crimes similar to those committed by others investigated in this period, including for his claims to having experienced revelations from both God and the esteemed hermit Gregorio López informing him about the foundation of a New Jerusalem. The court seemed initially suspicious of Zárate, but once he was placed in the inquisitorial prison, his jailer informed the court that he suspected Zárate to be "without possession of his judgment."[26] Unfortunately neither the jailer's assessment nor that of the doctor who examined Zárate at the court's order and diagnosed him as suffering from *flaqueza* (weakness), as indicated by his low heart rate, contain many details concerning how they formed their particular judgments of him. Based on their recommendations, however, the court concluded that Zárate was insane and sent him to Mexico City's hospital of San Hipólito, rather than convicting him as an alumbrado.

Inquisitors did not explicitly reveal their reasons for dismissing two of the other alumbrado cases—those of Juan Fernández and Manuel Fernández (no relation) in which witnesses described defendants as insane.[27] However, in both cases the accused parties were priests and therefore claimed membership in the social group that least threatened the inquisitorial court in its regulation of claims to mystical experiences. A similar explanation may explain the early-eighteenth-century dismissal of madre Paula Rosa de Jesús, a cloistered nun who thus posed a lesser social threat to the court than would an uncloistered beatas. In another case the inquisitors seem to have found the evidence of the "insane" actions of the accused party harmless enough that they did not deem it necessary to pursue the investigation. Their interview with a parishioner of the priest Antonio Moncada revealed only Moncada's propensity for making strange faces and sticking out his tongue to people.[28] In the 1796 case of María Ignacia the court dismissed the case because it suspected that the denouncer was harboring a grudge against the accused party.

The late-eighteenth-century trial of the nun Ana María La Cal, on the other hand, provides us with telling information about those situations in which the court could be persuaded to accept a description of an accused party as insane and therefore "innocent" and so dismiss charges of mystical fraud. Sor Ana María's confessor, fray José Castro, denounced her to the court because of the strange fits, visions, bouts of elevation, and "impure actions" she executed with the devil that many in the convent had observed. Fray José attested that he believed sor Ana María suffered from "a strong illusion," but he stated others thought her crazy (loca), possessed by the devil, or epileptic. He explained that several people had witnessed sor Ana María experience strange fits during which she spoke to an image of Saint Teresa, declaring "you were also crazy [loca] like me, if only everyone was like that." For his part, however, Castro stated that he believed the nun had been faking all her experiences.[29]

A surgeon who testified in the case said he knew sor Ana María had been diagnosed as suffering from "epilepsy because of the detention of her menstruation," a somewhat curious diagnosis because this symptom was normally associated with the illness of hysteria rather than epilepsy. Another doctor who also gave evidence in the trial, Luis Montaña (an enthusiastic supporter of enlightened medicine's introduction to New Spain), claimed that rather than being possessed or feigning mysticism, sor Ana María had been suffering from a "weakness in the brain," caused by hysteria.[30]

Five doctors who examined the nun came to similar diagnoses of her state. Despite their repeated appearances before the tribunal, however, the inquisitors ignored their evaluations and deduced that the nun had been faking either illness or demonic obsession. Her judges repeatedly characterized sor Ana María in their questions to witnesses as "an ilusa, even if some people have said of this person that she is crazy." At one point, sor Ana María's inquisitors noted that although the nun had exhibited symptoms that had led medical experts to conclude she was either hysteric or epileptic, they believed she was feigning all of these things "in malice."[31]

Sor Ana María's trial ended, however, with a remarkable reversal of this perception. In their concluding assessment of the nun, sor Ana María's judges dwelled on the fact that she had finally confessed that she had engaged in some acts of mystical trickery "out of confusion." With humility, they noted, she had confessed her guilt and had declared herself prepared to fulfill her Christian obligations. Given sor María's penitent state, her inquisitors were prepared to accept the idea that she had indeed been suffering from "powerful delirium and sickness and other pains."[32] Having accepted this diagnosis, inquisitor Bernardo Prado determined that she should be released from all negative ramifications of her actions and that her case should be suspended. In sor Ana María's trial, then, the court's acceptance of the medical assessment of her insanity—a label indicating her innocence—was predicated upon the nun's demonstration of her essential humility and obedience to the Inquisition. Once she became unthreateningly submissive, the court was able to declare her insane and release her from the ramifications of conviction as an ilusa.

In Ana de Zayas's late-seventeenth-century trial the officers of the Holy Tribunal executed an opposite reversal of their initial judgment of the defendant's sanity (guilt) and insanity (innocence). Zayas's inquisitors initially suspended the case against her due to her *falta de juicio* (lack of reason). Fifty days after passing this judgment, however, the court overturned its decision and ordered Zayas placed immediately in its secret cells. Her judges appear to have changed their minds about how to deal with Zayas when they learned that she had left her husband and was living apart from him. The inquisitors wrote to the local comisario instructing him to "inform himself with all clarity and distinction as to the reason or motive why the husband of the said woman allows his wife to live outside of his company."[33] After conducting extensive interviews into the reasons for Zayas's disobedient and unseemly decision to live apart from her husband, her inquisitors revised their earlier judgment and convicted Zayas for alumbradismo.[34]

In cases involving diabolic encounters, it was crucial that the court determine whether the accused had experienced demonic "obsession" or "possession," since each state carried such different implications. These trials contain many different examples of tests that clerics used to determine the nature of accused parties' diabolic experiences. Sometimes they attempted to determine if defendants had witnessed visions with their "corporal" or "interior eyes," revealing whether visions were divine, diabolic, or imaginary.[35] On other occasions they attempted to measure the strength of the devil's powers, ascertaining if the supposed spirits could distinguish between consecrated and ordinary wafers and between true relics and frauds. In several trials clerics employed the standards of testing for demonic obsession that Pope Paul V (1552–1621) had articulated. These constituted "the ability to speak in an unknown language . . . to know of distant and hidden things, and . . . to manifest superior physical force."[36]

Various clerics employed such testing in the early-eighteenth-century ilusa trial of Jeronymite nun Paula Rosa. Madre Paula's confessor, Miguel de Roxas, denounced the nun to the Inquisition in 1717 because of his suspicion of the trances, violent fits, and bouts of vomiting metal pegs, pendants, and nails that madre Paula had undergone. He also described an incident during which a force that madre Paula claimed was the devil had pegged her through the ears with nails to her bed's headboard. Although theologians could interpret such physical tormenting as evidence of the devil's presence, several priests concluded that in this case madre Paula had only feigned her interactions with the devil. Roxas testified that the nun had obviously faked her fits because it was widely known that she did not respect the sacrament of communion and had exhibited disobedience to her superiors in the convent. The court, after receiving Roxas's denunciation and at the order of Mexican archbishop José de Lanciego, dispatched a Carmelite priest, padre Pablo de Santa María, to examine madre Paula. In her first encounter with padre Pablo the nun expressed great dismay at meriting examination by one of the archbishop's attendants rather than by Lanciego himself. Aware of the distinctions the church perceived between people whom the devil had "obsessed" and those whom he had "possessed," madre Paula explicitly endeavored to convince padre Pablo that she had "not been possessed, but rather obsessed" by the devil.[37]

Padre Pablo attempted to ascertain the truth of her claim by applying a number of tests to the obsessing (or possessing) devil. In order to ascertain his strength, the priest asked the demon, who spoke through the nun's mouth, if he had actually entered madre Paula's interior, and if he had, how he had managed to assume complete control of her body. The priest then subjected madre Paula to a number of proofs designed to reveal if she had the powers normally acquired by those whom the devil occupied. He touched her with both sanctified and ordinary water and then with authentic and inauthentic relics to test her ability to distinguish between them. He also spoke to her in both French and Latin to see if she could comprehend these foreign languages. Madre Paula failed all tests, and padre Pablo concluded that she was therefore merely faking her interactions with the devil. A friar who had witnessed the testing, Andrés de San Miguel, supported his conclusions. San Miguel asserted, "There is only fiction in her, caused by the frailty that is often found in her sex."[38] Clerics also provided the court with extensive evidence about similar tests they conducted in the trials of María Felipa Viruete and fray Agustín Claudio. In the former case they argued that the defendant had been feigning obsession, and in the latter they declared that the devil had obsessed the accused.[39]

In all these cases priests who submitted evidence to the court strove to employ an almost scientific level of testing in their evaluations of the kind of demonic encounters accused parties had experienced. Inquisitors, nevertheless, gave these kinds of evaluations little credit when forming their opinions of the demonic experiences of the accused. In the trials of both madre Paula Rosa and María Felipa Viruete, in which clerics testified that the accused had been feigning their demonic interactions, the court neglected to pursue prosecution. Fray Agustín died in the secret cells of the Inquisition before his judges reached a final verdict in his case, but his calificadores' assessment that he had not been demonically obsessed suggests the court would not have found in his favor but would have prosecuted him despite a priest's contrary evidence.[40]

The Holy Office most often based its assessment of defendants' demonic encounters on evaluations of their moral character rather than on the standards used by clerics who gave evidence in court. Inquisitors automatically suspected people whom they perceived as having exercised their individual wills in seeking out the devil, while they released others when they believed the defendants had passively submitted to demonic forces. This observation explains the seeming paradox of the court's condemnation of ilusos for having faked all interactions with the devil, while at the same time convicting these same people for having contracted "explicit" or "implicit" pacts with the devil.[41]

The court also took a skeptical view of defendants who had displayed too much pride or self-confidence about their interactions with the devil or about their other religious activities. In a mid-eighteenth-century spiritual guide translated and published in Spain and circulating in Mexico, Portuguese Augustine Francisco de la Anunciacão wrote that "when the Devil . . . attempts to fabricate some false sign, he proceeds in the following manner: First, he plants in the heart the spirit of pride and vanity with which he instigates the desire in subjects to participate in high things; with great visions, revelations, ecstasies, etc. After that, a person begins to take pleasure in himself, and takes himself for learned, and after this, the devil easily tricks people . . ."[42] The most condemnable aspect of interaction with the devil was the self-confidence found in those who had encountered him and in their conception that they were capable of knowing and doing "high things."

Several ilusos expressed this very sentiment. During one of her appearances before the court, mid-seventeenth-century ilusa Josefa de San Luis Beltrán explained that many times while in mystical raptures she had seen visions of her patron saint, San Luis Beltrán. After a time, however, she realized that she was really having visions of the devil who had disguised himself as the saint. When the court questioned her as to how she had ascertained she was actually experiencing a vision of the devil, she stated that "when she saw this figure, her soul was raised in the spirit of pride and vainglory."[43] Several of the clerics and nuns who testified in the mid-eighteenth-century trial of sor Josefa Clara de Jesús, investigated for fits of demonic tormenting, linked sor Josefa's contact with the devil to her disobedient nature. Juana María de las Virgenes asserted that just before sor Josefa's first demonic encounter, "the madre maestra scolded her for having spoken back to her, and not having acted with total obedience and humility in the things required of her." Another nun declared that she thought Josefa Clara had herself inflicted the wounds she claimed the devil had given her because "that same day she had responded angrily to the madre maestra" and earlier had written to her confessor against her superior's will.[44]

Inquisitors based their judgments about accused parties' diabolic encounters on their interpretations of the moral qualities defendants exhibited. If the court saw these parties as humble and obedient subjects, they were likely to judge that their encounters with the devil had been essentially harmless. However, if those investigated posed some threat to the church—in terms, especially, of an arrogant or disobedient nature—the tribunal was likely to judge that the accused had experienced diabolic possession or had made a pact with the devil in defiance of God.

The Discourse of Medical and Spiritual Classification

Assessments of diabolic encounters remained prominent in Mexican iluso trials throughout the colonial period, but testimony that those accused of feigning mysticism were actually ill or insane also increased over the course of the eighteenth century. Doctors appeared before the tribunal with increasing frequency in the later eighteenth century, often supplying evidence that those accused of feigning paramystical episodes were, in fact, victims of epilepsy or hysteria. In this era a number of new influences from European science infiltrated New Spain's medical establishment. The period witnessed an augmentation of the state's participation in the regulation of medicine, the establishment of public health standards, an increase in hospital construction, and an expansion in the range and number of medical texts circulating in the colony.[45] Prior to the mid-eighteenth century, medical students' readings were restricted almost exclusively to the writings of Galen, Hippocrates, Avicenna, and Galileo, and their training focused on humoral theory. After midcentury, as the Enlightenment spread to Mexico, medical students began studying the work of a number of seventeenth- and eighteenth-century European physicians and scientists, including Lorenzo Bellini, Frederick Hoffman, Hermann Boerhaave, Johannes de Gorter, Andres Piquer, and, by the beginning of the nineteenth century, John Brown and Lazarus Riverius.[46]

Medical personnel were not alone in their exposure to these new influences. Clerics who appeared in the Mexican trials also demonstrated the appeal some of these new theories held for them. In Josefa Palacios's trial priest Mariano Iturria displayed his enthusiasm for a rationalist explanation of Palacios's extraordinary behavior. He wrote respectfully

Classification of Female Disorders ❀ 155

of contemporary physicians who attempted to banish "superstitious" beliefs that attributed such fits as Palacios experienced to "demonic" melancholy. According to Iturria, "neither blaspheming God and his saints, nor speaking a word or two in Latin, . . . nor having exceptional forces . . . nor breathing fire . . . nor pronouncing in a prophetic tone something that is then verified to be true; nor all this together nor any of it separately, is a sign of demonic possession, but rather most of the time reveals the existence of an extraordinary melancholic mania." Iturria rejected the medieval and early modern belief that the devil most often caused such fits and instead deduced that the physical illness of hysteria was responsible.[47]

Although Mexican medical thought underwent some transformations during the late eighteenth century, an older terminology and rationale clearly continued to exert a powerful influence on medical and clerical perceptions of mental and physical illness in this era. As Mexico entered the nineteenth century, earlier spiritual and moralistic discourses contin-ued to inform medical explanations of irregular behavior. Judgments of physical and psychological health were rooted in assessments of individ-uals' embodiment of virtue and of vice.

A medical tract that doctor Pedro de Horta wrote about an "epidemic" of epilepsy that swept the city of Puebla in the mid-eighteenth century illustrates the way in which Christian precepts influenced medical per-ception in this period. During the height of the epidemic, Horta wrote that Puebla's streets had teemed with citizens in the throes of violent convulsive fits who had contracted the disease. When the contagion reached Puebla's Jeronymite convent, many of the nuns were afflicted so severely that they were "almost continuously in the arms of death." Alarmed poblanos debated the origins of this frightening malady. "Some," Horta noted, "say that these diseases are only affected by natural causes; others believe they may be demonic; and of those from this camp, some think the cure would be exorcism and others do not. There are even some who affirm that they think that if the diseases are diabolic, the ill can not be cured by doctors, but only with confessors or exorcisors."[48]

The reason for the controversy over the most expedient means of curing those whom epilepsy had infected was that nobody was certain whether the disease had been caused by natural or supernatural forces. Horta, when first characterizing the illness, described it in almost strictly biological terms, defining it as "a forced, involuntarily, preternatural, violent, convulsive concussion of the nervo-membranous muscular parts of the entire body, accompanied by a privation of the senses, caused by a spasmodic tightening of the membranes that surround the brain, spinal chord and nerves, and by the subsequent influence of very violent animal spirits."[49]

Among the symptoms that Horta included in his list of those afflicted with epilepsy were lassitude, pain, heart palpitations, stomach noises, difficulty breathing, coldness in the limbs, lengthy urination, a sensation of coolness around the heart and brain, foaming at the mouth, tongue biting, rigidity in the limbs, crying and laughing fits, and speaking in unknown languages. [50] This list includes many examples of physical behavior also common to people experiencing mystical raptures or bouts of demonic possession or obsession.[51]

Besides describing epilepsy in ways that resembled contemporary characterizations of mysticism and diabolism, Horta's tract also linked the symptoms and sources of the disease to those associated with hysteria. In the eighteenth century much European medical literature viewed hysteria as an ailment caused by fluctuations in the uterus and drastic extremes in the frequency with which women engaged in sexual activities.[52] Horta associated epilepsy with hysteria in his treatise by writing that epilepsy seemed to "follow the mutations of the moon and of the times: and in women, it proceeds or follows menstruation." As was also common to many contemporary discussions of hysteria's causes, Horta wrote that overstimulation of the senses or emotions often brought on epilepsy in women. Epilepsy, he stated, could be caused in women because of "sudden and unexpected disturbances in the spirit, surprise, fear, rage, happiness, or joy. It can also be caused by the falling of the spirit, grief, intense thought, drinks that intoxicate, excessive heat and other things."[53]

Horta's diagnosis that overstimulation caused epilepsy in women re-sembles much contemporary literature on the causes of hysteria. The most extensive discussions of hysteria produced in Mexico during this period appeared in the pages of José Ignacio Bartolache's *Mercurio volante*, the first medical periodical published in the New World, which com-menced circulation in 1772. Bartolache, a doctor who had embraced the new directions of European science and rejected humoral teachings, dedicated one of the first issues of his periodical to the discussion of hysteria. Bartolache wrote that hysteria, a uniquely female malady, had reached "epidemic" proportions in New Spain, where it had afflicted 60 percent of laywomen and 80 percent of nuns. [54] The disease, he wrote, usually took root in the uterus (*matriz*), then spread to the brain, nerves, and muscles, and was common "among people of high and medium category, born and educated in the kingdom."[55]

Although he acknowledged hysteria first affected the uterus, Bartolache disputed hysteria's common contemporary association with female reproduction and sexuality. He argued that "the sick . . . continue to believe that the suppression and diminution of the menses is the cause of *la mala histérico* and other many sicknesses. But Doctors know . . . that to the contrary, this said suppression or diminution is only the effect of another sickness that must be cured." Bartolache reduced hysteria's causes to three principal points: "The first is the abuse of sweets and chocolate. The second is tight clothing, encouraging inaction and lack of exercise. The third is the perverse custom of going to bed and getting up late."[56] In addition to these factors, he deduced that the capital city's elevated altitude and high population density exacerbated the malady.

Many ideas expressed in the writings of other physicians whose work circulated in Mexico in the late eighteenth century and at the beginning of the nineteenth resembled those of Bartolache. One Mexican author, doctor Juan Manuel Vanegas, whose *Compendio de la medicina práctica* was published in New Spain in 1788, wrote in his discussion of obstetrics and gynecology that women who failed to conceive or lactate were likely to experience numerous grave medical repercussions including hysteria. Vanegas believed that a host of factors could lead to the suppression of the menses, including the "disposition of women's organs," their overall health, the climates in which they lived, the physical activities they engaged in, and the type of food they consumed. Disastrous repercussions could befall women who either did not become pregnant or who, once pregnant, failed to lactate. Vanegas also advised (using somewhat circular logic) that the "suppression of the menses" had a number of causes including contraction in the uterus caused by cold elements, the blockage of blood vessels of the uterus, impediments in the movement of blood (caused by sadness and dizziness), violent rages, and hysteria.[57]

John Brown, whose *Elements of Medicine* was translated and published in Mexico in 1802, wrote that injuries to the uterus most often caused hysteria and argued that excessive blood flow in women's menses could be caused by "lascivious thoughts and violent moral affections," overengagement in sexual activities, or overconsumption of stimulants or spicy food. He concluded that hysteria and epilepsy greatly resembled one another, writing that bouts of the former malady could be brought on by "excess in the pleasures of love."[58]

Lazarus Riverius, a seventeenth-century French physician whose work was also studied at the beginning of the nineteenth century in Mexico, adopted an opposing position on the question of the relationship of hysteria to sexual intercourse.[59] Reverting to one of the oldest ideas about the illness's cause, Riverius asserted that women's lack of sexual (or, more particularly, reproductive) activity could cause hysterical fits. Describing hysteria alternatively as "womb furie" and "the mother," Riverius advised marriage as a cure. In cases in which "the patient cannot be so conveniently married," however, he counseled "that the Genital Parts should then by a cunning Midwife be so handled and rubbed as to cause an Evacuation of the over-abounding Sperm."[60]

These medical sources permit us some insight into how physicians in the colony were taught to understand the illness of hysteria. They learned that it was a female disease usually afflicting affluent women. They were taught that hysteria was often caused by sensory decadence and might also be linked to moral depravity.[61] Many doctors would have read that hysteria's origin was related in some way to female sexuality and reproduction, but they may have been exposed to divergent views over whether excessive or insufficient sexual intercourse was most likely to induce hysteria. This medical literature bears a strikingly close resemblance, despite its derivation from new sources, to the spiritual directives the Catholic church had traditionally issued concerning women's means of achieving virtue and distancing themselves from the vices of Lucifer.

Theological and mystical guides of the seventeenth and eighteenth centuries propounded the central tenet that virtue consisted in avoiding the carnality associated with the diabolic temptations of gluttony, greed, and lasciviousness. José de Castillo Grajeda's 1692 biography of Catarina de San Juan, Puebla's celebrated seventeenth-century mystic of East Indian origin, illustrates how deprivation of fleshy indulgences demonstrated female morality. In his vida Castillo detailed a number of demonstrations of Catarina's incredible feats of virtue, including her practice of depriving herself the luxury of eating anything but the plainest of food, choosing to fast for much of her life on bread and water. If rich foods or sweets ever tempted her, Christ appeared before the holy woman, saying, "Catarina, what is happening? Does my mouth taste of metal and vinegar? Why do you want to try these other sweet things?"[62]

Although especially revering Christian figures who deprived themselves of all excessive carnal temptation, seventeenth- and eighteenth-century theology sometimes counseled that the virtuous should refrain from indulging in even the most minute of bodily pleasures. One promi-nent seventeenth-century author, Antonio de Molina, advised his readers that mortification of the flesh entailed "the study and virtuous care, with which man deprives himself for the love of God of the things that are conformed to the inclination of ruined nature, although they are licit, and embraces those that of the same nature are abhorrent and repellent."[63]

Virtuous people were to avoid sensual pleasures and allow only reason, spirit, and the superior part of the soul to govern their behavior. For Molina and his contemporaries, true mortification consisted in the de-privation of even minutely pleasurable things. He encouraged the faithful to deny themselves the joy of looking at sights including fields, rivers, and gardens, and he condemned "listening to dishonest music, smelling flowers, reading stories, or other things of this type." In order to rid themselves of all possible temptation by the devil, Christians should deprive themselves of any kind of stimulation, whether to the senses, imagination, emotions, or intellect: "Generally, each person must train their eyes away from all type of curiosity, wherever it is they wish to travel, and wherever they wish to enter, so that they not examine, nor see anything, except simply that which presents itself directly in front of them, or that which is necessary for that which they have to do, or deal with."[64]

For Molina, deprivation of the senses and the imagination paved the route toward union with God and away from the devil's temptations. In the late eighteenth-century, physicians also believed the same pro-scriptions held the key to both the prevention and cure of physical and mental illness, particularly in cases of female sufferers. Physicians wrote that excessive stimulation of the imagination and overindulgence of the senses, which Molina argued led people into the pathway of the devil's temptation, caused hysteria and other physical and mental disorders. They advised cures involving the deprivation of the mind and body from such excessive indulgence. In addition to counseling patients' avoidance of such stimulants as chocolate or spicy food, one early-nineteenth-century writer advised patients to restrain from drinking coffee. French physician Jean-Baptiste Louyer-Villermay, whose works circulated in Mexico, wrote that a female acquaintance had told him that she "was seized by a hysterical convulsion each time that she breakfasted upon a cup of *café au lait*."[65]

Conclusion

Various sectors of colonial Mexican society attempted in the late eigh-teenth century to introduce new discourses of hysteria and epilepsy into the classificatory vocabulary of female disorders. The officers of the Mexican Inquisition, however, rejected these new explanations for female disorderliness, preferring to persevere in their traditional practice of labeling women who experienced spastic fits, physical torment, or ecstatic swoons as feigners of mystical sanctity, often in combination with charges of diabolic possession. The competing labels physicians, laypeople, and clerics employed to describe these women's behavior would have exonerated them from the court's prosecution, but they still carried with them a stigma of deviancy. The court often ordered women classified as hysterical or epileptic to undergo treatment in reformatory institutions—hospitals or insane asylums—that may have been preferable to the recogimientos or poorhouses where those convicted of false mysticism were often sentenced to serve, but they were reformatory institutions nonetheless. Service of a sentence in one of these institutions may have only been marginally less unpleasant than confinement in the Inquisition's secret cells.

Those clerics and physicians who advocated the adoption of newly enlightened means of explaining aberrations in female behavior differed from their baroque predecessors in their view of society and its disorders. They understood social problems as corrigible through the application of reason and reform, whereas holders of the older baroque vision understood sickness and health in human physiology and wider societal organisms in terms of the need for the organic balance of humors. Despite this difference in the two models' perspectives of normalcy and aberration, an important set of constants underlay the new enlightened vision of social deviancy. The new medical literature of the eighteenth century, in its efforts to explain the origins of female—and societal—disorder, pointed to some of the very same factors that the older baroque traditions of the Counter-Reformation church had pinpointed.

The types of women that physicians labeled as "hysterical" and the reasons medical professionals produced for attaching such labels to women illustrate the consistency of this reasoning. Physicians and clerics who introduced the new vocabulary of hysteria into the inquisitorial court in the late eighteenth century pointed to three types of women whose behavior demonstrated they merited such classification: women who had fallen in social position, women accused of sexual promiscuity, especially with their social inferiors, and women who questioned the miracle of the Virgin Mary's sexual purity.

In Josefa Palacios's late-eighteenth-century trial, several ecclesiastics and doctors used the term *hysteric* to account for this beata's behavior. Their testimonies sometimes amounted to rationalist descriptions of the violent physical fits they had watched her experience, but these witnesses also intertwined observations about how other aspects of Palacios's history and practices had induced this condition in her. By the time of her trial, Palacios, a child born to "distinguished parents," had fallen into somewhat diminished economic circumstances. She declared that during her adult life she had worked as a seamstress and maid.[66] Such a reduction of economic prospects also applied to other women labeled as hysterics in the late colonial period, including Barbara de Echagaray. When this criolla laywoman appeared before the Holy Office in 1785, she described herself as a person of "noble descent" and asserted that her father had been a captain of "Dragones," a military unit in which her two uncles had also served.

As an adolescent, Echagaray continued, she had received education in dancing and other skills "appropriate to females of her status." When her trial opened, however, Echagaray had been forced to maintain herself by performing "women's offices" and by collecting alms from her relatives and acquaintances, although she was still wealthy enough at the outset of her trial to retain the services of a black servant. By the time her investigation entered its twelfth year, her situation had further deteriorated. José Saurez, the case's comisario, noted that she was "in such a state of misery and poverty that she has nothing other to care for herself beyond some little alms that she can acquire."[67]

Besides being women who had fallen in social status, many of those labeled as hysterics in the Mexican trials were women simultaneously accused of sexual promiscuity. In Josefa Palacios's trial cleric Iturria focused on her sexual crimes as a central factor in demonstrating her "catching" of hysteria. Several other witnesses concurred. Fray Matías de los Dolores commented to the court that he had heard of the "indecency" with which the beata and her confessor, Eusebio Villarejo, had comported themselves.[68] Similarly, in Barbara de Echagaray's trial her confessor, Pedro Ibarrarán, supplied evidence to the court about how Echaragay's history of sexual promiscuity secured his condemnation.[69] In Ana María La Cal's late-eighteenth-century trial, one witness who described the nun's lewd interactions with the devil testified that he had deduced that the *furor uterino* had afflicted sor Ana because she had not behaved in a manner "corresponding her state" but had engaged in "very obscene words and actions."[70]

Finally, many of the late-eighteenth-century mystical women labeled as hysterics were also people who had questioned the validity of the church's doctrine on Mary's perpetual virginity. In one late-eighteenth-century heresy trial a friar testified that his confessant, María del Castillo Espanda, had "gravely suffered from the illness of hysteria for seven months," and her state had impeded her from confessing and taking communion. When María appeared before the tribunal, she testified that besides failing to attend mass, she had committed other sins. She declared that she refused to believe "that the Virgin Mary Our Lady had been conceived in grace," and also that it was not true that Mary had been a virgin "during the birth, before, and after the birth," contesting instead that Mary had enjoyed sexual relations with her husband, José, eight times or more.[71] Espanda's words eschewed the text of the articles of the Christian faith popularly reproduced in Mexico.[72]

Several ilusas tried in the same period similarly questioned the doctrine of Mary's perpetual virginity. Barbara de Echagaray, for instance, confessed that she had believed that the Holy Spirit had not impregnated the Virgin Mary, but rather than she "had conceived by her chaste spouse." Echagaray also testified that she had been so fascinated with the story of the Virgin Mary that on one occasion, when meditating before her, she had "lifted up her clothes and put her hands on her stomach," contemplating what she had done.[73]

In this period, then, women who challenged the doctrine of Mary's perpetual virginity or those who were suspected of unchaste behavior might be classified as hysterical as well as heretical. This was particularly true if they were women who had either fallen in social class or failed to behave in a manner "corresponding to their states." Although various witnesses who appeared before the tribunal labeled women who engaged in such behavior as hysterical, the court of the Inquisition was not prepared, in most cases, to accept the validity of this new discourse of female deviancy that had begun circulating in New Spain's educated elite in the second half of the eighteenth century. The calificadores in Josefa Palacios's trial concluded that she was guilty of affecting sanctity and wrote that "it would be imprudent to attribute all or the majority of [her crimes] to hysteria." Although a variety of "impartials" had testified she had experienced hysteria, they argued that "the actions and words that she and her director attribute to the devil were their own, and freely engaged in."[74]

The source of the court's resistance to accepting the validity of these new categories of female deviancy lay in the connotations of innocence associated with illness and mental illness, as with the older category of demonic obsession. The officers of the Holy Office resisted accepting the new categories of female dysfunction. The discourse of female virtue and transgression that they had helped to shape in the seventeenth and eighteenth centuries, however, continued to influence the newly developed means of identifying hysterical women at the close of the colonial period. Since the mid-seventeenth century, in the context of both the growth of New Spain's mixed-race population and the inception of criollos' efforts to secure their own political, economic, and social legitimacy, three sets of concerns had underwritten the identification of those designated authentic and false mystics in New Spain. Anxieties about female chastity, "passing," and social mobility and the potential influences of African and Indian religious practices on the purity of colonial Catholicism had all served as important bases in the detection of false mystics in New Spain. In the last decades of the eighteenth century both Christian theological directives counseling isolation from excessive stimulation and racial concerns that had preoccupied elites for over a century exerted a profound influence on the colony's reception of the new medical and social ideologies of the European Enlightenment.

Conclusion

The Spirit and the Flesh

I n the midst of Ana de Aramburu's late-eighteenth-century Inquisition hearing, someone composed a scathing visual lampoon of her religious experiences and tacked it up to the door of the Orcolaga household where Aramburu was living at the outset of her trial (see figure 4). [1] Juan Domingo Gutiérrez, one of her former patrons, submitted the drawing to the court. The drawing depicts particular elements of Aramburu's religious practices that a number of witnesses described to the Holy Office during the course of her investigation and attacks her claims to spiritual and social authority in a number of ways. It illustrates some of the central tensions that characterized her trial, and those of other Mexican mystics.

As was common in miniature retablo paintings (paintings documenting miraculous occurrences that were popular in the colonial period and nineteenth century), the drawing features three representations of the central subject, Aramburu, engaged in three different activities. [2] Two men are also depicted, and all the figures have textual scrolls floating around them. The left-hand image of Aramburu shows her reclining on an elaborate canopied bed. Pictured in the midst of an ecstatic fit, she stretches her arms and legs rigidly out from her body in a position of partial levitation.

Two tiny demonlike creatures float behind her head and above the tips of her outstretched feet, and one scroll springing from the top of her head reads: "diabolic illusion." [3] The Aramburu figure standing in the middle of the drawing states, "crazy am I, and senseless." In the late eighteenth century laypeople, medical professionals, and clerics often testified to

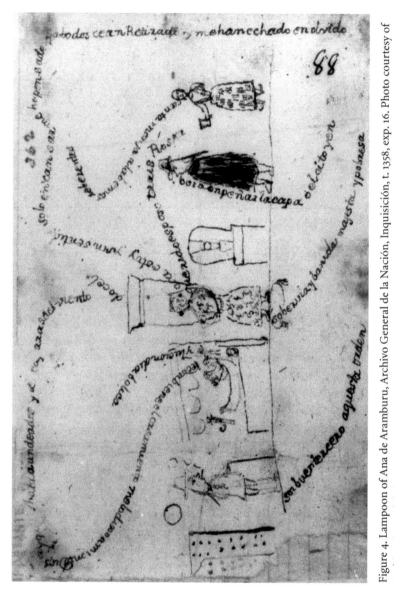

Figure 4. Lampoon of Ana de Aramburu, Archivo General de la Nación, Inquisición, t. 1358, exp. 16. Photo courtesy of Archivo General de la Nación, México.

the court that explanations of insanity or demonism might account for the unusual acts they had witnessed ilusos and alumbrados perform. During much of the colonial period judgments of diabolic obsession and assessments of physical or mental illness signified the innocence of afflicted parties. In most cases in which witnesses testified that the accused had experienced one or more of these states, however, officials of the Holy Office ignored such alternative explanations and deduced that defendants were guilty of "faking" mysticism. Inquisitors' resistance to adopting these alternative labels likely rested in their awareness that both illness and diabolism often implied the essential innocence of the afflicted parties. The court's rejection of these alternative explanations of defendants' behavior was often rooted in the evaluation of the quality of the individuals who had mystical experiences, rather than in the study of these experiences themselves.

A second caption that rises above the levitating figure in the image reads: "Marriage suits you; my God told me so." The central Aramburu figure also discusses marriage, asking "Dear husband, have you brought a ring?" These allusions to matrimony may relate to societal suspicion of Aramburu, who was a married woman living apart from her husband, or they may refer to her public reputation for working as a spiritual and social counselor to women in her community. One witness who testified in the trial remembered that Aramburu had offered counsel to one of the two daughters of her patron, Josefa Orcolaga, to marry and had advised the second to join a convent.[4] Although Aramburu, like many other ilusas in Mexico, secured the support of a network of spiritual and financial sponsors through her religious performances and social services, some members of her community obviously felt threatened that a woman such as she held power over others.

The references to marriage in the Aramburu drawing might also allude to the spiritual bonding that marked the highest phase of a true mystic's union with God. The drawing again mocks Aramburu's claims to achieving lofty mystical heights. Besides being an insane pretender to mystical union, the text that trails from below this central figure, reading "pride and vanity, majesty and poverty," scorns Aramburu's assertions of spiritual virtue. These four terms are a parody of the vows of poverty, humility, obedience, and chastity taken by nuns.[5] The court of the Holy Office judged that fraudulent mystics rejected these attributes. It saw them as undeservedly proud individuals who had deceitfully used religion to overcome poverty by securing financial sponsors for themselves. Some of these attitudes clearly existed in the wider body of the Mexican populace as well. The illustrator jeers at Aramburu's claim to piety in the text issuing from the right-hand image of Aramburu, reading "sing nun, we admire you reverently."

This figure extends a cup, likely for the collection of alms, to the back of a male figure. Like many other Mexican mystics, Aramburu supported herself partially through donations from her spiritual patrons and clients. The Inquisition looked askance at such sponsorship. It convicted ilusos or alumbrados who, like Aramburu, surrounded themselves with spiritual and financial supporters much more frequently than those who existed in isolation. The two men depicted in the drawing likely represent two of Aramburu's patrons. The attire of the man on the right suggests he was a priest. The man on the left, who stands smoking and leaning on his cane while he watches Aramburu undergo her ecstasy, might be a merchant. Priests and merchants were the groups who most often provided spiritual and material support to beatas' mystical spirituality. The merchant figure implies that he is one of Aramburu's devotees with his exclamation, "I am a good tercero of this order," suggesting that he has himself become a tertiary in a religious order founded by Aramburu herself. Despite her success in securing admiring followers, however, the lampoon indicates that Aramburu's fortunes have shifted. The trail of text bordering the picture's right-hand side states: "already everyone has withdrawn and has thrown me into oblivion." In all Aramburu's postures, and in the commentary contained in the drawing's texts, its creator depicts Aramburu as an unlikely candidate for "authentic" mystical experiences.

This illustrator concluded Aramburu was a charlatan, a fool, an insane or demonized person, and a beggar. The court of the Inquisition, however, often had a much more difficult time distinguishing between legitimate and fraudulent mystics. One of Catholicism's central theological quandaries lay at the heart of the Inquisition's judgments of authentic and false mysticism in colonial Mexico. In the iluso and alumbrado trials the court evaluated the veracity of individual manifestations of the spiritual world's communications to the material world. The Holy Office judged the orthodoxy of people whose religious experiences—visions, miracles, and ecstatic fits—entailed the physical embodiment of supernatural forces. In the context of the growth of Protestantism the Inquisition prosecuted alumbrados in sixteenth-century Spain because of the Catholic church's heightened suspicion of forms of religious expression, such as mystical recogimiento, that celebrated the possibility of individuals' direct relationship to God. The Catholic church, in this environment, grew wary of all forms of piety that appeared to detract from the supremacy of the worldly agents whom God had appointed. In the mid-sixteenth century, the Council of Trent responded to Protestantism by reinforcing the divine legitimacy of the clergy with its exclusive rights to possession of theological knowledge, performance of the sacraments, and supervision of religious celebrations and artistic productions.

The Inquisition's mandate to purge the Iberian peninsula of crypto-Jews also shaped its condemnation of Spanish alumbrados. It associated alumbrados' alleged disdain for the sacrament of the Eucharist and the mystery of the Incarnation with Judaism's rejection of the idea that the savior had already reappeared on earth. Spiritual-material controversies also shaped the Inquisition's perception of Spanish alumbrados in light of the rise of the antinomian heresies of quietismo and molinismo in the seventeenth century. Institutional Catholicism mistrusted people who claimed their souls had reached such a state of spiritual excellence that their bodies were incapable of sin. They perceived alumbrados as frauds who feigned mystical perfection only so that they might gratify their own flesh-bound desires.

The Mexican Inquisition's initial prosecution of alumbrados in the late sixteenth century perpetuated these Iberian concerns. However, beginning in the mid-seventeenth century, the prosecution of Mexican false mysticism began shifting to reflect the predominant concerns of groups within the viceroyalty of New Spain. Transformations in the way the tribunal labeled false mystics marked this shift. Starting in the mid-seventeenth century, officers of the Mexican Inquisition, as well as lay and clerical witnesses, gradually began to substitute the label *iluso* for *alumbrado* to designate those accused of false mysticism. Simultaneously the court and members of the public began associating alumbradismo less with a particular set of theological concepts, such as had defined alumbradismo in sixteenth- and early-seventeenth-century Spanish edicts, and more with the ecstatic fits detailed in Mexican edicts' descriptions of alumbradismo. The shift was also manifest in the new focus in the Mexican trials on defendants' contemptible acts of deluding susceptible admirers (patrons and clients) into believing they were true mystics.

Alumbradismo in New Spain (with the possible exception of the late-sixteenth-century cases) was never a coherent religious movement or sect whose adherents were united through participation in a common set of religious practices and beliefs. Individuals accused of these crimes expressed faith in an assorted body of spiritual ideas. Their beliefs included such diverse concepts as Pedro García de Arias's claim that all men were slaves held hostage to Christ's sacrifice and Ana de Zayas's assertion that she should not be held responsible for the sins of her husband. They ranged from fray Agustín Claudio's belief that the soundest means of demonstrating resistance to worldly temptation was to thrust oneself into the midst of heightened sinful enticements to María Cayetana Loria's doubts about Mary's untainted virginity. Many of their ideas expressed mystics' particular interpretations of humanity's appropriate relationship to God and to contemporary Catholic morality, but they did not represent a coherent body of religious thought uniting all those whom the church labeled *alumbrados.*

The Inquisition prosecuted alumbrados in Spain in part for their supposed disdain of the church's sacraments and rituals. Occasionally the Mexican tribunal condemned New World mystics for similar issues. Inquisitors accused fray Agustín Claudio of restricting his daughters of confession from confessing with other priests and suspected Ana de Aramburu of defiling the ceremony of the Eucharist by masturbating with the host. For the most part, however, Mexican mystics embraced the church's use of ritual, the sacraments, and the incorporation of sacred religious objects into spiritual ceremonies. They also enthusiastically adopted the adoration of the saints and the celebration of miraculous occurrences that institutional Catholicism endorsed as orthodox in colonial Mexico.

Many of their individual visions, the most predominant of their paramystical experiences, did contain challenges to—or modifications of—orthodox Catholic theology. The Catholic canon contains no episodes involving faithful Christians' necessary transformation into black people in order to achieve redemption, and no documentation that the Virgin Mary considered abortion before giving birth to the Savior. The content of the modifications that Mexican ilusos and alumbrados made to conventional theology was disturbing in itself. More alarming to the court, however, was mystics' presumption that they might use their own experiences of life to make such modifications. As in Getrudis Rosa Ortiz's trial, the court condemned mystics who used their own "discourse, conjectures, and imagination" to reinterpret orthodoxy.

If ilusos and alumbrados did not form a sect that posed a coherent theological challenge to Counter-Reformation Catholic orthodoxy, what or who were these people? Why did the Inquisition prosecute them over the two-hundred-year period from the late sixteenth century to the beginning of the nineteenth century? Most of the defendants in the Mexican trials were people of relatively humble economic status from urban centers in New Spain. The majority of them were criollos, although a minority were mulatos or mestizos. A significant portion of the men accused of false mysticism were members of the clergy suspected of supporting the mysticism of a female visionary, and the highest rates of conviction occurred among beata, beato, or ermitaño defendants. The Inquisition found ilusos' accumulation of supporters one of the most threatening aspects of their religious expressions. Supporters were disturbing both because they documented mystics' influence and power among a larger segment of the colonial population and because they suggested that wider portions of this populous than the one hundred people tried for iluminismo and alumbradismo were persuaded by the legitimacy of these mystics' alternative religious perspectives.

Colonial Mexico was, for the most part, a nonliterate, visually oriented society in which advanced theological education (the only kind available) was a privilege accessible only to an exclusive elite. In this context the Inquisition may have accurately perceived that a vast portion of New Spain's devout Christian population—repeatedly and inadvertently— engaged in the kinds of personal reinterpretations of Catholic orthodoxy documented in iluso and alumbrado trials. Mexican mystics succeeded in retaining patrons and clients because their spiritual expressions mirrored their supporters' religious beliefs. Perhaps a wide body of colonial Mexicans, like the mystics who were tried, integrated Catholic doctrine into the particularities of their own experiences, understanding Catholicism both as a means to adore God and to address the occasional crises and more frequent daily anxieties that troubled them, as they have troubled so many others across time and place.

Some understood Catholicism as a way of addressing grief over the premature death of a beloved friend or family member. Seventeenth-century beata María de la Encarnación addressed such grief, and accumulated supporters for her abilities, in her communications with the souls of the dead. Others may have used religion to manage unanticipated or unforthcoming pregnancies, as Getrudis Rosa Ortiz, Agustina Rangel, and other mystics did in their visions, miraculous cures, and herbal remedies for either unhappily pregnant women or women frustrated in their desire to conceive. For others, such as Teresa Romero, Pedro García, and Josefa Palacios, spirituality was in part a concrete means of addressing and overcoming domestic economic shortfalls. Finally, mystics such as Ignacio de San Juan Salazar, among many others (present and past), saw religion as a venue in which to express anger at illegitimate and immoral secular and sacred governors. In supporting local figures whose spiritual expressions addressed their own concerns, the population of colonial Mexico contested Spain's intended use of saint worship: as a means of indoctrinating and assuming colonial control of its New World territories.[6]

The court, then, in some instances accurately perceived the dangers of mystics' influences over the populace. However, in many other ways, the Holy Office failed to apprehend the nature of alumbrado and iluso piety. The Mexican Inquisition and the defendants' views of one another parallel the scenario of "Double Mistaken Identity" that Mexican ethnohistorians use to describe Catholic proselytizers' and indigenous people's misperceptions of one another's religious systems. According to James Lockhart, this scenario described Spaniards' and Nahuas' unspoken—and wildly inaccurate—presumption of sameness between their own religious beliefs and those of the other group. In this situation "each side takes it that a given form or concept is essentially one already known to it, operating in much the same manner as in its own tradition, and hardly takes cognizance of the other side's interpretation."[7]

"Double Mistaken Identity" can be usefully applied to the history of Mexican alumbradismo because it suggests how mistaken the Inquisition was in its perception of many aspects of the true nature of these mystics' religious practices. Although the mystics were ostensibly prosecuted for a religious heresy promoting interior religion, very few of their spiritual practices, in fact, involved such isolated contemplative spirituality. "Double Mistaken Identity" also partially explains why many ilusos and alumbrados persisted in having faith in their own orthodoxy even in the context of inquisitorial investigations. They perceived themselves to be true Christians and awaited the court's realization of this truth. There was no reason for Getrudis Rosa Ortiz to hide her divine revelations from the Holy Office (or from New Spain's viceroy or archbishop, for that matter). Since she was merely expressing sanctified Catholicism, she believed she had every right—indeed every obligation—to share her revelations with the institutions of orthodoxy in the series of letters she posted up around Mexico City's churches and convents and sent to the viceroyalty's highest administrators.

Mexican mystics who considered themselves orthodox may have believed they were following the dictates of Christianity to which they had been exposed. In sermons, vidas, catechisms, and religious art generated in seventeenth- and eighteenth-century New Spain, they learned that virtue lay in poverty, humility, and disdain for the world. The catechism produced by the Mexican Provincial Council taught colonial Mexicans that the flesh represented original sin, and that original sin was constantly reenacted when "disturbance of sensual appetites" threatened to overwhelm humans' rational souls. [8] In sermons they heard that to attain virtue, they should "discard the ancient vices of the flesh" and use penitence to deny "pride and the rebelliousness of blood." As one priest declared in his 1685 sermon, "as far as the body goes, we know that we have to care for it (seeing as we are born with this natural love of food) as if we are encharged with the tutoring of a pupil . . . that when necessary will be corrected with the whip."[9]

Colonial Mexicans learned to adore and admire Christ for the bodily suffering he had withstood in his sacrifice for humanity. [10] Ecclesiastics who regulated female convents repeatedly stressed the need for religious women to imitate Christ's poverty, asceticism, and chastity. [11] Many Mexican mystics, the majority of whom came from impoverished circumstances, believed the ideas endorsed by sources of religious orthodoxy all around them. If humility and poverty were virtuous, then who, in the social hierarchy of colonial Mexico, was better positioned to imitate Christ and receive God's mystical gifts than they themselves? Inquisitors may have been wary of claims to mystical authority that humble people espoused, but sound doctrinal support for their assumption of these positions appeared to exist.

One late-eighteenth-century ilusa nun, sor María Coleta de San José, described a vision to the court she had experienced: "I saw my body alone and without a soul and with many tiny worms and my soul was very high, I saw it as if it were placed in a reliquary . . . and I heard the voice of God who said that the worms were the bad inclinations that the body had, but they had not touched the soul which was already separate from the body."[12] Sor María Coleta clearly embraced the idea that virtue entailed the separation of spiritual from worldly concerns. Perhaps one reason why many other ilusos and alumbrados so readily embraced this concept was that their material circumstances were so miserable that the notion that they should distance themselves from their immediate surroundings was tremendously appealing. Seventeenth-century hermit Pedro García de Arias conveyed that this was true at least for him. In its list of the many heretical statements that García had apparently professed, the Inquisition included his declaration that "Jesus Christ condemned the labors of Martha as bad."[13] García referred to the episode in the Gospel of Luke when the sisters Mary and Martha received Christ in their house, and "Mary sat at Jesus' feet and heard his word, but Martha was cumbered about much serving." García may have simply been interpreting Christ's response to Martha's complaint about this situation in an extreme manner. Christ replied: "Martha, Martha, thou art careful and troubled about many things. But one thing is needful: and Mary hath chosen that good part which shall not be taken away from her."[14] But the hermit may also have been looking for biblical justification for the idea that physical labor, which he had no wish to continue performing, was not sacred in God's eyes. His inquisitors obviously disagreed, noting that in his proposition García had "condemned physical works in which the saints had busied themselves."[15]

Pedro García may have wondered why an idea that he derived from orthodox sources could be deemed heterodox by his inquisitors. In the context of colonial Mexico, as in many other settings, orthodoxy and heterodoxy were not absolute codes that judges simply accessed and applied to the cases before them. Rather than unchanging absolutes, orthodoxy and heterodoxy were (and are) mutually reinforcing constructions, only ever identifiable in contrast to one another and existing in a state of constant reformulation in response to the changing historical circumstances in which they exist.

In the historical context of seventeenth- and eighteenth-century Mexico, contraventions of secular conventions had a great deal of impact on the construction of spiritual orthodoxy. In many cases the court did not censure ilusos and alumbrados because of doctrinal matters but instead condemned their transgressions of social convention. The Mexican Inquisition targeted particular demographic groups for condemnation. Humble people who practiced their spirituality independently of clerical supervision—beatas, beatos, and ermitaños—were particularly suspect. The court also condemned women whose religious expressions broke from the traditionally feminized sphere of the paramystical and trod into the masculine realms of doctrinal or sacramental matters. The church was also incredulous of people who claimed to be mystics but who failed to embody the virtues of humility, obedience, and chastity. Finally, racial and religious tensions unique to New Spain's particular historical context shaped the court's prosecution of Mexican false mystics.

Beginning in the mid-seventeenth century and culminating in the late eighteenth century, peninsulares expressed heightened concern about the growth of the viceroyalty's mixed-race population, about the rising power of the criollo population, and about the possible influences Africans and Indians might exert on the Christian traditions of New Spain's population. All three sets of anxieties infused judges' and denouncers' concerns about practitioners of false mysticism. Their religious practices were scrutinized for signs of African or Indian influences. Like aspiring criollos, or mixed-race people, they were seen as individuals illegitimately posing as more powerful and valuable members of society than they had been designated by birth or deserved to become. The court—and those members of the public who supported the court's work—disdained and feared Mexican mystics because they were people who had succeeded in passing themselves off as something they were not. While ilusos and alumbrados were not rebels who self-consciously defied the doctrines of Catholicism, they did challenge the church's authority on one fundamental level. They asserted, in the face of convention, that they were creatures who were worthy of the receipt of bona fide mystical experiences. If they were resisting anything, it was the court's idea that their own experiences of the world disqualified them from assuming such positions.

Appendix 1

Database of Iluso and Alumbrado Trials in the Inquisición Ramo of the Archivo General de la Nación

Name	Date*	Ref. (tomo/exp.)	Ethnicity	Place	Accusation	Sentence
1 Juan Plata	1593	180/1	Spanish	Tlaxcala	Alumbrado, solicitación	Abjuración de levi, suspension from office, exile
2 Sor Agustina de S. Clara	1593	189/2	Spanish	Tlaxcala	Alumbrada	Abjuración de levi
3 Alonso de Espinosa	1593	209/6	Spanish	Tlaxcala	Alumbrado	?Proceso—fragment
4 Catalina de Lidueña	1593	209/6	Spanish	Tlaxcala, Puebla	Alumbrada, judaizer	?Proceso—fragment
5 Juan Núñez	1598	210/2–3	Spanish	México	Alumbrado	Abjuración de vehementi, reclusion, 6 yrs. service
6 Mariana de San Miguel	1598	210/3	Spanish	México	Alumbrada	Abjuraci'on de vehementi, 100 lashes, 10-yr. exile
7 Ana de Guillamas	1598	176/9	Spanish?	México	Alumbrada	?Proceso—fragment
8 Luis de Zárate	1598	218/3	Spanish	Tlaxcala, Toluca	Alumbrado	Proceso—dismissed due to insanity
9 Pedro de Coronado	1602	452/42	Portuguese	Oaxaca	Illusions	Testificación—not pursued

(continued)

Appendix 1 (*continued*)

	Name	Date[*]	Ref. (tomo/exp.)	Ethnicity	Place	Accusation	Sentence
10	Diego Phelipe	1628	364/7	Spanish	México	Alumbrado	Died during trial
11	Leonor Márquez	1649	432/12	Spanish	México, Puebla	Alumbrada	Proceso—apparently not pursued
12	Juan Romero Zapata	1649	432/12	Spanish	México, Puebla	Alumbrado	Proceso—apparently not pursued
13	Josefa de S. L. Beltrán	1649	432/11; 503/31 . . .	Spanish	México, Puebla	Alumbrada	Proceso—died during trial (negative calificación)
14	Teresa de Jesús	1649	432/14; 503/30 . . .	Spanish	México, Cholula	Alumbrada	200 lashes, abjuración de vehementi, 10-yr. reclusion
15	Nicolasa de S. Domingo	1649	432/5; 433/1	Spanish	México, Cholula	Embustera, false revelations	Abjuración de levi, 4 yrs. hospital service, 10-yr. exile
16	María de la Encarnación	1649	433/5; 503/58	Spanish	Puebla, México	Alumbrada	Proceso—died during trial (negative judgment)
17	José Bruñón de Vertiz	1649	443/2; 503/58, 63 . . .	Spanish	México	Alumbrado	Died during trial, burned in effigy

(*continued*)

Appendix 1 (*continued*)

	Name	Date[*]	Ref. (tomo/exp.)	Ethnicity	Place	Accusation	Sentence
18	Diego Pinto Bravo	1649	432/8	Spanish	Cholula	Alumbrado	Died during trial (negative judgment)
19	Pedro García de Arias	1651	505/1; 436/14	Spanish	México, Chimalixtac	Alumbrado	Burned at the stake
20	Salvador Victoria	1659	445/1	Spanish	México, Manila	Alumbrado, iluso	200 lashes, abjuración de levi, 6-yr. exile in Philippines
21	Juan Gómez	1659	1501/1	Portuguese	México	Blasphemer, alumbrado	Burned at the stake
22	Javier de Riquelme	1667	608/1	Spanish	Manila, México	Iluminado	Reprimanded
23	Juan Bautista Surero	1673	608/7	Spanish	Manila, México	Iluminado	Died during trial
24	Juan B. de Cárdenas	1673	623/1	Spanish	Puebla	Iluso, alumbrado	Abjuración de levi, deprived of habit, exile, reclusion
25	Agustina Rangel	1684	522/2; 673/32	Mestiza	Valladolid	Embustera, alumbrada	200 lashes, abjuración de levi, 8 yrs. in poor house
26	Petrona Rangel	1684	668/5	Mestiza	Valladolid	Embustera, superstición	Not pursued

(*continued*)

Appendix 1 (*continued*)

	Name	Date[*]	Ref. (tomo/exp.)	Ethnicity	Place	Accusation	Sentence
27	Tomasa Rangel	1684	668/6	Mestiza	Tarímbaro	Embustera, superstición	Not pursued
28	Manuel Fernández	1684	522/6	Portuguese	Puebla, Cholula	Alumbrado, heretical propositions	Información; qualified; apparently not pursued
29	Antonia de Ochoa	1686	538/1; 539/25; 694/5	Spanish	México	Alumbrada, embustera	Abjuración de levi, 2-yr. reclusion in recogimiento
30	Clemente de Ledesma	1687	671/2	Spanish	México	Iluso, alumbrado	Not pursued
31	Diego de Briçuela	1687	671/7	Spanish	México	Embustero, alumbrado	Documentation suggests not pursued
32	Bernardo de Ledesma	1687	664/5	Spanish	México	Iluso, alumbrado	Not pursued
33	María de San José	1687	450/13	Spanish	México	Ilusa, alumbrada	Not pursued
34	Franciso Romero	1687	450/14	Spanish	México	Iluso	Not pursued
35	Francisco Jordanes	1687	477/20	Spanish	México	Iluso, alumbrado	Testificación—not pursued
36	Francisco Anguino	1687	1551/31–32	Spanish	México	Alumbrado, embustero	Not pursued

(*continued*)

Appendix 1 (*continued*)

	Name	Date*	Ref. (tomo/exp.)	Ethnicity	Place	Accusation	Sentence
37	Francisca de Montero	1688	674/20	Mestiza	Orizaba	Ilusa	Not pursued
38	Francisco Navarro	1691	682/4	Spanish	Guatemala	Alumbrado	Documentation suggests not pursued
39	Tomasa Gonzáles	1692	685/11	Spanish?	Aguascalientes	Alumbrada	Not pursued
40	Ana de Zayas	1694	692/2	Spanish	Puebla	Ilusa, alumbrada	Sentenced
41	Francisca de los Angeles	1694	693/5	Mestiza	Querétaro	Alumbrada	Not pursued
42	Pedro Antonio	1693	693/11	Mulato?	Oaxaca	Alumbrado	Died during trial
43	Juana la Cuculteca	1696	697/11	Spanish?	Gauadalajara	Alumbrada, estafadora	Documentation suggests not pursued
44	Antonio Moncada	1697	536/1	Spanish	Chalco, México	Alumbrado	Not pursued
45	Diego Martín Davila Pinzón	1699	542/7	Spanish	Toluca, México	Alumbrado, iluso, embustero . . .	Qualified but not sentenced
46	Juan Felix de Luna	1699	711/1	Spanish	México	Molinismo, alumbrado . . .	1-yr. exile from Mexico and Madrid, reclusion
47	Diego Martínez de Arce	1699	710/68	Spanish	México	Iluso	Qualified but no documentation of sentence

(*continued*)

Appendix 1 (*continued*)

	Name	Date*	Ref. (tomo/exp.)	Ethnicity	Place	Accusation	Sentence
48	Juan Fernández	1699	543/9	Spanish	México	Iluso	Not pursued
49	Juan Luis de Torres	1700	716/5	Spanish	México	Alumbrado	Dismissed due to illness
50	Ignacio de S. J. Salazar	1709	743/1	Mestizo	México, Puebla	Alumbrado, embustero	Died during trial (relapso—negative judgment)
51	Agueda de Salas	1709	1286/14	Spanish	Mérida	Alumbrada	Documentation suggests not pursued
52	Diego Fernández	1709	1286/14	Spanish	Mérida	Alumbrado	Documentation suggests not pursued
53	María Manuela Picazo	1712	748/1	Spanish	México	Alumbrada, ilusa . . .	Abjuración de levi, reclusion
54	María India Colorada	1713	753/fols. 642–53	Indian	México	Ilusa, embustera	Relegated to the Provisorato del ordinario
55	Baltasar Núñes de los Reyes	1713	753/2; 730/ ?/331 fols.	Spanish	Puebla, México	Alumbrado, iluso . . .	Abjuración de levi, 200 lashes, exile, recogimiento
56	Catalina	1715	760/3	Spanish	México	Ilusa, hipócrita	Not pursued
57	Madre P. R. de Jesús	1717	767/9	Spanish	México	Ilusa	Not pursued

(*continued*)

Appendix 1 (*continued*)

	Name	Date*	Ref. (tomo/exp.)	Ethnicity	Place	Accusation	Sentence
58	Marta de la Encarnación	1717	788/24; 799/8	Castiza	Puebla	Ilusa, embustera, hipócrita . . .	Abjuración de levi, 200 lashes, exile, reclusion
59	Beatriz de Jesús las Flores	1723	806/5	Spanish	Querétaro	Ilusa	Not pursued
60	María Felipa Viruete	1723	793/2	Spanish?	Guadalajara	Ilusa	Not pursued
61	Getrudis Rosa Ortiz	1723	805/1–2	Mestiza	México	Ilusa	Died during trial (negative calificación)
62	Agustín Claudio	1738	867/1–3	Spanish	México	Alumbrado, molinismo, solicitante	Died during trial (negative judgment)
63	Phelipe Alvarez	1739	1316/2	Spanish	Querétaro	Calvinisto, molinismo . . .	Guilty
64	Juan Antonio Zumalde	1743	891/1	Spanish	México	Alumbrado, molinismo	Guilty
65	María de Jesús	1745	820/15	Spanish	Zacatecas, Celaya	Ilusa	Apparently not pursued
66	?	1746	900/4	Mulata	Puebla	Ficciones, ilusiones	Not pursued

(*continued*)

Appendix 1 (*continued*)

	Name	Date*	Ref. (tomo/exp.)	Ethnicity	Place	Accusation	Sentence
67	José de Betancourt	1746	900/4	Spanish	Puebla	Ficciones, ilusiones	Not pursued
68	Sor Josefa C. de Jesús	1747	816/34	Spanish?	México	Ilusa, embustera	Not pursued
69	Ana María de Santo Domingo	1748	885/25	Spanish?	México	Ilusa, embustera	Not pursued
70	Josefa de Aguirre	1751	934/4	Spanish	Querétaro	Ilusa, embustera	Not pursued
71	José Castillo	1752	952/1	Spanish	México	Molinismo	Not pursued
72	Nicolás de Landeta	1753	981/10	Spanish	México	Alumbrado	Not pursued
73	Antonia	1753	981/10	Spanish	México	Ilusa, alumbrada	Not pursued
74	José Armengol	1760	1087/3	Spanish	Atlixco	Molinismo	Not pursued
75	Alonso G. de Terreros	1761	1088/6	Spanish	Querétaro	Molinismo	Died during trial (negative judgment)
76	Miguel Pinilla	1762	1088/7	Spanish	Querétaro	Molinismo	Not pursued
77	Saintiago Díaz	1762	1088/7	Spanish	Querétaro	Molinismo	Not pursued
78	María Guadalupe Rivera	1765	1078/2	Spanish	Querétaro	Ilusa	Abjuración de vehementi, 6-yr. reclusion
79	Bruno del Puerto	1767	1063/1	Spanish?	Puebla	Molinismo	Not pursued

(*continued*)

Appendix 1 (*continued*)

	Name	Date[*]	Ref. (tomo/exp.)	Ethnicity	Place	Accusation	Sentence
80	Bartolomé de la S. Trinindidad	1770	1158/2	Spanish	México, San Luis Potosí	Molinismo	Denuncia—Not pursued
81	Sor M. Coleta de S. José	1774	1172/7	Spanish	Oaxaca	Alumbrada	Died during trial (negative calificación)
82	Andrés M. Quintana	1774	1172/7	Spanish	Oaxcaa	Alumbrada	Apparently not pursued
83	José F. de Arayo	1775	1182/5	Spanish	Querétaro	Molinismo, solicitación	Sentenced
84	María Cayetana Loria	1778	1173; 1258/19	Mulata	Ixmiquilpan, México	Molinismo, alumbrada, ilusa . . .	Reclusion, exile
85	Ángel Vázquez	1778	1173; 1258/19	Spanish	Ixmiquilpan, México	Molinismo, alumbrado, iluso . . .	Deprived of office, 10-yr. exile, reclusion
86	Sebastián . . . Francisco	1784	1239/3	Spanish	Toluca	Iluso	Reprimanded
87	Lorenzo de la Concepción	1784	1239/3	Spanish	Toluca	Iluso	Reprimanded
88	María Josefa . . . Peña	1784	1239/3	Spanish	Toluca	Ilusa	Died before trial started

(*continued*)

Appendix 1 (*continued*)

	Name	Date[*]	Ref. (tomo/exp.)	Ethnicity	Place	Accusation	Sentence
89	Barbara de Echagaray	1785	1251/1; 1344/9 . . .	Spanish	Puebla, Jalapa	Heregía mixta, ilusa	Reprimanded, 10-yr. exile, reclusion
90	Sor Ana María La Cal	1788	1246/5	Spanish	Atlixco	Ilusa	Not pursued
91	Josefa Palacios	1788	1291/1; 1325/13	Spanish	México, Pachuca	Ilusa	Abjuración de levi, 10-yr. exile, reclusion
92	Eusebio Villarejo	1788	1291/1; 1325/13	Spanish	México, Pachuca	Iluso	Abjuración de vehementi, deprived of office, reclusion
93	María A G. Lozano	1790	1312/2	Spanish	Teolotlan, México	Hipócrita, ilusa . . .	Reprimanded, abjuración de levi, exile, hospital service
94	Pedro de Jesús	1792	1276/7	Spanish	Toluca, México	Iluso	Not pursued
95	Jaime de Santa Teresa	1792	1283/24	Spanish	México	Iluso	Increase of previous reclusion sentence
96	Antonio Rodríguez	1794	1331/3; 1408/7	Spanish	México	Iluso	Deprived of office, exile, reclusion
97	María Rita Vargas	1794	1418/13, 17	Spanish	México	Ilusa	Reclusion, service, exile
98	María Lucia Celis	1794	1418/13, 17	Mestiza	México	Ilusa	Reclusion, service, exile

(*continued*)

Appendix 1 (*continued*)

	Name	Date*	Ref. (*tomo/exp.*)	Ethnicity	Place	Accusation	Sentence
99	Sor María Ignacia	1796	1349f/30	Spanish?	México	Ilusa	Not pursued
100	Ana de Aramburu	1799	805/2; 1358/16/ 1419/1	Spanish?	México, Toluca	Ilusa, alumbrada	Exile, reclusion
101	M. Micaela de San José	1801	1189/35; 1419/5 . . .	Spanish	México	Ilusa, false revelations	Incomplete documentation; apparently not pursued
102	José M. Estevez	1801	1189/35; 1419/5 . . .	Spanish	México	Solicitante, false revelations	Incomplete documentation; apparently not pursued

* Indicates when case opened.

Note: Database does not include the cases of three isolated early-sixteenth-century iluso trials, those of Catalina Hernández, determined guilty of "some illuminism" and sent back to Spain by the Episcopal Inquisition; Gerónimo de Mercado, tried in the 1560s; and a Franciscan beata, María de la Concepción, investigated in 1575. I also do not treat the cases of Pedro Menendez de Llano and Gabriel de Vozmediano, whose trials were also tangentially related to illuminismo.

Appendix 2

Database of Selected Eighteenth-Century Embustero Trials in the Inquisición Ramo of the Archivo General de la Nación

	Name	Date*	Ref. (tomo/exp.)	Ethnicity	Place	Accusation	Sentence
1	José Guyaquin	1712	843/7	Spanish	Oaxaca	Adivino, embustero	Not pursued
2	Teresa de Jesús	1714	758/30	Mulata	Chiametla	Embustera	100 lashes
3	María Rentería	1715	759/fs. 388–97	Mestiza	Zacatecas	Embustera	100 lashes
4	Francisca de los Reyes	1715	760/14	Mestiza	Puebla, México	Embustera	Apparently not pursued
5	Vicente de Torres	1715	760/39	Mulato	Chiapa	Embustero	Sentenced
6	José Elias Venegas	1715	760/27	Mestizo	México	Embustero	Died befote trial completed
7	Rosa María de Salazar	1716	552/37	Mestiza	Zinacantepeque	Supersticiosa, embustera	Incomplete documentation; apparently sentenced
8	Pedro Anastacio	1717	800/14	Negro	San Juan Zitácuaro	Embustero, supersiticoso . . .	250 lashes

(continued)

Appendix 2 (*continued*)

	Name	Date[*]	Ref. (tomo/exp.)	Ethnicity	Place	Accusation	Sentence
9	Josefa de Villafaña	1717	767/3	Spanish	Oaxaca	Embustera	Reprimanded
10	María de Escobar	1717	767/30	Mestiza	Izaqualtipan	Curandera, embustera	Not pursued
11	Miguel de los Angeles	1717	767/18–19	Mulato	Charcas	Adivino supersticioso, embustero	Sentenced
12	Carlos de Segura	1718	751/20	?	Puebla	Embustero	Sentenced
13	Getrudis	1719	769/14	Mestiza	Oaxaca	Embustera	Not pursued
14	María F. Mendivil	1719	920/18	Spanish	México	Embustera, fingidora . . .	Incomplete documentation
15	Sebastián Hernández	1720	781/54	Negro	Zacatecas	Embustero, curandero . . .	Sentenced
16	Michaela Catalana	1720	781/26	Mulata	México	Supersticiosa, embustera	Apparently not pursued
17	Salvador Vargas	1724	908/29	Spanish	?	Embustero	Not pursued

(*continued*)

Appendix 2 (*continued*)

	Name	Date[*]	Ref. (tomo/exp.)	Ethnicity	Place	Accusation	Sentence
18	Inés Gonzáles	1727	817/34	Mulata	Guatemala	Embustera, supersticiosa	200 lashes
19	María Rosa	1733	844/4	Mulata	México	Embustera, supersticiosa . . .	50 lashes, hospital service
20	Salvador Vargas	1733	845/11	Spanish	Querétaro	Hipócrita, embustero . . .	Apparently not pursued
21	Phelipa Zafra	1736	812/26	?	Mérida	Supersticiosa, embustera	25 lashes, reprimand
22	Luzía Berruete	1743	826/54	Spanish	Zultepec	Embustera	Apparently not pursued
23	María García	1742	793/fols. 132–39	Mestiza	Temascaltepec	Adivinadora, embustera	Not pursued
24	María de los Dolores	1744	902/1	Mulata	Querétaro	Supersticiosa, embustera	Not pursued
25	Michaela de Contreras	1745	892/6	Indian?	Paso del Río del Norte	Supersticiosa, embustera	Apparently not pursued
26	Manuel	1748	902/3	Mestizo	Mérida	Supersticioso, embustero	Not pursued

(*continued*)

Appendix 2 (*continued*)

	Name	Date[*]	Ref. (tomo/exp.)	Ethnicity	Place	Accusation	Sentence
27	José J. G. Gonzáles	1752	868/fs. 295–305	Indian	Chilapa	Supersticioso, embustero	Warning
28	José Antonio Hernández	1784	1210/4	Spanish	México	Supersticioso, embustero . . .	Incomplete documentation; apparently not pursued
29	José M. de Ayala	1797	941/20	Spanish	México?	Blasfemo heretical, embustero . . .	Incomplete documentation
30	María Manuela Sanabria	1793	1364/3	Spanish?	México	Embustera, sacrílega . . .	Incomplete documentation

[*] Indicates when case opened.

Notes

Introduction

1. Bravo, *Ana Rodríguez de Castro y Aramburu*, 26. Her judges referred to her as "la Aramburu" throughout her trial, so I have adopted this title. Aramburu's complete trial is housed in the Archivo General de la Nación, Mexico City (hereafter AGN), Inquisición, tomo 1358, expediente 13, folios 158–68; exp. 16, fols. 272–487; t. 1361, exp. 2, fols. 184–252; t. 1419, exp. 1, fols. 1–130; exp. 2, fols. 131–45; t. 1543, exp. 19, fols. 340–406. For further discussion of Aramburu's case, see "The Power of the Spider Woman: The Deluded Woman and the Inquisition" in Franco, *Plotting Women*, 55–76. Unless otherwise noted, all translations from Spanish are mine. I have modernized most Spanish names and spelling.
2. Bravo, *Ana Rodríguez de Castro y Aramburu*, 26, 25.
3. Bravo, *Ana Rodríguez de Castro y Aramburu*, 25.
4. Bravo, *Ana Rodríguez de Castro y Aramburu*, 79.
5. AGN, Inq., t. 1543, exp. 19, fols. 394v, 400v.
6. AGN, Inq., t. 1419, exp. 1, fols. 118v–119. Twenty leagues equals roughly one hundred kilometers or sixty miles.
7. AGN, Inq., t. 1419, exp. 1, fols. 126, 128, 137, 144.
8. My understanding of the conferred rather than inherent nature of "deviancy" here parallels Kai Erickson's interpretation of unorthodox religious practices in seventeenth-century New England. See Erickson, *Wayward Puritans*. Histories of the persecution of alumbrados in sixteenth- and seventeenth-century Spain have traditionally focused on theological issues. The foundational works on Spanish alumbrados are Márquez, *Los alumbrados*; Andrés Martín, *Los recogidos*; Huerga, *Historia de los alumbrados*; Imirizaldu, *Monjas y beatas*; Surtz, *Guitar of God*; and Hamilton, *Heresy and Mysticism*.

9. Paz, "Spanish Spirituality's Mid-Sixteenth-Century Change," 423–24; Andrés Martín, "Alumbrados, Erasmians, 'Lutherans' and Mystics," 457–94; and Hamilton, *Heresy and Mysticism*, 71.

10. For a parallel reading of the Inquisition's predominant concerns in the context of colonial Guatemala, see Few, *Women Who Live Evil Lives*.

11. For further discussion of this theme as reflected in the writings of New Spanish nuns, see Sampson Vera Tudela, *Colonial Angels*.

12. I take Ginzburg's fine work on early modern Italy, *Cheese and the Worms*, as a model for how to use inquisitorial records to approach the examination of non-elite mental framework. In the context of colonial Latin America, several important studies have been produced on the spirituality of the elite, but less research is available on the religious practices of non-elite urban populations. Publications abound, for example, on the ideas of the celebrated seventeenth-century Jeronymite nun Juana Inés de la Cruz; see, among others, Merrim, *Feminist Perspectives*. On the writings of other celebrated Iberian and colonial nuns, see Arenal and Schlau, *Untold Sisters*; Myers, *Word from New Spain*; Myers and Powell, "*Wild Country.*" There are also a number of excellent works on the social history of plebeian populations in colonial Mexico, including Boyer, *Lives of the Bigamists*.

13. For classic discussions of the hierarchy of peninisulares, criollos, and castas, see Mörner, *Race Mixture*; Chance, *Race and Class in Colonial Oaxaca*; Israel, *Race, Class, and Politics*. For more recent revisions of the degree to which seventeenth-century Mexico's plebeian population accepted this hierarchy and how it functioned, see Cope, *Limits of Racial Domination*; Lewis, *Hall of Mirrors*.

14. The *Pragmática*, applied to the colonies in 1778, decreed that children had to receive parental approval of marriage choices until the age of twenty-five. For a discussion of the history of the impact of the policy on the colony, see Seed, *To Love, Honor, and Obey*. For further discussion on challenges to elite racial and social control in the eighteenth century, see Twinam, *Public Lives, Private Secrets*.

15. For a discussion of plebeian conceptions of honor, including its Christian connotations, see Johnson and Lipsett-Rivera, *Faces of Honor*.

16. Kathryn Burns's study of Cuzco's convents contains a comprehensive discussion of the complex connections between religious piety and social status in colonial Latin America. See *Colonial Habits*.

17. Gutiérrez discusses the significant impact the *Reconquista* had on shaping Spanish American masculinity in *When Jesus Came*, 176–206.

18. Rodríguez G. de Ceballos, "Uso y funciones," 102.

19. Giles, *Women in the Inquisition*, 11. See also Franco, *Plotting Women*, 55–56.

20. AGN, Inq., t. 743, exp. 1, fols. 288, 162, 165. Given the timing of his trial, it is likely that in this revelation Salazar was referring to the death of the last

Hapsburg king, Charles IV, whose heirless death was one of the central causes of the War of Spanish Succession (1701–13).

21. AGN, Inq., t. 805, exp. 2, fol. 68v.

22. AGN, Inq., t. 788, exp. 24, fol. 144.

23. AGN, Inq., t. 623, exp. 1, fols. 7v, 9, 91v.

24. AGN, Inq., t. 1501, exp. 1, fol. 2v.

25. AGN, Inq., t. 805, exp. 1, fol. 13v.

26. On the female tradition of mystical Christianity in the medieval period, see Bynum, *Holy Feast and Holy Fast.*

27. AGN, Inq., t. 1291, exp. 1, fols. 145–48; Bravo, *Ana Rodríguez de Castro y Aramburu,* 112; AGN, Inq., t. 1543, exp. 19, fol. 400v.

28. Medina, *Historia del tribunal,* 306–7.

29. AGN, Inq., t. 1331, exp. 3, fol. 63.

30. AGN, Inq., t. 1291, exp. 1, fol. 34.

31. AGN, Inq., t. 743, exp. 1, fols. 353v, 13. French feminist Luce Irigaray argues that mystical expressions feminize the men who participate in them. See Franco, *Plotting Women,* 6.

32. Bravo, *Ana Rodríguez de Castro y Aramburu,* 121, 125.

33. AGN, Inq., t. 805, exp. 1, fol. 17; underlining in the original.

34. For examples of these kinds of interpretations in Latin American history and in the wider body of cultural theory and history, see Stern, *Secret History of Gender;* Gutiérrez, *When Jesus Came;* Few, *Women Who Live Evil Lives;* Butler, *Gender Trouble;* Stallybrass and White, *Politics and Poetics of Transgression.*

35. For an example of this kind of approach, see Velasco, *Demons, Nausea, and Resistance.*

36. For an early conceptualization of this theoretical approach, see Natalie Zemon Davis's landmark essay, "Women on Top," in *Society and Culture,* 124–51.

37. For a recent discussion of the debates surrounding such cultural history, see the collection of essays in a special edition of the *Hispanic American Historical Review,* "Mexico's New Cultural History: *Una Lucha Libre?*" 79, no. 2 (May 1999).

38. Caroline Walker Bynum's essay "Women's Stories, Women's Symbols: A Critique of Victor Turner's Theory of Liminality" in *Fragmentation and Redemption,* 27–51, addresses some difficulties entailed by this type of interpretation in a thorough and thought-provoking manner.

39. Franco, *Plotting Women,* 57.

40. Franco, *Plotting Women,* 75. Ruth Behar makes a similar argument in her discussion of sexual witchcraft in the Mexican inquisition. See "Sexual Witchcraft," 197. Laura Lewis also includes Steve Stern, Irene Silverblatt, and Alejandra Cárdenas in her discussion of writers who embrace a "resistance" reading of such religious practices. Lewis, *Hall of Mirrors,* 232–33, n. 5.

41. Franco, *Plotting Women,* 59.

42. For a discussion of the influences of Saint Teresa of Avila on the writings of one Mexican ilusa, see Jaffary, "Tratado espiritual." Antonio Rubial García analyses another body of such writings in "Josefa de San Luis Beltrán," 161–77. Other ilusas who were copious writers included Ana de Zayas and sor María Coleta de San José.

43. For discussions of seventeenth- and eighteenth-century theological debates in Mexico over the concept of Immaculate Conception and differing institutional views of the vileness of menstrual blood, see "Gender Control in the Era of the Counter-Reformation" on pp. 59–63 of this work and "The Court's Determination of Illness, Insanity, or Demonism" on pp. 147–55.

44. Alberro, "La licencia vestida de santidad," 232–33.

45. Daniel Dwyer's dissertation, which focuses on alumbrados in seventeenth-century Mexico, pays greater attention to the spiritual aspects of the religious practices engaged in by these men and women. Dwyer's conclusion that ilusos and alumbrados were social deviants produced by a society in social turmoil, however, is also unsatisfactory. See Dwyer, "Mystics in Mexico."

46. On the racial dimensions of late colonial Mexico City, see Seed, "Social Dimensions of Race," 569–606.

47. Boyer, *Lives of the Bigamists*, 21.

48. While I believe that the inquisitorial court played a determinative role in creating the heresy of false mysticism in Mexico, I do not concur with Lewis's bolder argument regarding witchcraft in Mexico. Neither of us views the religious deviants we examine in terms of "autonomous realms of resistance." However, I disagree with her contention that practices that did not conform to the sanctioned realm merely "derived from the hegemonic" or were primarily a product of Spanish ideology projected onto Indian practices. See Lewis, *Hall of Mirrors*, 7, 172–74.

1. Production of Orthodoxy and Deviancy

1. Bujanda, "Recent Historiography," 226. The classic works on the history of the Spanish Inquisition include Lea, *History of the Inquisition*; Kamen, *Inquisition and Society*. See also the three-volume collection edited by Pérez Villanueva and Escandell Bonet, *Historia de la Inquisición*; Alcalá, *Spanish Inquisition*.

2. The historiography on the Mexican inquisition is extensive. Henry Charles Lea, José Toribio Medina, and Julio Jiménez Rueda wrote pioneering works, while Richard Greenleaf, Solange Alberro, and Richard Boyer have produced some of the more recent well-known work on the Mexican tribunal. On the history of the Peruvian court, see René Millar Carvacho. For recent treatment of witchcraft investigations in New Spain, see Few, *Women Who Live Evil Lives*; Lewis, *Hall of Mirrors*.

3. See Moreno de los Arcos, "New Spain's Inquisition," 23–36; Greenleaf, "Inquisition and the Indians," 138–67.

4. Lewis, *Hall of Mirrors*, 39.

5. Papal bulls had awarded the Spanish crown the power of patronato real, the right to appoint all officers of the secular church, in 1501 and 1508.

6. For a discussion of Philip's crises at that time and their effect on the founding of the colonial courts, see Pérez Villanueva and Escandell Bonet, *Historia de la Inquisición*, 1:713.

7. For more details on the links between international and local political tensions and the prosecution of Judaizers and other heretics in the peak years of the Mexican court's operation, see Curcio-Nagy, "Faith and Morals," 169. On the New Spanish tribunal's concerns with casta, Indian, and African religious practices, see Few, *Women Who Live Evil Lives*.

8. Boyer, *Lives of the Bigamists*, 17. Juan Miguel Blázquez records that cases against 144 Lutherans, 405 crypto-Jews, and 6 Muslims were prosecuted in Mexico during the entire colonial period. *La inquisición en América*, 289.

9. Alberro, dealing with only the period until 1700, records that 34.4 percent of the crimes the court prosecuted were minor religious crimes, 18.8 percent were for "magic and witchcraft," 14.8 percent were heresy trials, 13.2 percent were for sexual transgressions, and the remaining 16.5 percent were for idolatry, heterodox tendencies, and solicitation. *Inquisición y sociedad*, 205.

10. Greenleaf, "Historiography of the Mexican Inquisition," 271. Lay people initiated the investigations of over one quarter of the total Mexican iluso and alumbrado trials.

11. The Mexican Tribunal sent regular reports (*relaciones*) back to the Suprema summarizing its activities. It was upon these materials, housed in Madrid's National Historical Archives Library, that many early historians of the Mexican Inquisition, including José Toribio Medina, based their research.

12. Alberro, *Inquisición y sociedad*, 23–29.

13. Drawing on Durkheim, Kai Erickson argues that judicial bodies create deviancy in the population because deviancy serves the useful social purpose of binding members of societies to one another in contradistinction to deviants. See *Wayward Puritans*, 14.

14. AGN, Inq., t. 1349, exp. 30, fol. 4.

15. Among others, Villa Alta denounced fray Francisco Jordanes, AGN, Inq., t. 477, exp. 20, fols. 194–222; fray Clemente de Ledesma, AGN, Inq. t. 671, exp. 2, fols. 5–17; don Francisco Romero de Quevedo AGN, Inq., t. 450, exp. 14, fols. 557–68; fray Diego de Briçuela, AGN, Inq., t. 671, exp. 7, fols. 49–58; and fray Bernardo de Ledesma, AGN, Inq., t. 644, exp. 5, fols. 472–518.

16. AGN, Inq., t. 463, exp. 8, fols. 281–393.

17. See Alberro, *Inquisición y sociedad*, 53–60, regarding familiares' social status backgrounds and aspirations.

18. Three of the ilusos and alumbrados investigated in this book were tortured over the course of their trials.

19. AGN, Inq., t. 505, exp. 1, fol. 193.
20. AGN, Inq., t. 505, exp. 1, fol. 195v, 195; emphasis in the original.
21. Alberro calculated that between 1522 and 1700 the various incarnations of the Mexican Inquisition (regular, episcopal, and independent) processed approximately twelve thousand cases, with fewer than two thousand of these pertaining to the post-1570 independent tribunal. *Inquisición y sociedad*, 168. For statistics regarding the Spanish Inquisition's various tribunals, see Contreras and Henningsen, "Forty-four Thousand Cases," 100–129.
22. Historians have underrepresented the existence of the numbers of these cases, particularly in the later colonial period. Lewis A. Tambs claimed in 1965 that only one such case was tried in the eighteenth century. See his "Inquisition in Eighteenth-Century Mexico," 180. Dwyer located many of the same seventeenth-century trials as are discussed here, but with regard to the late colonial period he wrote: "Occasionally the charge was bandied about in the eighteenth century but with less and less frequency." "Mystics in Mexico," 240.
23. Five cases span over a decade; two cases are nearly eight hundred folios long, two fill nearly five hundred folios, eight fill over two hundred folios, and four fill over one hundred folios.
24. Greenleaf, "Historiography of the Mexican Inquisition," 270. Alberro's findings for the period up to 1700 roughly concur. *Inquisición y sociedad*, 192, 205.
25. Greenleaf, "Historiography of the Mexican Inquisition," 270.
26. For a discussion of the impact of humanist thought on Spanish spirituality, see Bataillon, *Erasmo y España*. On Spain's climate of intellectual liberty in the early sixteenth century and its subsequent repression, see Cruz and Perry, *Culture and Control*.
27. For a comprehensive discussion of recogimiento's various formulations—as a theological concept, a virtue, and an institutional praxis—see van Deusen, *Between the Sacred and the Worldly*. For a discussion on Osuna's development of the theological concept, see 18–20.
28. Van Deusen, *Between the Sacred and the Worldly*, 19–20.
29. See Kamen, *Spanish Inquisition*, 86; Paz, "Spanish Spirituality's Mid-Sixteenth-Century Change," 423–24; Andrés Martin, "Alumbrados, Erasmians, 'Lutherans' and Mystics," 457–94.
30. Giles, *Women in the Inquisition*, 5, 10.
31. Members of tertiaries, or "third orders," were people who were regulated by a particular order but who received much less supervision than cloistered nuns or friars. Their members took many of the same vows as nuns and friars but did not formally profess. Some members were reclusive, but others circulated publicly. In some periods the term was used interchangeably with the terms *beata* and *beato*, people living either alone or in communities who had taken

religious vows but who had even less affiliation with an order than tertiaries. Many female beatas had not become nuns because they had been unable to afford the dowry required for admission to a convent. Most of the Mexican beata alumbradas were of the most independent and unsupervised variety.

32. Regarding the distinction between recogimiento and dejamiento, see Llorca Vives, *La Inquisición española*; Ahlgren, *Teresa of Avila*, 14–19; Dwyer, "Mystics in Mexico," 9; van Deusen, *Between the Sacred and the Worldly*, 18.

33. Márquez reproduces the edict in its entirety in an appendix in *Los alumbrados*, 229–38. Jiménez Rueda published a copy of the 1574 edict in *Herejías y supersticiones*, 11.

34. Contreras and Henningsen, "Forty-four Thousand Cases," 114.

35. Hamilton, *Heresy and Mysticism*, 65–75. See also Jiménez Rueda, "La secta de los alumbrados," 9; Márquez, *Los alumbrados*, 112. In Spain the only major heresy about which the Inquisition failed to project anxieties in its prosecution of alumbrados seems to have been moriscos. Angel A. Amy Moreno and Pierre Duviols have argued that the New World's indigenous population came to replace the Moors in terms of Spanish anxieties about religious conversion. See Duviols, *La lutte contre les religions autochtones*; Amy Moreno, "Spanish Treatment of Moriscos."

36. On the links between the Inquisition's association of alumbradismo with Lutheranism, see Alcalá, "María de Cazalla," 98–99. For further discussion of the connections between the founders of the alumbrado tradition and conversos, see Nieto, "Franciscan *Alumbrados*," 3–16.

37. "Edicto de los alumbrados de Toledo. Toledo, 23 de septiembre de 1557." Reproduced in Márquez, *Los alumbrados*, 231. Chapter 26 of this edict also refers specifically to Lutheran heresies.

38. Márquez, *Los alumbrados*, 233.

39. The quotations from Alcaraz's trial come from Hamilton, *Heresy and Mysticism*, 70.

40. For more extensive discussions of this group of late-sixteenth-century trials, see Dwyer, "Mystics in Mexico," 44–94; Huerga, *Historia de los alumbrados*, 3:593–779. A similar linking of Spanish to Mexican alumbradismo had occurred in the 1530s when Catalina Hernández, one of the beatas Archbishop Zumárraga requested be sent to the new colony to assist in the conversion of Indian women, had been returned to Spain under the suspicion of engaging in "some illuminism." This suspicion coincided with the conviction in Toledo of one of her friends, Francisca Hernández, for the same crime. Dwyer, "Mystics in Mexico," 47–48; van Deusen, *Between the Sacred and the Worldly*, 28, 202 n.80.

41. AGN, Inq., t. 180, exp. 1, fols. 10–15, 6.

42. Jiménez Rueda, *Herejías y supersticiones*, 144. López's spirituality was also celebrated in Spain. Seventeenth-century mystical writer Miguel de Molinos

described López as a *gran místico* in his 1675 work *Guía espiritual*. When the Inquisition banned this work shortly after publication, López's spirituality was subject to greater scrutiny as well. Rubial García, *La santidad controvertida*, 109. For more information on López's spiritual practices, see Bilinkoff, "Francisco Losa," 115–28.

43. AGN, Inq., t. 180, exp. 1, fol. 20.

44. Huerga, *Historia de los alumbrados*, 3:861. Huerga reproduces significant portions of the sixteenth- and seventeenth-century alumbrados' trials from Spain's Archivo Histórico Nacional.

45. Jiménez Rueda, *Herejías y supersticiones*, 151; Dwyer, "Mystics in Mexico," 31, 50.

46. For a published reproduction of portions of San Miguel's trial in English, see Holler, "Spiritual and Physical Ecstasies," 77–100. See also Holler, "More Sins than the Queen," 209–28.

47. AGN, Inq., t. 210, exp. 3, fol. 351v.

48. Francisco Losa published the first biography of López in 1613. In 1617 Alonso de Remón, the Spanish playwright and chronicler of the Mercedarian Order, rewrote Losa's work and published it in Spain, and in 1642 the professional hagiographer Luis Muñoz published Losa's biography with some editorial additions and dedicated it to Juan de Palafox, who was one of the chief promoters of López's canonization. Chocano Mena, "Colonial Scholars," 352, 359–60.

49. Dwyer, "Mystics in Mexico," 75–76.

50. AGN, Inq., t. 210, exp. 2, fols. 74v–75.

51. Huerga, *Historia de los alumbrados*, 3:884.

52. AGN, Inq., t. 176, fol. 67.

53. For further information on Carvajal and the crypto-Jewish community in New Spain, see Liebman, *Enlightened*. For a discussion of theologians' ongoing spiritual preoccupations in seventeenth-century Peru, see Silverblatt, "New Christians and New World Fears."

54. AGN, Edictos de la Inquisición, t. 2, fol. 78. See also t. 1, fols. 23, 27; t. 2, fol. 101.

55. The Mexican court also convicted a Guatemalan priest, Gerónimo Larios, in 1621 for feigning sanctity and for claiming the ability to speak with saints, but they never referred to him as an alumbrado. AGN, Inq., t. 219, exp. 1, fols. 1–565.

56. Alberro discusses the trial of one of these sisters, Teresa de Jesús, in *Inquisición y sociedad*, 493–99, and in "La licencia vestida de santidad."

57. Alberro also discusses the relación of Ochoa's trial in *Inquisición y sociedad*, 500–507.

58. AGN, Inq., t. 1173, exp. 1; t. 1258, exp. 19, fols. 175–303.

59. Guilhem, "La Inquisición," 191.

60. AGN, Inq., t. 743, exp. 1, fol. 7v.

61. This distinction is outlined by Jiménez Rueda, *Herejías y supersticiones*, 161.
62. This occurs, for example, in the trials of Ana de Aramburu, AGN, Inq., t. 1358, exp. 14; and María Rita Vargas and María Lucía Celis, AGN, Inq., t. 1418, exp. 17.
63. AGN, Inq., t. 176, exp. 9, fols. 66–68.
64. AGN, Inq., t. 760, exp. 3, fols. 97–104.
65. AGN, Inq., t. 760, exp. 3, fol. 100.
66. Julio Jiménez Rueda, one of the pioneering historians on the religious expressions in Mexico's colonial period, wrote, regarding such paramystical phenomena, that "there is a state of conscience in the seventeenth century that singularly favors these illusions, which in terms of the characteristic ideas of the baroque period are perfectly explainable." *Historia de la cultura*, 122.
67. Jiménez Rueda, *Historia de la cultura*, 122.
68. See Griffiths and Cervantes, *Spiritual Encounters*, 15–18.
69. Griffiths and Cervantes, *Spiritual Encounters*, 19–24. Missionaries in New Spain placed particular stock in the use of the sacrament of confession. See Gruzinski, "Individualization and Acculturation," 96–117.
70. Sampson Vera Trudela, *Colonial Angels*, 78, 15–16.
71. Bilinkoff, introduction to Greer and Bilinkoff, *Colonial Saints*, xiv.
72. Rubial García, "Tierra de prodigios, 358. For further discussion of Counter-Reformation religious practices in colonial Mexico, see García Ayluardo and Ramos Medina, *Manifestaciones religiosas*; Rubial García, *La santidad controvertida*; Ramos Medina, *Místicas y descalzas*; Taylor, *Magistrates of the Sacred*; Brading, *First America*.
73. Rubial García, "Tierra de prodigios," 360.
74. For discussions of mystical religious practices, see Weinstein and Bell, *Saints and Society*; Certeau, *Mystic Fable*; Christian, *Local Religion*; Arenal and Schlau, *Untold Sisters*; Weckmann, *Medieval Heritage of Mexico*.
75. Bynum, *Fragmentation and Redemption*, 186. See also McNamara, "Rhetoric of Orthodoxy," 9–27. Although women have the strongest history of association with affective mystical spirituality, men have also participated in meditative approaches to mysticism.
76. Muriel de la Torre, *Cultura femenina novohispana*.
77. For a discussion of New World hagiography, see Morgan, *Spanish American Saints*.
78. Pardo, *Vida y virtudes heróycas*. Subsequent biographies of María de Jesús Tomelín were published in 1683 and 1756. For further discussion of the recording of her biography, see "Writers in Spite of Themselves: The Mystical Nuns of Seventeenth-Century Mexico," in Franco, *Plotting Women*, 3–22.
79. Rubial García, *La santidad controvertida*, 86.
80. Godínez was the Hispanicized name of an Irish Jesuit, Michael Wadding,

who taught theology at Mexico City's college of San Pedro and Pan Pablo. Franco, *Plotting Women*, 193 n. 8. Godínez wrote a guide to mystical theology, *Practica de la theologia mystica*, in which he extensively discussed the dangers of confusing genuine mysticism with the heretical illusions of alumbrados.

81. Pirate attacks were feared in the sixteenth and seventeenth centuries not only for the physical and economic damage they might inflict on the Spanish colonies but also for the Protestant beliefs they were believed to introduce among those who were conquered. Franco, *Plotting Women*, 9–11, 68.

82. For further discussion of the features of orthodox vidas in colonial Mexico, see Rubial García, *La santidad controvertida*, 73–75.

83. Maravall, *Culture of the Baroque*, 19, 27, 36.

84. In Europe the baroque era is generally considered to have ended nearer the beginning of the eighteenth century, but in the New World its life was extended by another half century. See Brading, "Tridentine Catholicism," 5.

85. For more detailed discussion of the development of criollo identity in colonial Latin America, see Brading, *First America*; Pagden, "Identity Formation," 51–93.

86. Leonard, *Baroque Times*, ix–x, 38.

87. Weinstein and Bell, *Saints and Society*, 161–62.

88. Greer and Bilinkoff, *Colonial Saints*, xvii–xviii; Myers, "Redeemer of America," 251, 259, 272; Taylor, "Mexico's Virgin of Guadalupe," 281.

89. Rose, whose cult was extremely popular in Mexico as well as Peru, was canonized in 1671. For a discussion of her canonization and cult, see Glave, "Santa Rosa de Lima," 1:53–70; Millones and Maza, *Una partecita del cielo*; Flores Araoz et al., *Santa Rosa de Lima*. Regarding the development of the cult of Guadalupe, see Lafaye, *Quetzalcóatl and Guadalupe*; Taylor, "Virgin of Guadalupe," 9–33; Poole, *Our Lady of Guadalupe*; Brading, *Mexican Phoenix*.

90. Rubial García, "Tierra de prodigios," 362–63. See also Brading, *First America*, 349.

91. Rubial García describes the ecclesiastical hierarchy of New Spain's efforts to have miracles and saintly figures recognized by the Catholic Church's central authorities in *La santidad controvertida*.

92. Brading, *First America*, 350.

93. See Osowski, "Saints of the Republic"; Villaseñor Black, "St. Anne Imagery," 3–29.

94. Lorenzana, *Concilios provinciales primero*, 45.

2. Mystical Spirituality in Colonial Mexico

1. AGN, Inq., t. 788, exp. 25, f. 453. *Castiza* referred to someone who had one Spanish and one mestizo parent. *Embustera* meant a feigner, a trickster.

2. AGN, Inq., t. 788, exp. 25, fol. 178. The medal might well have been one of the medallions nuns wore as part of their profession costume.

3. AGN, Inq., t. 788, exp. 25, fols. 289–99, 180v.

4. AGN, Inq., t. 788, exp. 25, fol. 254v.

5. AGN, Inq., t. 788, exp. 25, fols. 155–157v.

6. AGN, Inq. t. 799, exp. 8, fol. 179.

7. Martha Few found a similar pattern in the context of colonial Guatemala. See *Women Who Live Evil Lives*, 3, 5, 108, 110–15.

8. Cook and Borah, *Essays in Population History*, 181.

9. Boyer, "Mexico in the Seventeenth Century," 455–78.

10. Cook and Borah, *Essays in Population History*, 198. Gonzalo Aguirre Beltrán's figures differ. He calculated 75 percent indigenous, 1 percent Spanish, and 24 percent casta in 1646. *La población negra de México*, 219.

11. Aguirre Beltrán, *La población negra de México*, 225; Cook and Borah, *Essays in Population History*, 221–23.

12. Florescano and Gil Sánchez, "La época de las reformas borbónicas," 520; Aguirre Beltrán, *La población negra de México*, 231.

13. For a discussion of Mexico City's population based on the 1811 census, see Klein, "Demographic Structure of Mexico City," 66–93.

14. Seed, "Social Dimensions of Race," 569–606.

15. Stern, *Secret History of Gender*, 37.

16. Arrom, *Women of Mexico City*, 7–8.

17. Robles, "Diario de sucesos notables," fols. 414, 416.

18. Viqueira Albán, *Propriety and Permissiveness*, 10, 11.

19. Robles, "Diario de sucesos notables," fols. 417, 450, 454.

20. Robles, "Diario de sucesos notables," fol. 417. The third Mexican Provincial Council, deeming bullfights irreverent, banned clerics from attending them, but this provision was often overlooked.

21. See AGN, Inq., t. 721, exp. 32, fols. 462–70; t. 740, exp. 3, fols. 54–68.

22. AGN, Inq., t. 743, exp. 1, fol. 162.

23. AGN, Inq., t. 805, exp. 1, fols. 96, 56v, 65v, 66.

24. Alonso de Peralta, the inquisitor who tried the cases of the first Mexican ilusos in the late sixteenth century, for instance, was the first Mexican inquisitor born in the New World.

25. Seed, "Social Dimensions of Race," 580.

26. See Gibson, *Aztecs under Spanish Rule*, 158–65; and Lockhart, *Nahuas after the Conquest*, 130–40.

27. Susan M. Socolow, introduction to Hoberman and Socolow, *Cities and Society*, 7.

28. On the growth of such anxieties, see Seed, *To Love, Honor and Obey*; Voekel, "Peeing on the Palace," 183–208.

29. Voekel, "Peeing on the Palace," 185.

30. Seed, " Social Dimensions of Race," 572. See also Haslip-Viera, "Underclass," 285–312.

31. Norman F. Martin, "Pobres, mendigos, y vagabundos," 108, 110, 108.
32. AGN, Inq., t. 432, fol. 287. A number of other cases, such as those of María Manuela Picazo, Marta de la Encarnación, and Pedro García, also document mystics' financial desperation.
33. For information on poverty's predominance among unmarried people, see Arrom, "Desintegración familial y pauperización," 119–31.
34. AGN, Inq., t. 753, exp. 2, fol. 249.
35. AGN, Inq., t. 522, exp. 2, fol. 142v.
36. AGN, Inq., t. 1291 exp. 1, fol. 182.
37. AGN, Inq., t. 805, exp.2, fols. 230–230v.
38. Cope, *Limits of Racial Domination*, 29–32.
39. On interracial mixing and popular culture in the eighteenth century, see Viqueira Albán, *Propriety and Permissiveness*.
40. Cope, *Limits of Racial Domination*, 21.
41. Arrom, *Containing the Poor*, 157.
42. For a discussion of the operation of patron and client networks in terms of employment and social mobility, see Cope, *Limits of Racial Domination*.
43. Besides patronizing mystics, people from a variety of backgrounds also frequented other types of spiritual or physical healers in colonial Mexico. Both wealthy and poor Spanish women used the services of Indian midwives, and people of all races and classes consulted Indian and African curanderos. For further discussion, see Megged, "Magic, Popular Medicine and Gender," 189–207; Quezada, *Enfermedad y maleficio*.
44. Agustina Rangel, a mestiza tried in the 1680s, had clients from a variety of ethnic backgrounds, including Petrona Castro, a mestiza, Juana de Abalos, a mulata, and Inés de Bustos, a Spanish woman married to a merchant of *pulque* (fermented maguey alcohol). AGN, Inq, t. 522, exp. 2, fols. 95, 110, 120.
45. Such arrangements were common to the promotion of mystical women. The success of Rose of Lima's campaign for canonization was in some part due to the substantial patronage she received from the powerful Gonzalo de la Maza family.
46. Members of the Mexican elite patronized María de la Encarnación, Getrudis Rosa Ortiz, and Ignacio de San Juan Salazar.
47. Bravo, *Ana Rodríguez de Castro y Aramburu*, 41, 94, 26, 41–42, 59.
48. Huntington Library (HL), Mexican Inquisition Papers, Bruñón de Vertiz, fols. 58, 143.
49. HL, Mexican Inquisition Papers, Bruñón de Vertiz, fols. 150–155v. The marquesado del Valle referred to in these trial documents is likely that portion of Coyoacán, southwest of the colonial capital, that along with Tacubaya formed a portion of Cortés's enormous 1529 land grant. See Gerhard, *Guide to the Historical Geography*, 100–102.
50. Josefa de San Luis Beltrán, one of María's sisters, also had an extensive network

of supporters. Many other ilusas, including Antonia de Ochoa, Marta de la Encarnación, and Juana la Culteca, also received financial support in exchange for their religious work.

51. Richard Kagan examined the pragmatic side of a mystic's need to secure powerful sponsorship in early-seventeenth-century Spain. See *Lucrecia's Dreams*.

52. For a discussion of Isabel's life, see Ramos Medina, *Imagen de santidad* and *Místicas y descalzas*.

53. The Inquisition also initiated proceedings against many other clerics for their support of Mexican mystics, including José de Bruñón Vertiz, Javier de Requelme, Juan Bautista Surero, Francisco Jordanes, Clemente de Ledesma, Bernardo de Ledesma, Ángel Vázquez, Sebastián de San Francisco, Lorenzo de la Concepción, Antonio Rodríguez, and Eusebio Villarejo. The court, however, did not normally pursue mystics' lay patrons or clients.

54. AGN, Inq., t. 1173, exp. 6, fols. 122–23.

55. AGN, Inq., t. 816, exp. 34, fol. 277.

56. AGN, Inq., t. 816, exp. 34, fol. 270v.

57. AGN, Inq., t. 816, exp. 34, fols. 287v, 288.

58. See Lavrin, "Ecclesiastical Reform of Nunneries," 183–202.

59. On the curtailment of women's secular and sacred activities during in Counter-Reformation Spain, see Cruz and Perry, *Culture and Control*; Perry, *Gender and Disorder*.

60. Cruz and Perry, *Culture and Control*, xviii.

61. Holler, "I, Elena de la Cruz," 158. For further discussion of the Counter-Reformation's impact on female religiosity, see Lavrin, "Women and Religion in Spanish America," 42–53; Ranft, "Key to Counter Reformation," 7–25.

62. *Concilio provincial mexicano IV*, lib. 3, titulo 18, capítulo 3, p. 156.

63. Alberro, *La actividad del Santo Oficio*, 129–30.

64. For discussions of notions of male and female honor in colonial Mexico, see Seed, *To Love, Honor, and Obey*; Gutiérrez, *When Jesus Came*; Johnson and Lipsett-Rivera, *Faces of Honor*.

65. Mary Elizabeth Perry, "Magdalens and Jezebels in Counter-Reformation Spain," in Cruz and Perry, *Culture and Control*, 124.

66. The classic work on the importance of female honor—defined as chastity—in colonial Spanish America is Martínez Alier, *Marriage, Class and Colour*.

67. For further discussions of the cult of Guadalupe, see Poole, *Our Lady of Guadalupe*; Lafaye, *Quetzalcóatl and Guadalupe*; Taylor, "Virgin of Guadalupe," 9–33; Brading, *Mexican Phoenix*.

68. These events are immortalized in Cayetano Javier de Cabrera y Quintero's 1746 work *Escudo de Armas de México*, published the year Guadalupe was decreed co-patron (along with Saint Joseph) of Mexico.

69. For a discussion of indigenous saint cults, see Osowski, "Saints of the Republic."

70. Brading, *First America*, 338. Santiago's full title, "Santiago Matamoros," carries with it the connotation of Spain's earlier religious preoccupations with repressing the Islamic population of the Peninsula.

71. Taylor, *Magistrates of the Sacred*, 280.

72. Glave, "Santa Rosa de Lima," 53–70.

73. Morgan, "Saints, Biographers and Creole Identity," 153, 169.

74. Morgan, "Saints, Biographers and Creole Identity," 58.

75. Chocano Mena, "Colonial Scholars," 330, 326–27. Pope Alexander VII (1655–67) issued a decree invalidating the doctrine later in the seventeenth century, but it continued to have its detractors in Mexico.

76. AGN, Inq., t. 180, exp. 1, fol. 241; t. 210, exp. 3, fol. 318; t. 218, exp. 3, fol. 12.

77. Such visions also occurred in the trials of Josefa de San Luis Beltrán, Antonio Moncada, Agustín Claudio, and Getrudis Rosa Ortiz.

78. This description comes from her husband's testimony but is verified by several other witnesses who appeared in the trial of her confessor. HL, Mexican Inquisition Papers, Bruñón de Vertiz.

79. The following ilusos experienced visions of souls in purgatory: María de la Encarnación, Antonia de Ochoa, María de San José, Pedro Antonio, María Manuela Picazo, Ignacio de San Juan Salazar, Marta de la Encarnación, Getrudis Rosa Ortiz, Josefa de Aguirre, María Josefa Peña, sor María Coleta de San José, Barbara de Echagaray, Josefa Palacios, and María Gonzales Lozano. Antonia de Ochoa, Diego Martín, Juan de Luna, María Manuela Picazo, Catalina, Marta de la Encarnación, Getrudis Rosa Ortiz, Josefa Palacios, sor María La Cal, and María Gonzales Lozano all stated they could foresee their own or others' deaths.

80. AGN, Inq., t. 503, exp. 2, fol. 107.

81. HL, Mexican Inquisition Papers, Bruñón de Vertiz, fols. 42, 155v.

82. Among these mystics receiving supernatural signs were Antonia de Ochoa, AGN, Inq., t. 788, exp. 1, fol. 144v; a lay ilusa, also called Antonia, t. 981, exp. 10, fols. 141–45; and sor María Coleta de San José, t. 1172, exp. 7, fol. 74.

83. AGN, Inq., t. 522, exp. 2, fols. 95, 98, 63.

84. AGN, Inq., t. 805, exp. 1, fols. 85, 89v. Teresa Romero and Josefa de San Luis Beltrán also used relics in their supernatural fits. AGN, Inq., t. 432, exp. 8, fols. 159v–160.

85. AGN, Inq., t. 806, exp. 5, fols. 349v, 385v.

86. AGN, Inq., t. 788, exp. 24, fol. 300.

87. AGN, Inq., t. 805, exp. 1, fol. 99v.

88. Few, *Women Who Live Evil Lives*, 55.

89. For further discussion of food consumption and deprivation, see Bynum, *Holy Feast and Holy Fast*.

90. A number of the Mexican ilusos, including Marta de la Encarnación, Getrudis

Rosa Ortiz, María Rita Vargas, Josefa Palacios, and Ignacio de San Juan Salazar, followed rigorous fasting disciplines.

91. AGN, Inq., t. 748, exp. 1, fol. 78.
92. Ramírez Leyva, *María Rita Vargas*, 144, 162.
93. AGN, Inq., t. 788, exp. 24, fol. 231.
94. AGN, Inq., t. 1291, exp. 1, fol. 85v.
95. Bravo, *Ana Rodríguez de Castro y Aramburu*, 86.
96. Bravo, *Ana Rodríguez de Castro y Aramburu*, 54. Ana María de la Colina also declared that Aramburu would often experience such intense conversations with the Holy Spirit that she would interrupt them only to "ask for a cigar" (59).
97. Bravo, *Ana Rodríguez de Castro y Aramburu*, 77, 78, 167.
98. AGN, Inq., t. 432, exp. 8, fol. 148v.
99. HL, Mexican Inquisition Papers, Bruñón de Vertiz, 164, 165.
100. AGN, Inq., t. 538, exp. 2, fol. 95.
101. AGN, Inq., t. 445, exp. 1, fols. 1–370. Salvador Victoria is labeled "fray Sebastián Victoria" on the introductory page of his trial but is called "Salvador" throughout the rest of the case. Luis de Zárate and Juan Plata, tried in 1589, had also seen visions.
102. AGN, Inq., t. 623, exp. 1, fols. 1–185.
103. AGN, Inq., t. 711, exp. 1, fols. 1–277. Diego Martín, another early-eighteenth-century layman who predicted the deaths of his acquaintances, was not convicted. AGN, Inq., t. 542, exp. 7, fols. 547–93. The court dismissed the case of Antonio Moncada, a late-seventeenth-century layman who also claimed to have experienced visions and ecstasies. AGN, Inq., t. 536, exp. 1, fols. 1–5.
104. AGN, Inq., t. 743, exp. 1, fols. 1–408.
105. Among the 102 Mexican cases only 3 involved members of the clergy who claimed paramystical powers. The court dismissed the charges against all three men. They had been implicated in the investigation of the late-seventeenth-century alumbrada Antonia de Ochoa.
106. AGN, Inq., t. 820, exp. 15, fols. 296–321.
107. See "Writers in Spite of Themselves: The Mystical Nuns of Seventeenth-Century Mexico" in Franco, *Plotting Women*, 4–22; Sampson Vera Tudela, *Colonial Angels*, 35–54.
108. AGN, Inq., t. 1173, fols. 7–45. Several other ilusas, including Getrudis Rosa Ortiz and María Josefa, were also investigated in considerable part because of the spiritual tracts they produced.
109. Pelagius was the Latinized name of a fifth-century British lay monk who denied the doctrine of original sin and believed humanity was capable of good without the help of divine grace. Jansen's *Augustinas*, published in 1640 and banned by the Inquisition in 1653, criticized the Jesuits' emphasis on human

action and responsibility and defended Saint Augustine's writings arguing in favor of the idea of absolute predestination and the power of God's grace.

110. AGN, Inq., t. 692, exp. 2, fol. 173v.

111. Some of these writings are contained in AGN, Inq., t. 692, exp. 2, fols. 257–62.

112. AGN, Inq., t. 692, exp. 2, fol. 262. Zayas's original reads: "*Vela, en silencio profundo / batalla, como valiente / volarás, que es evidente / vivir, sin amor de mundo. / Vela, porque si no te hablo / no es efecto de locura, / porque mi fe te asegura / que he de desafiar al diablo. / Vela porque se descarne / tu afecto, y me quieras bien / no tengas esto a desdén / que el espíritu no es carne.*"

113. AGN, Inq., t. 753, exp. 2, fols. 200–374.

114. AGN, Inq., t. 1239, exp. 3, fol. 339. For more information about the trial, see Jaffary, "Tratado espiritual." Spanish laywoman Barbara de Echagaray, sentenced in 1799 for *ilusa y heregía mixta*, is also accused of having assumed responsibility for her own spiritual direction as well as of that of her niece. AGN, Inq., t. 1251, exp. 1, fol. 100.

115. AGN, Inq., t. 538, exp. 1, fol. 131. The text that Ocoha owned, *Contemptu mundi*, was likely a tract originally composed by Thomas Kempis that Luis de Granada translated from Latin to Spanish and published in the early sixteenth century. Granada, "Contemptus mundi," 380–430.

116. AGN, Inq., t. 538, exp. 1, fol. 156.

117. Further references to Teresa's writings are contained in the trials of Josefa de San Luis Beltrán, AGN, Inq., t. 432, exp. 8, fol. 114; María Rita Vargas, in Ramírez Leyva, *María Rita Vargas*, 108; and Josefa Palacios, AGN, Inq., t. 1291, exp. 1, fol. 43.

118. AGN, Inq., t. 1239, fols. 145–58, 192–99, 231–32, 255–321.

119. AGN, Inq. t. 1503, exps. 1–3. A listing of the visions contained in these stations is recorded in exp. 1, fol. 20.

120. AGN, Inq., t. 1351, exp. 14, fol. 305.

121. AGN, Inq., t. 503, exp. 17, f. 185v.

122. References to these and other saints are found in AGN t. 503, exp. 31, fol. 7v; t. 760, exp. 3, fol. 98v; t. 743, exp. 1, fol. 232; t. 748, exp. 1, fol. 71v; t. 748, exp. 1, fol. 71v; t. 805 exp. 1, fol. 58–59; t. 1291, exp. 1, fol. 89v; t. 788, exp. 24, fol. 144v. Both Antonia de Ochoa and Pedro Antonio owned copies of Loyola's *Exercisios Espirituales*.

123. Sor María de Jesús de Agreda became close confidante of Philip IV during the 1640s and 1650s. She was also the celebrated author of a multivolume biography of the Virgin Mary entitled *La Mística Ciudad de Dios*. References to her writings are contained in the trials of Josefa de San Luis Beltrán, AGN, Inq., t. 432 exp. 8, fol. 114; María Rita Vargas, in Ramírez Leyva, *María Rita Vargas*, 108; Josefa Palacios, AGN, Inq., t. 1291, exp. 1, fol. 43.

124. AGN, Inq., t. 748, exp. 1, fol. 89v. This was also true in the cases of the ilusas "Catalina," AGN, Inq., t. 760, exp. 3, fols. 97–104; "Antonia," AGN, Inq., t. 981,

exp. 10, fols. 141–45; and Ana de Aramburu, Bravo, *Ana Rodríguez de Castro y Aramburu*, 178.

125. AGN, Inq., t. 505, exp. 1, fols. 1–550, and t. 436, exp. 41, fols. 6v–7v. Juan Gómez had attempted to become a Franciscan friar, and Juan Bautista de Cárdenas had tried to become a Carmelite but did not have the financial resources necessary to pay for this venture. Salvador de Victoria had been a Capuchine friar in Spain, but he had been disciplined for disobedience and had then escaped from his monastery. During much of his inquisition trial in Mexico, he denied ever having had an affiliation with the Capuchines.

3. Evaluation of True and False Mysticism

1. Fray Agustín's lengthy case fills two volumes of Inquisition documents: AGN, Inq., t. 867, parts 1 and 2, fols. 1–377, 378–709.

2. AGN, Inq., t. 867, fols. 5, 8, 49v, 60, 87v, 88, 98–116.

3. AGN, Inq., t. 867, fols. 282v, 283, 283v. They also concluded other aspects of his practice were not heretical on fols. 284v, 286v.

4. AGN, Inq., t. 867, fols. 286, 291, 295.

5. AGN, Inq., t. 867, parts 1 and 2, fols. 446v, 658v; underlining in the original.

6. Ochoa's trial is located in AGN, Inq., t. 539, exp. 25, fols. 326–40, and t. 538, exp. 1, fols. 1–308.

7. AGN, Inq., t. 538, exp. 1, fol. 5.

8. AGN, Inq., t. 539, exp. 25, fol. 377.

9. Pardo, *Vida y virtudes heróycas*, 14.

10. Sigüenza y Góngora, *Parayso occidental*, 92. Madre Marina's biography contains a second parallel to that of the Mexican alumbrados in that she engaged in a lively correspondence with the hermit Gregorio López in the mid-sixteenth century.

11. AGN, Inq., t. 1173, exp. 1, fol. 24.

12. Ramírez Leyva, *María Rita Vargas*, 146.

13. Valdés, *Vida admirable y penitente*, 286.

14. References to Godínez's *Practica* are made, for example, in AGN, Inq., t. 793, exp. 1, fol. 145; t. 743, exp. 1, fol. 7; t. 748, exp. 1, fol. 36.

15. References to Arbiol's work are contained in AGN, Inq., t. 867, exp. 1, fols. 287, 479; t. 816, fol. 299.

16. The tract written by fray Francisco, who likely served the court as a theological qualifier, is located in AGN, Inq., t. 1480, exp. 4, fols. 131–51. Other contemporary guides dealing with these issues include Luis de la Peña, preface to fray Sebastián de Santander y Torres's *Vida de la venerable madre María de S. Joseph*; fray Francisco Anunciacão, *Vindicias de la virtud*; Joseph de Bayarta, *Práctica de las tres vías místicas*. Fifteenth-century theologian Jean Gerson developed one of the earliest codes for the detection of authentic mysticism

as a device for testing the veracity of the religious experiences of Joan of Arc. See Boland, *Concept of Discretio Spirituum*.

17. Godínez, *Practica de la theologia mystica*, 380, 431; Peña, preface to Santander y Torres, *Vida de la venerable madre Maria de S. Joseph*, 7. Seventeenth-century fray Francisco de Guevara of Mexico City's Santo Domingo convent also endorsed this idea in his translation of the vida of a sixteenth-century Italian beata, María Raggi. *Libro de la vida de la bendita Soror Maria Raggi, Beata Professa de la Orden Tercera de S. Domingo* (1632, Mexico City), 101v–102.

18. Godínez, *Practica de la theologia mystica*, 383–84. Peña articulated the same idea in his preface to Santander y Torres, *Vida de la venerable madre María de S. Joseph*, 7.

19. AGN, Inq., t. 176, exp. 9, fol. 68.

20. AGN, Inq., t. 753, exp. 2, fols. 210, 318; Inq., t. 210, exp. 3, fols. 310–310v.

21. AGN, Inq., t. 1078, exp. 2, fols. 96v, 108v. An early-eighteenth-century beato, Juan Bautista de Cárdenas, also made this claim, arguing that God and not only the devil could tempt humans. AGN, Inq., t. 623, exp. 1, fol. 90.

22. AGN, Inq., t. 692, exp. 2, fol. 172v.

23. AGN, Inq., t. 505, exp. 1, fols. 379v–380.

24. AGN, Inq., t. 445, exp. 1, fol. 164.

25. AGN, Inq., t. 805, exp. 1, fols. 13v, 14.

26. AGN, Inq., t. 805, exp. 1, fol. 14, 17v.

27. Museo Nacional de Antropología (MNA), 4a Serie, Doc. Varios, leg. 91, caja 26, doc. 5, fol. 22, "Instrucción Pastoral del Illmo: Señor Don Francisco Xavier de Lizana Beaumont, Arzobispo de México."

28. Morgan, *Spanish American Saints*, 29; Burke, "How to Be a Counter-Reformation Saint," 45.

29. Rubial García, *La santidad controvertida*, 36, 42.

30. Burke, "How to Be a Counter-Reformation Saint," 45–55.

31. The production of these hagiographies peaked between 1650 and 1770. Morgan, "Saints, Biographers and Creole Identity," 39.

32. Rubial García, *La santidad controvertida*, 165.

33. Arbiol, *Desengaños mysticos*, 78.

34. Godínez, *Practica de la theologaa mystica*, 436, 389. See also Peña, preface to Santander y Torres, *Vida de la venerable madre María de S. Joseph*, 7.

35. See Lavrin, "Women in Convents," 250–77; Burns, *Colonial Habits*.

36. Teresa wrote: "We may also imitate the saints by striving for solitude and silence, and many other virtues that will not kill our wretched bodies [*negros cuerpos*] which insist on controlling us so that they may disorder the soul." Santa Teresa de Jesús, *Libro de la vida* in *Obras completas*, 1, XII:9, 664.

37. Arbiol, *Desengaños mysticos*, 11.

38. AGN, Inq., t. 505, exp. 1, fols. 358–60, 369. Further examples of condemnation for this kind of evidence are contained in other iluso and alumbrado trials:

AGN, Inq., t. 743, exp. 1, fols. 28v, 89; t. 788, exp. 24, fol. 191, and t. 543, exp. 9, fol. 105.

39. AGN, Inq., t. 805, exp. 1, fols. 20–21, 2. Other examples of this kind of assessment are found in AGN, Inq., t. 816, exp. 34, fol. 299; t. 210, exp. 3, fol. 373; t. 219, exp. 1, fol. 389v; t. 503, exp. 23, fol. 211, exp. 30, fol. 258; t. 1480, exp. 4, fol. 139v.

40. Ignacio de San Juan Salazar's calificación indicates the court would likely have also convicted him, but he and one other beato both died during his trial proceedings.

41. Van Deusen, "Defining the Sacred," 445.

42. The same was also true for the three women who wore Dominican habits, the four who wore Carmelite habits, the two who wore Augustinian habits, and the one beata who wore a Mercedian habit.

43. Ramírez Leyva, *María Rita Vargas*, 28.

44. Iwasaki Cauti, "Mujeres al borde," 75.

45. Diego Pérez expressed such ideas in *Aviso de gente recogida*. Fray Clemente de Ledesma, one of the original spiritual supporters of late-seventeenth-century beata Antonia de Ochoa expresses a cleric's negative attitudes toward lone beatas in *Compendio de las excelencias*.

46. AGN, Inq., t. 806, exp. 5, fol. 342.

47. Lorenzana, *Concilios provinciales*, titulo 13, "De los regulares y de las monjas," 288.

48. *Concilio provincial mexicano IV*, libro 3, titulo 16, "De los regulares y de las monjas," 152.

49. Published in the *Gazeta de México* (February 2, 1790), tom 4: 3, 19.

50. For further discussion on contemporary associations between beatas and trickery, see Sampson Vera Tudela, *Colonial Angels*, 39.

51. Rubial García, *La santidad controvertida*, 96.

52. AGN, Inq., t. 445, exp. 1, fol. 89.

53. AGN, Inq., t. 445, exp. 1, fols. 62–62v, 289.

54. AGN, Inq., t. 623, exp. 1, fol. 298; t. 445, exp. 1, fol. 224; t. 1501, exp. 1, fol. 379.

55. Weinstein and Bell write that the church has always been more concerned with appraising the virtue of candidates for canonization than in any other supernatural indications of sanctity. *Saints and Society*, 141–43.

56. Godínez, *Practica de la theologia mystica*, 382. See also 385, 389. Arbiol and others express similar views: Arbiol, *Desengaños mysticos*, 77; Bayarta, "Práctica de las tres vías místicas," 208; Peña, preface to Santander y Torres, *Vida de la venerable madre María de S. Joseph*, 5.

57. AGN, Inq. t. 748, exp. 1, fols. 189, 192.

58. AGN, Inq., t. 805, exp. 2, fol. 191.

59. Arbiol, *Desengaños mysticos*, 78, 81.

60. AGN, Inq., t. 692, exp. 2, fols. 177v–178. The court made a similar assessment of Josefa Palacios, AGN, Inq., t. 1291, exp. 1, fols. 190–190v.

61. AGN, Inq., t. 799, exp. 9, fol. 206v.

62. AGN, Inq., t. 692, exp. 2, fol. 195v.

63. In 63 out of the total 102 iluso and alumbrado cases analyzed (62 percent of the cases), the accused either demonstrated or attested to literacy. In cases involving members of the institutional church, I have deduced literacy. Defendants attested to illiteracy in only 4 cases. No information on this matter is available in the other 35 cases.

64. Holler, "I, Elena de la Cruz," 150. Holler also writes that in the era of the conquest the Spanish crown had deemed reading particularly dangerous among colonial Latin America's "lower orders." Charles V issued an edict prohibiting Indians from reading fiction in 1531 (147).

65. The trials contain numerous references to theological tracts that defendants had either studied from or owned. The Romero sisters stated in their trial, for example, that their father had read to them the lives of Saint Teresa de Jesús and Isabel de Jesús. Pedro García de Arias owned *Precio de la gracia* by Juan Rodríguez. Salvador Victoria was familiar with the writings of Gregorio López. Antonia de Ochoa owned a number of theological tracts besides her *Contemptus mundi*, including *Los exercisios espirituales* by Ignacio Loyola and *Un combate espiritual*, likely authored by Lorenzo Scupoli. Pedro Antonio also owned a copy of Loyola's *Exercises*. Marta de la Encarnación had read the lives of San Juan de la Cruz and Santa Brigida, and María Guadalupe Rivera owned some of Augustine's writings and a treatise entitled *Aborrecimiento de pecado mortal*. Josefa Palacios owned *El Director de las almas, Máximas eternas, Conbate espiritual, Verdadera saviduría, Cristiana de Dutari,* and *Breve explicación de los principios mysteriosos,* among many other tracts. Sor Ana María La Cal had read the lives of San Juan de la Cruz, Santa Teresa, and Santa Coleta. María Josefa de la Peña demonstrated her familiarity with Teresa's *Interior Castles* in imitating them in her own writing. Ana de Aramburu also alludes to familiarity with this work.

66. AGN, Inq., t. 1173, exp. 5, fol. 3v.

67. AGN, Inq., t. 1173, exp. 5, fol. 3v, 4.

68. Regarding the European background on the prosecution against quietism, see Knox, *Enthusiasm.*

69. The papacy condemned Molinos's *Guía espiritual* in 1688, thirteen years after its publication, partially because of the text's emphasis on the passive nature of the soul and partially because of personal scandals that tainted Molinos's reputation.

70. AGN, Inq., t. 692, exp. 2, fol. 171v.

71. Pelagius was a fifth-century theologian who upheld that humanity possessed total freedom of will and was therefore completely responsible for its own sins. The court also connected María Manuela's heresies to quietist beliefs. AGN, Inq., t. 749, exp. 1, fol. 117v.

72. AGN, Inq., t. 753, exp. 2, fol. 310. The court also associated Núñez's contemporary, Marta de la Encarnación, with molinismo. AGN, Inq., t. 788, exp. 9, fol. 177v.

73. Rubial García, *La santidad controvertida*, 68.

74. See Brading, *Church and State* and "Tridentine Catholicism," for a thorough account of this process. See also Taylor, *Magistrates of the Sacred*, 19, 23, 265–300.

75. Rubial García, *La santidad controvertida*, 43. See also Larkin, "Splendor of Worship," 404–42.

76. Brading, *Church and State*, 163–69.

77. Bravo, *Ana Rodríguez de Castro y Aramburu*, 121.

78. AGN, Inq., t. 1173, fol. 293. Such attitudes are also expressed by the court's calificadores in their evaluation of the late-eighteenth-century case of Barbara de Echagaray. AGN, Inq., t. 1251, exp. 1, fol. 419.

79. On Indian nuns, see Lavrin, "Indian Brides of Christ," 225–60. On Indian clerics, see Taylor, *Magistrates of the Sacred*, 516–17, 522; Ricard, *Spiritual Conquest of Mexico*.

80. For further details on the cult of La China Poblana, see Myers, "Testimony for Canonization," 270–95.

81. Morgan, *Spanish American Saints*, 123, 124, 138.

82. A similar phenomenon is also evident in the debate surrounding the establishment of the first convent for Indian nuns in Mexico, Corpus Christi, in 1724, which determined that admission would be granted only for women of the indigenous elite, whose parents were removed from the taint of all suspicions of idolatry. See Lavrin, "Indian Brides of Christ," 242.

83. The Inquisition banned public adoration of the images of Catarina de San Juan in an edict in 1791. AGN, Edictos de la Inquisición, t. 1, fol. 14.

84. This is a neglected question in the historiography of the Inquisition in the colonial world, but Bartolomé Escandell Bonet does make a similar observation in "Sociologica Inquisitorial Americana," in Pérez Villanueva and Escandell Bonet, *Historia de la Inquisición*, 3:869–71. See also Gruzinski, *Man-Gods in the Mexican Highlands*; Cervantes, *Devil in the New World*; Osowski, "Saints of the Republic."

85. Giles, *Women in the Inquisition*, 8.

86. See Sampson Vera Tudela, *Colonial Angels*, 81, 84, for further discussion of Spanish fears of indigenous culture and its possible influences on Catholicism and Christians.

87. AGN, Inq., t. 805, exp. 1, fols. 214v–215.

88. Lorenzana, *Concilios provinciales*, capítulo 5, 45. The Council voiced similar concerns in the 1585 Third Council Meeting. *Concilio III provincial mexicano*, capítulo 6, "De los Hechiceros," 375.

89. Sampson Vera Tudela, *Colonial Angels*, writes that the rediscovery of evidence

of indigenous idolatry in New Spain and Peru in the seventeenth century refueled fears of indigenous religion.

90. John Carter Brown Library (JCBL, "Disertaciones," fol. 257. Judith Laikin Elkin has argued, along similar lines, that the Inquisition's intensive mid-seventeenth-century prosecution of Jews under charges of idolatry was due both to the court's perception that Indians had introduced idolatrous practices among the Jewish population as well as to missionaries' displaced frustration over their inability to prosecute Indians within the jurisdiction of the Inquisition after 1571. See Laikin Elkin, *Imagining Idolatry*.

91. For further discussions of these traditions in colonial Mexico, see Quezada, *Enfermedad y maleficio*; Aguirre Beltrán, *Medicina y magia*.

92. For a discussion of the concept of *tonalli*, see López Austin, *Human Body and Ideology*, 204–36.

93. López Austin, *Human Body and Ideology*, 216, 227.

94. This is the position argued by Aguirre Beltrán in *Medicina y magia*.

95. López Austin, *Human Body and Ideology*, 206.

96. AGN, Inq., t. 767, exp. 10, fols. 216, 221v.

97. Behar, "Sexual Witchcraft, Colonialism," 178–206.

98. AGN, Inq., t. 743, exp. 1, fols. 27, 354v, 355.

99. HL, Mexican Inquisition Papers, Bruñón de Vertiz, fol. 125.

100. This type of transformation occurs in the trials of Getrudis Rosa Ortiz, AGN, Inq., t. 805, exp. 1, fols. 34–34v; Ignacio de San Juan Salazar, AGN, Inq., t. 743, exp. 1, fol. 352v; and Marta de la Encarnación, AGN, Inq., t. 788, exp. 1, fol. 14.

101. AGN, Inq., t. 432, exp. 8, fol. 167v.

102. Jiménez Rueda, "El proceso de una seuda iluminada," III: 405.

103. AGN, Inq., t. 1489, exp. 4, fol. 133. On the role of religious art and its promotion by the post-Tridentine church in the context of colonial Mexico, see Loreta López, "Familial Religiosity and Images," 26–49.

104. AGN, Inq., t. 753, fols. 642–53. No witnesses knew María's surname, and all referred to her as "La India Colorada" (bright red or ribald Indian). I am grateful to Ed Osowski for sharing this case with me. The case appears in the Inquisition's records because the Provisorato notified the Holy Office that it should try María's mestizo, mulato, and Spanish clients for supporting her heretical practices.

105. Pipilzintli, according to the nineteenth-century Mexican historian José Antonio de Alzate, referred to the seeds of cannabis plants. Bartolache, *Mercurio volante*, 73 n. 7.

106. Lewis, *Hall of Mirrors*, 95–97.

107. Cope, *Limits of Racial Domincation*, 125–60.

108. Browne, "When Words Collide," 108. An extensive literature exists regarding the colonial church's fears about the Indian population's possibly "faked"

adoption of Christianity throughout the colonial period. For central Mexico, see Burkhart, *Slippery Earth*, and Lockhart, *Nahuas after the Conquest*.

109. The General Edict of the Faith published in New Spain, after warning listeners about alumbradismo, described the dangers of other "Diverse Heresies." These included invoking the devil, being witches, or "mixing sacred things with profane ones." AGN, Inq., t. 436, exp. 13, fol. 227v.

110. AGN, Inq., t. 868, fols. 295–305.

111. AGN, Inq., t. 781, exp. 54, fols. 609–44.

112. AGN, Inq., t. 1480, exp. 4, fol. 133v.

113. AGN, Inq., t. 1480, exp. 4, fols. 133v–134.

114. Martha Few also found that the Inquisition's fear of deviant religious practitioners grew in proportion to expansion of the mixed-race population. *Women Who Live Evil Lives*, 30.

4. Visions of Ilusos and Alumbrados

1. AGN, Inq., t. 805, exp. 1, fol. 31.

2. AGN, Inq., t. 805, exp. 1, fol. 31.

3. AGN, Inq., t. 805, exp. 1, fols. 32, 69, 12v.

4. Sor María de Jesús de Agreda, author of *Escuela mystica de María Santissima* (see figure 1) described her mystical visions in which she traveled in the spirit to New Mexico and Texas. See Colahan, *Visions of Sor María de Agreda*.

5. AGN, Inq., t. 805, exp. 1, fols. 20v, 22–25. 79.

6. See Taylor, "Virgin of Guadalupe"; Luisa Elena Alcalá, "Imagen e historia: La representación del milagro en la pintura colonial," in *Los siglos de oro*, 108.

7. The painting now hangs in the Catedral de Nuestra Señora de la Asunción in Tlaxcala, Mexico. For a reproduction, see *Los siglos de oro*, 185.

8. For an excellent treatment of the development of casta paintings in colonial Latin America, see Katzew, *New World Orders*.

9. Juan Rodríguez Juárez's (1675–1728) *San Francisco Javier bendiciendo nativos* (Franz Meyer Museum, Mexico City) represents a black man in this way. Villaseñor Black notes that non-Spanish characters generally appear in Mexican religious art as servants. "St. Anne Imagery," 17.

10. AGN, Inq., t. 805, exp. 1, fol. 3.

11. AGN, Inq., t. 805, exp. 1, fol. 10v.

12. AGN, Inq., t. 805, exp. 1, fols. 12, 225v.

13. In our own times it has become tantamount to blasphemy to refer to the Guadalupe image as a "painting," but this is what it was called in the colonial period when artist Miguel Cabrera and subsequent appraisers verified that the piece had not been formed by human hands. HL, Collection Mexico (Viceroyalty), Lorenzana, *Oración á Nuestra Señora de Guadalupe*. On the Guadalupe cult, see Lafaye, *Quetzalcóatl and Guadalupe*; Poole, *Our Lady of Guadalupe*; Brading, *Mexican Phoenix*.

14. Rodríguez G. de Ceballos, "Uso y funciones," 89, 90. For a discussion of the role of religious art in the spiritual ideology of elite laypeople, see Loreto López, "Familial Religiosity and Images," 26–49, and "Devil, Women, and the Body," 181–99.

15. Chazal, "Arte y mística del barroco," 23–24; Rodgríguez G. de Ceballos, "Uso y funciones," 103; Lorenzana, *Concilios provinciales*, capítulo 34, p. 91.

16. Villaseñor Black, "St. Anne Imagery," 21.

17. Vargaslugo, "La obra de arte," 18.

18. For discussions of baroque painting's influences on mysticism, see *Arte y mística*.

19. AGN, Inq., t. 748, exp., 1, fol. 89v. Mary is often pictured in these colors in colonial art, including in her apparition as the Virgin of Guadalupe.

20. Vargaslugo, "La obra de arte," 84.

21. AGN, Inq., t. 748, exp., 1, fol. 89v. Other explicit references to visual representations' influences on alumbrado visions are documented in the trials of Getrudis Rosa Ortiz, AGN, Inq., t. 805, exp. 1, fols. 45v, 79, 95v; and Salvador Victoria, AGN, Inq., t. 445, exp. 1, fols. 172–73.

22. For general treatments of colonial Mexican art, see Tovar de Teresa, *México Barroco*; Toussaint, *Colonial Art in Mexico*; Weismann, *Art and Time in Mexico*; Maza, *Los retablos dorados*.

23. JCBL, Núñez de Miranda, "Sermón de Santa Teresa de Jesús."

24. JCBL, Núñez de Miranda, "Sermon de Santa Teresa de Jesús," fol. 1.

25. JCBL, Núñez de Miranda, "Sermon de Santa Teresa de Jesús," fols. 2, 3.

26. *Catecismo para uso de los párrocos*, 14, 42, 44.

27. Regarding the circulation of this work, see Josefina Muriel de la Torre, *Las mujeres de Hispanoamérica*, 315; for an analysis of María de Jesús de Agreda's texts, see Colahan, *Visions of Sor María de Agreda*.

28. María Rita Vargas and Josefa Palacios both read Agreda's writings, and they were likely not the only mystics tried who were familiar with it. Ramírez Leyva, *María Rita Vargas*, 108; AGN, Inq., t. 1291, exp. 1, fol. 43.

29. María de Jesús de Agreda, *Escuela mystica de María Santissima*, 129.

30. For an example see the writings of eighteenth-century nun Sebastiana de la Santísima Trinidad. Sampson Vera Tudela, *Colonial Angels*, 111.

31. Bravo, *Ana Rodríguez de Castro y Aramburu*, 68. Similarly "orthodox" descriptions are found in the trials of Marta de la Encarnación, AGN, Inq., t. 788, exp. 25, fol. 205; María Picazo, t. 748, exp. 1, fol. 78; and Beatriz de Jesús las Flores, t. 806, exp. 5, fol. 350.

32. Ramírez Leyva, *María Rita Vargas*, 144.

33. Ramírez Leyva, *María Rita Vargas*, 161, 162; emphasis in the original.

34. Ramírez Leyva, *María Rita Vargas*, 162. On Mexican artists' propensity for depicting gory scenes of the Passion, see Clara Bargellini, "Cristo en el arte barroco," in *Arte y mística*, 43–47. Mexico's Museo del Virreinato houses an

anonymous *Ecce Homo* painting that can be viewed from the front and back and that depicts Christ in an equally devastated state.

35. Ramírez Leyva, *María Rita Vargas*, 163.

36. See MacCormack, *Religion in the Andes*, 20–25.

37. Bynum, "Women Mystics and Eucharistic Devotion," in *Fragmentation and Redemption*, 119–50. One anonymous seventeenth-century painting entitled *San Bernardo de Claraval* (Museo del Virreinato, Tepotzotlán, México), for example, portrays a seated Virgin Mary squirting a stream of her breast milk to the sanctified Bernardo.

38. Teresa de Jesús, *Libro de la vida*, in *Obras completas*, 1:587–877.

39. The Juárez work hangs in the Museo del Virreinato. Another version of it, possibly by the same painter, hangs in the Carmen Convent in San Angel.

40. Teresa de Jesús, *Libro de la vida*, in *Obras completas*, 1:xxiv:13, 775.

41. Bravo, *Ana Rodríguez de Castro y Aramburu*, 52, 99. A similar criticism—that interactions with Christ had been too *quotidienne*—is found in the qualifiers' judgment of Marta de la Encarnación, AGN, Inq., t. 799, exp. 9, fol. 206v; and in their assessment of Josefa Palacios's portrayal of God's means of addressing her as "reverendísimo" and of making a "miserable human have the properties of a God," AGN, Inq., t. 1019, exp. 2, fols. 190–190v.

42. See Gruzinski, *Man-Gods in the Mexican Highlands*.

43. The representation of human flaws in the divine world is recurrent in the writings and statements of other ilusos and alumbrados, such as those by mid-seventeenth-century hermit Pedro García de Arias, late-seventeenth-century beato Juan Bautista de Cárdenas, and late-eighteenth-century beata María Guadalupe Rivera.

44. Ramírez Leyva, *María Rita Vargas*, 122.

45. This is hardly surprising given the importance of miraculous Marian images in Mexico's religious history. See discussions of her role in Taylor, *Magistrates of the Sacred*, 277–300; Nebel, *Santa María Tonantzín*.

46. AGN, Inq., t. 805, exp. 1, fols. 48v–49.

47. Villaseñor Black notes, however, that many Mexican paintings of the scene differ from peninsular representations in that they depict realistic details of the postpartum scene. "St. Anne Imagery," 19.

48. AGN, Inq., t. 1173, exp. 1, fol. 28.

49. AGN, Inq., t. 1258, exp. 19, fol. 214v.

50. The suggestion of a coupling between Jesus Christ and the Virgin Mary does belong to a tradition within ecclesiastically endorsed iconography. See Warner, *Alone of Her Sex*, 121–33.

51. AGN, Inq., t. 522, exp. 2, fol. 112.

52. AGN, Inq., t. 522, exp. 2, fol. 104.

53. AGN, Inq., t. 1246, exp. 5, fol. 124. See also his appearance before the court, fol. 129.

54. AGN, Inq., t. 1246, exp. 5, fols. 155v, 130.

55. Unorthodox discussions of the Virgin Birth are also found in the trials of Barbara de Echagaray, AGN, Inq., t. 1251, exp. 1, fol. 5; Mariana de San Miguel, AGN, Inq., t. 210, exp. 3, fol. 310; Ana de Aramburu, Bravo, *Ana Rodríguez de Castro y Aramburu*, 94; and María Manuela Picazo, AGN, Inq., t. 748, exp. 1, fol. 276.

56. Burns, *Colonial Habits*, 21.

57. The partos reservados component of the Poor House, originally founded in 1763, was created in 1774. See Karchmer Krivistsky, "La ginecología y la obsetrica," 282.

58. AGN, Bandos, t. 24, exp. 55, fol. 143.

59. On the practice of illegitimacy in colonial Spanish America, see Twinam, *Public Lives, Private Secrets*; Calvo, "Concubinato y mestizaje," 203–12; and Asunción Lavrin, "Sexuality in Colonial Mexico: A Church Dilemma," in Lavrin, *Sexuality and Marriage*, 47–92.

60. Proposition thirty-four of sixty-five statements that Pope Innocent XI prohibited states "that it was licit to procure an abortion of the animation of the fetus." *Explicación de las sesenta y cinco proposiciones*, 37; AGN, Bandos, t. 24, exp. 55, fol. 143.

61. AGN, Inq., t. 788, exp. 24, fols. 405v, 406, 503v.

62. AGN, Inq., t. 522, exp. 2, fol. 114v.

63. AGN, Inq., t. 522, exp. 2, fols. 114v, 116v.

64. Franco, *Plotting Women*, 59–60.

65. AGN, Inq., t. 1231, exp. 1, fols. 152, 20, 86, 160–160v.

66. Alberro discusses the examples of Teresa Romero and one of her contemporaries, Juana de los Reyes, in this regard in *Inquisición y sociedad*, 493–99, 508–25.

67. Jiménez Rueda, "El processo de una seudo iluminada 1649," 217, 389, 394.

68. MNA, Colección Antigua, Inquisición, t. 2–29, fol. 14.

69. See Cervantes, *Devil in the New World*; Loreto López, "Devil, Women, and the Body," 188; Franco, *Plotting Women*, 20. For an example of a mystical vision in which demonic forces are associated with darkness, see the visions of sor Sebastiana Josefa de la Santísima Trinidad. Sampson Vera Tudela, *Colonial Angels*, 111.

70. Examples of such conventional associations with blacks occur in the trials, for instance, of Marta de la Encarnación, AGN, Inq., t. 788, exp. 24, fol. 189; t. 816, exp. 34, fol. 274v; and Ignacio de San Juan Salazar, AGN, Inq., t. 743, exp. 1, fols. 54, 216.

71. See Bynum, *Holy Feast and Holy Fast*; Bell, *Holy Anorexia*.

72. AGN, Inq., t. 805, exp. 1, fol. 34.

73. AGN, Inq., t. 805, exp. 1, fols. 34, 34v.

74. Bynum, *Holy Feast and Holy Fast*, 218, 257.

75. AGN, Inq., t. 805, exp. 1 fols. 41v–42. Black slaves often threatened to renege on God, as Joan Bristol argues, in order to bring the abusive behavior of their masters to the attention of the Inquisition. Bristol, "Negotiating Authority in New Spain." See also Villa-Flores, "To Lose One's Soul," 435–68.

5. Classification of Female Disorders

1. AGN, Inq., t. 1019, exp. 1, fols. 1, 3.
2. In the original passage, *"que se cagaba en la Sagrada comunión."* AGN, Inq., t. 1019, exp. 1, fols. 163v, 5v, 1; emphasis in the original.
3. HL, Trial of fray Eusbeio Villarejo, "El señor inquisitor fiscal," fol. 7v.
4. HL, Papers of Joseph Bruñón de Vertiz, fol. 13; emphasis in the original.
5. AGN, Inq., t. 1019, exp. 1, fols. 8, 122, 145, 145v.
6. AGN, Inq., t. 1019, exp. 1, fols. 2v, 3.
7. AGN, Inq., t. 1019, exp. 1, fols. 67v, 12v–18.
8. AGN, Inq., t. 1019, exp. 1, fol. 189v, 217v.
9. On the history of cross associations between female mysticism and mental illness, see Mazzoni, *Saint Hysteria*.
10. Epilepsy is not discussed in colonial Mexico's earliest medical texts. It is absent, for instance, in Farfán's *Tractado breve de anothomia y chirurgia* (1579) and Alonso López de Hinojos's *Summa y recopilación de cirugía* (1578). The disease began to appear in medical tracts published or circulated in New Spain in the eighteenth century, as in Horta, *Informe medico-moral*. Horta was head physician in Puebla's Hospital Real del Señor San Pedro.
11. AGN Inq., t. 1312, exp. 2, fol. 4v.
12. AGN, Inq., t. 1251, exp. 1, fols. 384v, 426. The trial of Salvador Victoria also contains similar evidence. AGN, Inq., t. 445, exp. 1, fol. 319. For further discussion of the perception of innocence associated with insanity, see Sacristán, *Locura y disidencia*, 18.
13. Convictions for demonic possession or for having made pacts with the devil accompanied, for instance, the sentences against Josefa de San Luis Beltrán, Augustina Rangel, Marta de la Encarnación, Barbara de Echagaray, and Josefa Palacios.
14. Salmerón, *Vida de la venerable madre Isabel*, 26.
15. José de Bayarta, priest, librarian, and author of a mid-eighteenth-century theological treatise concerning the three paths to divine union with God, also discussed the distinction between demonic possession and obsession. Fondo Reservado de la Biblioteca Nacional (FRBN), Bayarta, *Práctica de las tres vías místicas*, fol. 164.
16. Cervantes, *Devil in the New World*, 106, 101.
17. AGN, Inq., t. 1251, exp. 1, fol. 14v, 42, 55v.
18. AGN, Inq., t. 1251, exp. 1, fols. 47, 50, 313, 386, 69–69v. Many other iluso and alumbrado trials, including those of Mariana de San Miguel and María de

la Encarnación, contain such evidence of the overlapping perceptions of defendants' states.

19. AGN, Inq., t. 716, fols. 279v, 302, 307, 308, 309.

20. AGN, Inq., t. 716, fol. 328.

21. Two of the cases—those of sor Josefa Clara and sor Ana María La Cal, which are discussed subsequently in the text—also contain perceptions of the accused party also being either insane or demonized. The third case, that of María de San José, a peer of Antonia de Ochoa's, was likely not pursued because the notoriety of Ochoa's contemporary trial overshadowed the court's interest in pursuing a case against San José. San José was also much less threatening to the church since she had far fewer followers than Ochoa.

22. AGN Inq., t. 788, exp. 24, fol. 492.

23. Farfán, *Tractado breve de medicina*, 54. Two of the other most widely used tracts were Alonso López de Hinojos, *Suma y recopilación de cirugía* (1595) and Juan de Barrios, *Verdadera medicina, cirugía y astrología* (1607).

24. Lanning, *Royal Protomedicato*, 334.

25. *Boerhaave's Aphorisms concerning the Knowledge and Cure of Diseases*, 387. This view was also proffered in an early-nineteenth-century tract printed in Spain that circulated in Mexico. Vigarous, *Curso elemental de las enfermedades*, 64.

26. AGN, Inq., t. 218, exp. 3, fol. 37.

27. AGN, Inq., t. 543, exp. 9, fols. 95–107; t. 522, exp. 6, fols. 330–64.

28. AGN, Inq., t. 536, exp. 1, fol. 4.

29. AGN, Inq., t. 1246, exp. 5, fols. 129–31.

30. AGN, Inq., t. 1246, exp. 5, fols. 137, 148v. Montaña, a professor of botany at Mexico's Real y Pontificia Universidad, formed a secret medical academy in Mexico dedicated to the diffusion of new European medical practices. He also translated the medical tract of Scottish physician John Brown into Spanish and helped arrange for its publication as *Elementos de medicina del doctor Juan Brown* in Mexico. Martha Eugenia Rodríguez, "La medicina científica," 182.

31. AGN, Inq., t. 1246, exp. 5, fol. 139.

32. AGN, Inq., t. 1246, exp. 5, fol. 164.

33. AGN, Inq., t. 692, exp. 2, fols. 273, 266.

34. The conclusion of Zayas's case is not contained in the AGN documents. However, Medina notes that a woman named Ana de Zayas was a *penitenciado* (condemned by the Inquisition) in the late seventeenth century. *Historial del tribunal*, 364.

35. They applied this test, for example, in the 1598 trial of Mariana de San Miguel. AGN, Inq., t. 210, exp. 3, fol. 366.

36. AGN, Inq., t. 793, fol. 144v.

37. AGN, Inq., t. 767, exp. 10, fols. 216, 221v, 223.

38. AGN, Inq., t. 767, exp. 10, fols. 224v, 228v.

39. AGN, Inq., t. 793, exp. 2, fol. 144v; t. 867, exp. 1, fol. 282.

40. AGN, Inq., t. 867, exp. 1, fol. 282.

41. As it did, for instance, in its sentence of Marta de la Encarnación. AGN, Inq., t. 799, exp. 8, fol. 178. Josefa Palacios, the late-eighteenth-century "hysterical" beata, dared to point out to her inquisitors the illogic of such assessments: "Since all I have done is seen as fiction and trickery, I could not have had a pact, or commerce with the devil," she told the court. AGN, Inq., t. 1291, exp. 1, fol. 198.

42. Anunciacão, *Vindicias de la virtud*, 199.

43. MNA, Colección Antigua, Inquisición, t. 2–29, fol. 140v.

44. AGN, Inq., t. 816, exp. 34, fols. 273, 274–274v. The association between feigning mysticism and disobedience is also illustrated in the eighteenth-century trials of Antonia de Ochoa. AGN, Inq., t. 538, exp 1., fols. 118v, 170v; María Marta Picazo, AGN, Inq., t. 748, exp. 1, fol. 189, and Marta de la Encarnación, AGN, Inq. t. 788, exp. 24, fols. 193–193v, 194v, 347v.

45. For discussions of the history of New Spain's eighteenth-century medical establishment, see Lanning, *Royal Protomedicato*; Flores y Troncoso de Asís, *Historia de la medicina*; Mendiola Gómez, "Historical Synthesis of Medical Education," 88–96.

46. Regarding Enlightenment influences on Mexican medical practice, see Martha Eugenia Rodríguez, "La medicina científica," 181–93; Mathes, "Libros novo-hispanos de medicina," 55–69; Risse, "Medicine in New Spain," 12–63; Fajardo Ortiz, *Los caminos de la medicina colonial*; Hernández Sáenz, *Learning to Heal*.

47. AGN, Inq., t. 1291, exp. 1, fol. 67v.

48. Horta, *Informe médico-moral*, 2.

49. Horta, *Informe médico-moral*, 3.

50. Horta, *Informe médico-moral*, 5–7.

51. Bynum, *Fragmentation and Redemption*, 186. See also McNamara, "Rhetoric of Orthodoxy," 9–27.

52. For a comprehensive survey of the historical development of hysteria, see Micale, *Approaching Hysteria*. See also Gilman, *Hysteria beyond Freud*; and Veith's classic, *Hysteria*.

53. Horta, *Informe médico-moral*, 7.

54. Bartolache, *Mercurio volante*, 43.

55. Bartolache, *Mercurio volante*, 43.

56. Bartolache, *Mercurio volante*, 47, 45.

57. Vanegas's writings are quoted extensively in Nicolás León's history of Mexican obstetrics, *La obstétrica en México*. For Vanegas's discussion of suppression of the menses, see 133.

58. John Brown, *Élémens de médecine* (Paris, 1805), 390, 533, 425. I was unable to locate the Mexican edition of the work, so I have used a French translation.

59. Flores y Troncoso de Asís wrote that Riverius's writings had been incorporated

into the curricula of Mexico's medical school by 1825, if not earlier. Flores y Troncoso de Asís, *Historia de medicina*, 2:105.

60. Rivierius, *Practice of Physick*, 419.

61. These were views also supported by European scholars, including Boerhaave and Hoffman, whom Mexican physicians were reading in the late eighteenth and early nineteenth centuries. Micale, *Approaching Hysteria*, 155.

62. Castillo Grajeda, *Compendio de la vida y virtudes*, 22. This is also a central theme of the vida of the celebrated hermit of Chalma, fray Bartolomé de Jesús. FRBN, Sicardo, *Interrogatorio de la vida y virtudes*, Colección Lafraugua 1389, fol. 284.

63. Molina, *Exercisios espirituales*, 53.

64. Molina, *Exercisios espirituales*, 53, 73.

65. Louyer-Villermay, *Traité des maladies nerveuses*, 32–33. This work forms part of the collection in the Fondo Reservado in Mexico City's Biblioteca Nacional. María Cristina Sacristán assures me that its presence in this collection indicates that it was studied by the colony's medical professionals.

66. AGN, Inq., t. 1291, exp. 1, fol. 121.

67. AGN, Inq., t. 1251, exp. 1, fols. 135, 103v, 114.

68. AGN, Inq., t. 1291, exp. 1, fols. 155v, 159, 2.

69. AGN, Inq., t. 1251, exp. 1, fol. 9.

70. AGN, Inq., t. 1246, exp. 5, fol. 148v.

71. AGN, Inq., t. 1242, exp. 6, fols. 27, 29. María del Castillo Espanda was tried for heresy, but not for falsifying mysticism.

72. A contemporary version of the second article reads: "To believe that the Holy Virgin Mary, being herself a virgin before the birth, in the birth, and after the birth." Arbiol, *Explicacion breve*, 17.

73. AGN, Inq., t. 1251, exp. 1, fol. 5.

74. AGN, Inq., t. 1251, exp. 1, fol. 116.

Conclusion

1. Franco discusses this drawing in *Plotting Women*, 75.

2. See Calil Zarur and Lovell, *Art and Faith in Mexico*.

3. The tailed creatures in the drawing resemble the devils depicted in a drawing from a contemporary Inquisition trial. See the illustration in Behar, "Sex and Sin, Witchcraft," 44.

4. Bravo, *Ana Rodríguez de Castro y Aramburu*, 75.

5. Saint Brigida had apparently seen a vision of the Virgin Mary, who told her that women must shun pride and vanity that the devil encouraged in those who wore ostentatious clothing. Clemente de Ledesma, *Vida espiritual Comun*, 79.

6. For further discussion of this point, see Bilinkoff, introduction to Greer and

Bilinkoff, *Colonial Saints*, xiv, and Villaseñor Black, "St. Anne Imagery," in Greer and Bilinkoff, *Colonial Saints*, 23.

7. Lockhart, *Nahuas after the Conquest*, 445.
8. *Catecismo para uso de los párrocos*, 342.
9. Mendoza Ayala, *Impression mysteriosa*, fol. 10v.
10. Miguel Godínez advised the virtuous to meditate primarily upon Christ's passion in order to unite with God. Pardo, *Vida y virtudes heróycas*, 68–69.
11. HL, Collection Mexico (Viceroyalty), Lorenzana, "A las religiosas de los conventos."
12. AGN, Inq., t. 1172, exp. 7, fol. 155.
13. AGN, Inq., t. 505, exp. 1, fol. 382v.
14. Luke 10: 39–40, 41–42.
15. AGN, Inq., t. 505, exp. 1, fol. 382v. Francisco Losa also referred to this story in his 1613 biography of Greorgio López, where he noted that many people were suspicious of López because he dedicated himself almost exclusively to the contemplative life: "it is not new for Martha to complain because of Mary." See Losa, *La Vida que Hizo el Siervo*, 24.

Glossary

adivino. Diviner

alguacil. Bailiff

alumbrado. Illuminist

auto de fe. The Inquisition's ceremony of public condemnation

beata. Lay pious woman who took informal religious vows

beaterio. Community of *beatas*

cacique. Hereditary Indian governor

calendario. Calendar of religious celebrations

calificador. Theological evaluator for the Inquisition

cartilla. Christian reader

casta. Mixed-race person

castizo. Person with one *mestizo* and one Spanish parent

cofradía. Confraternity

comisario. Local judge of the Inquisition

consultor. Expert in theology and canon law who counseled the tribunal's inquisitors

converso. Jewish convert to Christianity

corridas de toros. Bullfights

criollo. Spaniard born in the New World

curandero. Healer

dejamiento. A mystical state involving the abandonment of the will

doctrina. Parish

edictos de fe. Edicts of the faith

embaucadora. Trickster, swindler

encomendero. Holder of private rights to Indian labor and tribute

engañadora. Fraud

embustero. Feigner, deceiver

encantador. Spell-maker, charmer

energúmena. Mad woman

ermitaño. Hermit

falta de juicio. Out of one's mind

familiares. Spies (officers of the Inquisition)

fiscal. Prosecutor

hacienda. Large agricultural estate

hechicería. Spell-making or witchcraft

hechizo. Spell

iluso. Deluded one

limeño. Citizen of Lima, Peru

limpieza de sangre. Cleanliness of the blood

loco. One who is insane

locura. Insanity

luteranos. Lutherans

mestizo. Person of mixed Indian and Spanish descent

morisco. Muslim convert to Christianity

mozo. Boy

mulato. Person of mixed African and Spanish descent

pardo. Person of mixed African and Spanish descent; Spaniards considered pardos darker skinned than mulatos

peninsulares. Spaniards born on the Iberian peninsula

pipilizintli. Cannabis seeds

poblano. Person from the city of Puebla

proceso. Inquisitorial trial

provisor. Chief ecclesiastical judge in a bishopric

recogimiento. Act of contemplation; house of spiritual reform for women

relaciones. Reports

religioso lego. Lay brother

retablo. Altarpiece

soltera. Single woman

sortílego. Sorcerer

supersticioso. Superstitious

tercero. Member of a third religious order

tonalli. Spirit, soul

vergüenza pública. Public shame

vida. Spiritual biography

Bibliography

Unpublished Primary Sources
Archivo General de la Nación (AGN), Mexico City
    Bandos
    Edictos de la Inquisición
    Inquisición

Museo Nacional de Antropología (MNA), Mexico City
    Colección Antigua
    Inquisición
    Doc. Varios

Fondo Reservado de la Biblioteca Nacional (FRBN), Mexico City
    Bayarta, Joseph de. *Práctica de las tres vías místicas.* Mexico City, 1751. MS 388
        [666].
    Sicardo, Fray Joseph. *Interrogatorio de la vida y virtudes del venerable hermano*
        fray Bartolomé de Jesús María. . . . Colección Lafragua 1389.

John Carter Brown Library (JCBL), Providence, Rhode Island
    "Disertaciones que el asistente real Dn. Antonio Joaquín Rivadeneira escrivió
        sobre los puntos que dieron a consultar por el Concilio 4.0 Mexicano."
        Codex Sp. 52.
    Núñez de Haro y Peralta, Alonso. "Cartas pastorales y edictos," No. 19.
    Núñez de Miranda, Antonio. "Sermón de Santa Teresa de Jesús. . . ." 1678.

Huntington Library (HL), San Marino, California
MEXICAN INQUISITION PAPERS
    Abecedario de Relaxados, reconciliados y penitenciados. . . . Series 1, vol. 2. HM
        35096.

Inventario de los Expedientes del Extinguido Tribunal de la Inquisición. . . . Series 1, vol. 1. HM 35095.

Papers relating to the case of Joseph Bruñón de Vertiz. Series 1, vol. 33, parts 1 and 2. HM 35127.

Trial of fray Eusbeio Villarejo for apostasy. HM 35140.

Published Primary Sources

Agreda, María de Jesús de. *Escuela mystica de Maria Santissima en la mystica ciudad de Dios en las doctrinas.* Mexico City: Joseph Bernardo de Hogal, 1731.

Anunciacão, Francisco. *Vindicias de la virtud, y escarmiento de virtuosas en los publicos castigos de los hipócritas dado por el Tribunal del Santo Oficio.* Madrid, 1754.

Arbiol, Antonio de. *Desengaños mysticos a las almas detenidas o engañadas en el camino de la perfeccion. . . .* 1705. Reprint, Barcelona, 1772.

———. *Explicacion breve de todo el sagrado texto de la doctrina cristiana. . . .* Mexico City, 1731.

Bartolache, Josef Ignacio. *Mercurio volante con noticias importantes i curiosas sobre varios asuntos de física i medicina.* No. 6 (November 25, 1772).

Boerhaave's Aphorisms concerning Knowledge and Cure of Diseases. Translated from the last Edition Printed in Latin at Leyden, 1728. London, 1735.

Bravo, Dolores. *Ana Rodríguez de Castro y Aramburu, ilusa, afectadora de santos, falsos milagros, y revelaciones divinas: Proceso inquisitorial en la Nueva España (Siglos XVIII y XIX).* Mexico City: Universidad Autónoma Metropolitana, 1984.

Brown, John. *Élémens de médecine.* Paris, 1805.

Castillo Grajeda, José del. *Compendio de la vida y virtudes de la venerable Catarina de San Juan.* Puebla, Mexico, 1692.

Catecismo para uso de los párrocos: Hecho por el IV. Concilio provincial mexicano. . . . Mexico City, 1772.

Concilio provincial mexicano IV, celebrado en la ciudad de México el año de 1771. Querétaro, Mexico: Imprenta de la Escuela de Artes, 1898.

Concilio III provincial mexicano, celebrado en México el año de 1585. Mexico City: Eugenio Maillefert y Compañía, 1859.

Eimeric, Nicolau, and Francisco Peña. *El manual de inquisidores.* 1376. Reprint, Barcelona: Atajos, 1996.

Farfán, Fray Agustín. *Tractado breve de anothomia y chirurgia. . . .* Mexico City, 1579.

———. *Tractado breve de medicina.* 1592. Reprint, Madrid: Ediciones de Cultura Hispánica, 1944.

Gazeta de México 4, no. 3 (February 2, 1790).

Godínez, Miguel. *Practica de la theologia mystica.* Seville, 1682.

Granada, Luis de. "Contemptus mundi: Menosprecio del mundo y imitación de Cristo." In *Biblioteca de autores españoles tomo tercero Obras del v.p.m. fray Luis de Granada*, 380–430. Madrid: Real Academia Española, 1945.

Horta, Pedro de. *Informe medico-moral de la penosissima y rigorosa enfermedad de la epilepsia, que a pedimento de la M.R.M. Alexandra Beatriz de los Dolores.* . . . Madrid, 1763.

Jiménez Rueda, Julio. "El proceso de una seudo iluminada 1649." *Boletín del Archivo General de la Nación* 7 (1946) no. 1: 35–72, no. 2: 217–42, no. 3: 387–442.

Ledesma, Clemente de. Compendio de las excelencias de la *Serafica sagrada Tercera orden.* . . . Mexico City, 1690.

León, Luis de. *La perfecta casada.* 1586. Reprint, Madrid: Taurus, 1987.

López de Hinojosos, Alonso. *Suma y recopilación de cirugía.* . . . Mexico City, 1578.

Lorenzana, Francisco Antonio. *Concilios provinciales primero y segundo, celebrados en la muy noble, y muy leal ciudad de México.* . . . Mexico City, 1769.

———. *Oración á Nuestra Señora de Guadalupe Compuesta por el Illmo Señor D. Francisco Antonio de Lorenzana.* Mexico City, 1770.

———. "A las religiosas de los conventos de nuestra filiación, y á todas las esposas de Jesu-Christo." Mexico City, 1769.

Losa, Francisco. *La Vida que Hizo el Siervo de Dios Gregorio Lopez, en algunas lugares de esta Nueva España.* . . . Mexico City, 1613.

Louyer-Villermay, Jean-Baptiste. *Traité des maladies nerveuses ou vapeurs et particulièrement de l'hystérie et de l'hypocondrie.* Paris, 1816.

Mendoza Ayala, Juan de. *Impression mysteriosa de las llagas de N. redemptor en el cuerpo del seraphin humano.* Mexico City, 1686.

Molina, Antonio de. *Exercicios espirituales de las excelencias, provecho, y necesidad de la oración mental.* . . . Barcelona, 1776.

Pardo, Francisco, Diego Osorio de Escobar y Llamas, and Matéo de la Cruz. *Vida y virtudes heróycas de la madre María de Jesus, religiosa profesa en el Convento de la limpia concepción de la Virgen María.* . . . Mexico City, 1676.

Pérez, Diego. *Aviso de gente recogida.* . . . Madrid, 1678.

Quiroga, Domingo de. *Compendio breve de la vida, y virtudes de la v. Francisca de Carrasco del Tercer Orden de Sto. Domingo.* Mexico City, 1729.

Ramírez Leyva, Edelmira. *María Rita Vargas, María Lucía Celis: Beatas embaucadoras de la colonia.* Mexico City: Universidad Nacional Autónoma de México, 1988.

Recopilacion de leyes de los reynos de las Indias. Madrid: Ivlian de Paredes, 1681.

Rivère, Lazare. *The Practice of Physick, in Seventeen Several Books.* London, 1655.

Robles, Antonio de. "Diario de sucesos notables, escrito por el licenciado D. Antonio de Robles y comprende los años de 1665 a 1703." In *Documentos para la historia de Méjico.* Mexico City: Imp. de J. R. Navarro, 1853–57.

Salmerón, Pedro. *Vida de la venerable madre Isabel de la Encarnacion carmelita descalza, natural de la Ciudad de los Angeles.* Mexico City, 1675.

Santander y Torres, Sebastián de. *Vida de la venerable madre Maria de S. Joseph.* . . . Seville, 1725.

Sigüenza y Góngora, Carlos de. *Parayso occidental plantado y cultivado por la liberal beneficia mano de los muy catholicos, y poderosos reyes de España.* . . . Mexico City, 1684.

Teresa de Jesús, Santa. *Obras completas.* Fr. Efrén de la Madre de Dios and Fr. Otilio del Niño Jesús, eds. 3 vols. Madrid: Biblioteca de autores cristianos, 1951–59.

Valdés, Joseph Eugenio. *Vida admirable y penitente de la V.M. sor Sebastiana Josepha de la SS. Trinidad.* . . . Mexico City, 1765.

Vigarous, Joseph Marie Joachim. *Curso elemental de las enfermedades de las mugeres.* . . . Madrid, 1807.

Viguera, Baltazar de. *La fisiologia y patologia de la muger.* . . . Madrid, 1827.

Vives, Juan Luis. *Libro llamada instrucción de la mujer cristiana.* 1524. Reprint, Juan Justiniano, trans. Madrid: Signo, 1936.

Secondary Sources

Aguirre Beltrán, Gonzalo. *Medicina y magia: El proceso de aculturación en la estructura colonial.* Mexico City: Instituto Nacional Indigenista, 1963.

———. *La población negra de México, 1519–1810: Estudio etnohistórico.* 2nd ed. Mexico City: Fondo de Cultura Económica, 1972.

Ahlgren, Gillian T. W. "Negotiating Sanctity: Holy Women in Sixteenth-Century Spain." *Church History* 64, no. 3 (September 1995): 373–88.

———. *Teresa of Avila and the Politics of Sanctity.* Ithaca: Cornell University Press, 1996.

Alberro, Solange. *La actividad del Santo Oficio de la Inquisición en Nueva España, 1571–1700.* Mexico City: Fondo de Cultura Económica, 1982.

———. "La Inquisición como institución normativa." In Seminario de historia, *Introducción a la historia de las mentalidades,* 231–57.

———. *Inquisición y sociedad en México, 1571–1700.* Mexico City: Fondo de Cultura Económica, 1988.

———. "La licencia vestida de santidad: Teresa de Jesús, falsa beata del siglo xvii." In *De la santidad a la perversión o de porqué se cumplía la ley de Dios en la sociedad novohispana,* ed. Sergio Ortega, 219–37. Mexico City: Grijalbo, 1986.

———. "Noirs et mulatres dans la société coloniale mexicaine d'après les Archives de l'Inquisition: XVIe–XVIIe siècles." *Cahiers de Amerique Latine* 17 (1978): 57–87.

Alcalá, Angel. "María de Cazalla: The Grievous Price of Victory." In Giles, *Women in the Inquisition,* 98–118.

———. *The Spanish Inquisition and the Inquisitorial Mind.* Boulder CO: Social Science Monographs, 1987.

Amy Moreno, Angel A. "The Spanish Treatment of Moriscos as a Model for the Treatment of Native Americans." PhD diss., Boston University, 1999.

Ancilli, Ermanno. *Diccionario de espiritualidad.* 3 vols. Barcelona: Editorial Herder, 1987.

Andrés Martín, Melquiades. "Los alumbrados de Toledo en el Cuarto abecedario espiritual o Ley de amor de Francisco Osuna (1530)." *Archivo Ibero-Americano* 41 (1981): 459–80.

———. "Alumbrados, Erasmians, 'Lutherans' and Mystics: The Risk of a More Intimate Spirituality." In A. Alcalá, *Spanish Inquisition*, 457–94.

———. *Los recogidos: Nueva visión de la mística española (1500–1700).* Madrid: Fundación Universitaria Española, 1975.

Arenal, Electa, and Stacey Schlau. *Untold Sisters: Hispanic Nuns in Their Own Works.* Trans. Amanda Powell. Albuquerque: University of New Mexico Press, 1989.

———. "Leyendo yo y escribiendo ella: The Convent as Intellectual Community." *Journal of Hispanic Philology* 13 (1989): 214–29.

Arrom, Silvia Marina. *Containing the Poor: The Mexico City Poor House, 1774–1871.* Durham: Duke University Press, 2000.

———. "Desintegración familial y pauperización: Los indigentes del Hospicio de Pobres de la ciudad de México, 1795." In *Familia y vida privada en la historia de iberoamérica,* ed. Pilar Gonzalbo Aizpuru and Cecilia Rabell Romero, 119–31. Mexico City: El Colegio de México, 1996.

———. "Historia de la mujer y de la familia latinoamericana." *Historia Mexicana* 42, no. 2 (1992): 379–418.

———. "Marriage Patterns in Mexico City, 1811." *Journal of Family History* 3, no. 4 (Winter 1978): 376–91.

———. *The Women of Mexico City, 1790–1857.* Stanford: Stanford University Press, 1985.

Arte y mística del barroco. Exh. Cat. Mexico City: El Colegio de San Ildefonso, Consejo Nacional para la Cultura y las Artes, 1994.

Bartra, Roger. *El siglo de oro de la melancolía: Textos españoles y novohispanos sobre las enfermedades del alma.* Mexico City: Universidad Iberoamericana, 1998.

Bataillon, M. *Erasmo y España: Estudios sobre la historia espiritual del siglo XVI.* Mexico City: Fondo de Cultura Económica, 1966.

Beezley, William, Cheryl English Martin, and William French. *Rituals of Rule, Rituals of Resistance: Public Celebrations and Popular Culture in Mexico.* Wilmington DE: Scholarly Resources Books, 1994.

Behar, Ruth. "Sex and Sin, Witchcraft and the Devil in Late-Colonial Mexico." *American Ethnologist* 14, no. 1 (February 1987): 34–54.

——. "Sexual Witchcraft, Colonialism, and Women's Powers: Views from the Mexican Inquisition." In Lavrin, *Sexuality and Marriage*, 178–206.

——. "The Visions of a Guachichil Witch in 1599: A Window on the Subjugation of Mexico's Hunter-Gatherers." *Ethnohistory* 34, no. 2 (Spring 1987): 115–38.

Bell, Rudolph. *Holy Anorexia*. Chicago: University of Chicago Press, 1985.

Bennassar, Bartolomé, ed. *Inquisición española: Poder político y control social*. 2nd ed. Barcelona: Editorial Crítica, 1981.

Bilinkoff, Jodi. *The Avila of Saint Teresa: Religious Reform in a Sixteenth-Century City*. Ithaca: Cornell University Press, 1989.

——. "Francisco Losa and Gregoria López: Spiritual Friendship and Identity Formation on the New Spain Frontier." In Greer and Bilinkoff, *Colonial Saints*, 115–28.

——. "A Spanish Prophetess and Her Patrons: The Case of María de Santo Domingo." *Sixteenth-Century Journal* 23, no. 1 (1992).

Blázquez, Juan Miguel. *La inquisición en América: 1569–1820*. Santo Domingo, Dominican Republic, 1994.

Boland, Paschal. *The Concept of Discretio Spirituum in John Gerson's "De Probatione Spirituum" and "De Distinctione Verarum Visionum a falsis."* Washington DC: Catholic University of America Press, 1959.

Bossy, John. *Christianity in the West, 1400–1700*. New York: Oxford University Press, 1975.

——. "The Counter-Reformation and the People of Catholic Europe." *Past and Present* 47 (May 1970): 51–70.

Boyer, Richard. *Lives of the Bigamists: Marriage, Family, and Community in Colonial Mexico*. Albuquerque: University of New Mexico Press, 1995.

——. "Mexico in the Seventeenth Century: Transition of a Colonial Society." *Hispanic American Historical Review* 57 (1977): 455–78.

Brading, David A. *Church and State in Bourbon Mexico: The Diocese of Michoacán, 1749–1810*. Cambridge: Cambridge University Press, 1994.

——. *The First America: The Spanish Monarchy, Creole Patriots, and the Liberal State, 1492–1867*. Cambridge: Cambridge University Press, 1993.

——. "Government and Elite in Late Colonial Mexico." *Hispanic American Historical Review* 53 (1973): 389–414.

——. *Mexican Phoenix: Our Lady of Guadalupe: Image and Tradition across Five Centuries*. Cambridge: Cambridge University Press, 2001.

——. "Tridentine Catholicism and Enlightened Despotism in Bourbon Mexico." *Journal of Latin American Studies* 15 (1983): 1–22.

Bristol, Joan Cameron. "Negotiating Authority in New Spain: Blacks, Mulattos, and Religious Practice in the Seventeenth Century." PhD diss., University of Pennsylvania, 2001.

Brown, Judith. *Immodest Acts: The Life of a Lesbian Nun in Renaissance Italy*. New York: Oxford University Press, 1986.

Brown, Peter. *The Cult of the Saints: Its Rise and Function in Latin Christianity.* Chicago: University of Chicago Press, 1981.

———. *The Body and Society: Men, Women, and Sexual Renunciation in Early Christianity.* New York: Columbia University Press, 1988.

Browne, Walden. "When Words Collide: Crisis in Sahagún's *Historia universal de las cosas de la Nueva España.*" *Colonial Latin American Historical Review* 5, no. 2 (Spring 1996): 101–49.

Bujanda, Jesús M. de. "Recent Historiography of the Spanish Inquisition (1977–1988): Balance and Perspective." In Perry and Cruz, *Cultural Encounters,* 221–47.

Burke, Peter. "How to Be a Counter-Reformation Saint." In *Religion and Society in Early Modern Europe, 1500–1800,* ed. Kaspar von Greyerz, 45–55. London: German Historical Institute, 1984.

Burkhart, Louise. *The Slippery Earth: Nahua-Christian Moral Dialogue in Sixteenth-Century Mexico.* Tucson: University of Arizona Press, 1989.

Burns, Kathryn. *Colonial Habits: Convents and the Spiritual Economy of Cuzco, Peru.* Durham NC: Duke University Press, 1999.

Butler, Judith. *Gender Trouble: Feminism and the Subversion of Identity.* New York: Routledge, 1990.

Bynum, Caroline Walker. *Fragmentation and Redemption: Essays on Gender and the Human Body in Medieval Religion.* New York: Zone Books, 1991.

———. *Gender and Religion: On the Complexity of Symbols.* Boston: Beacon Press, 1986.

———. *Holy Feast and Holy Fast: The Religious Significance of Food to Medieval Women.* Berkeley: University of California Press, 1987.

———. *Jesus as Mother: Studies in the Spirituality of the High Middle Ages.* Berkeley: University of California Press, 1982.

Caciola, Nancy. "Through a Glass, Darkly: Recent Work on Sanctity and Society." *Comparative Studies in Society and History* 38, no. 2 (April 1996): 301–9.

Calil Zarur, Elizabeth Netto, and Charles Muir Lovell. *Art and Faith in Mexico: The Nineteenth Century Retablo Tradition.* Exh. Cat. Albuquerque: University of New Mexico Press, 2001.

Calvo, Thomas. "Concubinato y mestizaje en el medio urbano: El caso de Guadalajara en el siglo XVII." *Revista de Indias* 44, no. 173 (1984): 203–12.

Caro Baroja, Julio. *Las brujas y su mundo.* Madrid: Revista de Occidente, 1961.

———. *Las formas complejas de la vida religiosa: Religión, sociedad, y carácter en la España de los siglos XVI y XVII.* Madrid: Akal, 1978.

———. *Vidas mágicas e inquisición.* 2 vols. Madrid: Taurus, 1967.

———. *Inquisición, brujería y criptojudaísmo.* Madrid: Ariel, 1970.

Castañeda, Carmen. *Violación, estupro y sexualidad: Nueva Galicia, 1790–1821.* Mexico City: Editorial Hexágono, 1989.

Castañeda Delgado, Paulino, and Pilar Hernández Aparicio. *La Inquisición de Lima, 1570–1655*. Madrid: Editorial Deimos, 1989.

Certeau, Michel de. *The Mystic Fable*, vol. 1: *The Sixteenth and Seventeenth Centuries*. Chicago: University of Chicago Press, 1992.

Cervantes, Fernando. *The Devil in the New World: The Impact of Diabolism in New Spain*. New Haven: Yale University Press, 1994.

Chazal, Gilles. "Arte y mística del barroco." In *Arte y mística del barroco*, 17–28.

Chance, John. *Race and Class in Colonial Oaxaca*. Stanford: Stanford University Press, 1978.

Chanau, Pierre, "Inquisition, et vie quotidienne dans l'Amérique espagnol du XVIIée siécle." *Annales, E.S.C.* 2 (1956): 228–36.

Chocano Mena, Magdalena. "Colonial Scholars in the Cultural Establishment of New Spain." PhD diss., State University of New York, Stonybrook, 1994.

Christian, William. *Apparitions in Late Medieval and Renaissance Spain*. Princeton: Princeton University Press, 1981.

———. *Local Religion in Sixteenth-Century Spain*. Princeton: Princeton University Press, 1981.

Coatsworth, John. "The Limits of Colonial Absolutism: The State in Eighteenth-Century Mexico." In *Essays in the Political, Economic and Social History of Colonial Latin America*, ed. Karen Spalding, 35–51. Newark: University of Delaware Press, 1982.

Cohn, Norman. *The Pursuit of the Millennium*. New York: Harper and Row, 1961.

Colahan, Clark. *The Visions of Sor María de Agreda: Writing, Knowledge, and Power*. Tucson: University of Arizona Press, 1994.

Contreras, Jaime, and Gustav Henningsen. "Forty-four Thousand Cases of the Spanish Inquisition (1540–1700): Analysis of a Historical Databank." In Henningsen and Tedeshci, *Inquisition in Early Modern Europe*, 100–129.

Cook, Sherburne F., and Woodrow Borah. *Essays in Population History*, vol. 2: *Mexico and the Caribbean*. Berkeley: University of California Press, 1974.

Cope, R. Douglas. *The Limits of Racial Domination: Plebeian Society in Colonial Mexico City, 1660–1720*. Madison: University of Wisconsin Press, 1994.

Cosío Villegas, Daniel, and Bernardo García Martínez. *Historia general de México*, 4 vols. Mexico City: El Colegio de México, 1976.

Cruz, Anne J., and Mary Elizabeth Perry. *Culture and Control in Counter Reformation Spain*. Minneapolis: University of Minnesota Press, 1992.

Cuevas, Mariano, S.J. *Historia de la Iglesia en México*. Mexico City: Editorial Porrúa, 1924.

Curcio-Nagy, Linda. "Faith and Morals in Colonial Mexico." In Meyer and Beezley, *Oxford History of Mexico*, 151–82.

Davis, Natalie Zemon. *Society and Culture in Early Modern France*. Stanford: Stanford University Press, 1975.

Deans-Smith, Susan. *Bureaucrats, Planters and Workers: The Making of the Tobacco Monopoly in Bourbon Mexico*. Austin: University of Texas Press, 1992.

Douglas, Mary. *Purity and Danger: An Analysis of Concepts of Pollution and Taboo*. London: Routledge, 1966.

Duviols, Pierre. *La lutte contre les religions autochtones dans le Pérou coloniale; "l'extirpation de l'idolâtrie," entre 1532 et 1660*. Lima: Institut français d'etudes andines, 1971.

Dwyer, Daniel. "Mystics in Mexico: A Study of Alumbrados in Colonial New Spain." PhD diss., Tulane University, 1995.

Eich, Jennifer Lee. "Mystic Tradition and Mexico: Sor María Ana Agueda de San Ignacio." PhD diss., University of California, 1992.

Erickson, Kai T. *Wayward Puritans: A Study in the Sociology of Deviance*. New York: Macmillan, 1966.

Fajardo Ortiz, Guillermo. *Los caminos de la medicina colonial en Iberoamérica y las Filipinas*. Mexico City: Universidad Nacional Autónoma de México, 1996.

Farriss, Nancy. *The Crown and Clergy in Colonial Mexico, 1759–1821: The Crisis of Ecclesiastical Privilege*. London: Athlone, 1968.

Few, Martha. *Women Who Live Evil Lives: Gender, Religion, and the Politics of Power in Colonial Guatemala*. Austin: University of Texas Press, 2002.

Flores Araoz, José, et al. *Santa Rosa de Lima y su tiempo*. Lima: Banco de Crédito de Perú, 1995.

Flores y Troncoso de Asís, Francisco. *Historia de la medicina en México desde la época de los indios hasta el presente*. 4 vols. 1886. Reprint, Mexico City: Instituto Mexicano del Seguro Social, 1982.

Florescano, Enrique, and Isabel Gil Sánchez. "La época de las reformas borbónicas y el crecimiento económico, 1750–1808." In Cosío Villegas and García Martínez, *Historia general de México*, vol. 2. 183–302.

Florescano, Enrique, et al. *La clase obrera en la historia de Mexico City: De la colonia al imperio*. Mexico City: Siglo XXI, 1980.

———. *Precios de maíz y crisis agrícolas en México, 1708–1810*. Mexico City: El Colegio de México, 1969.

Foucault, Michel. *Discipline and Punish: The Birth of the Prison*. New York: Vintage Books, 1979.

———. *Madness and Civilization: A History of Insanity in the Age of Reason*. New York: Vintage Books, 1973.

Franco, Jean. *Plotting Women: Gender and Representation in Mexico*. New York: Columbia University Press, 1989.

García Ayluardo, Clara, and Manuel Ramos Medina. *Manifestaciones religiosas en el mundo colonial americano*. 2 vols. Mexico City: Condumex, 1993.

Geertz, Clifford. *The Interpretation of Cultures: Selected Essays*. New York: Basic Books, 1973.

Gerhard, Peter. *A Guide to the Historical Geography of New Spain.* Rev. ed. Norman: University of Oklahoma Press, 1993.

Gibson, Charles. *The Aztecs under Spanish Rule, 1519–1810.* Stanford: University of Stanford Press, 1964.

Giles, Mary E., ed. *Women in the Inquisition: Spain and the New World.* Baltimore: Johns Hopkins University Press, 1999.

Gilman, Sander L. *Hysteria beyond Freud.* Berkeley: University of California Press, 1993.

Ginzburg, Carlo. *Clues, Myths, and the Historical Method.* Baltimore: Johns Hopkins University Press, 1989.

———. *The Cheese and the Worms: The Cosmos of a Sixteenth-Century Miller.* New York: Penguin, 1982.

———. *Ecstasies: Deciphering the Witches' Sabbath.* New York: Pantheon, 1991.

Glave, Luis Miguel. "Santa Rosa de Lima y sus espinas: La emergencia de mentalidades urbanas de crisis y la sociedad andina (1600–1630)." In García Ayluardo and Ramos Medina, *Manifestaciones religiosas,* 53–70.

Gonzalbo Aizpuru, Pilar. *Familias novohispanas: Siglos XVI al XIX.* Mexico City: El Colegio de México, 1991.

———. "Hacía una historia de la vida privada en la Nueva España." *Historia Mexicana* 42, no. 2 (1992): 353–77.

———. *Las mujeres en la Nueva España: Educación y vida cotidiana.* Mexico City: El Colegio de México, 1987.

Gonzalbo Aizpuru, Pilar, and Cecilia Rabell Romero. *Familia y vida privada en la historia de Iberoamérica.* Mexico City: El Colegio de México, 1996.

Greenleaf, Richard. "Historiography of the Mexican Inquisition: Evolution of Interpretations and Methodologies." In *Cultural Encounters,* ed. Perry and Cruz, 248–76.

———. "The Inquisition and the Indians of New Spain: A Study in Jurisdictional Confusion." *Americas—A Quarterly Review of Latin American Cultural History* 22, no. 2 (July 1966): 138–67.

———. "The Mexican Inquisition and the Enlightenment, 1763–1805." *New Mexico Historical Review* 41 (1966): 181–96.

———. *The Mexican Inquisition of the Sixteenth Century.* Albuquerque: University of New Mexico Press, 1969.

———. "The Inquisition in Eighteenth-Century New Mexico." *New Mexico Historical Review* 60, no. 1 (Spring 1985): 29–60.

Greer, Alan, and Jodi Bilinkoff, eds. *Colonial Saints: Discovering the Holy in the Americas.* New York: Routledge, 2003.

Griffiths, Nicholas, and Fernando Cervantes, eds. *Spiritual Encounters: Interactions between Christianity and Native Religions in Colonial America.* Lincoln: University of Nebraska Press, 1999.

Grundmann, Herbert. *Religious Movements in the Middle Ages: The Historical*

Links between Heresy, the Mendicant Orders, and the Women's Religious Movement in the Twelfth and Thirteenth Century. 1935. Reprint, Notre Dame IN: University of Notre Dame Press, 1995.

Gruzinski, Serge. La guerra de las imágenes: De Cristóbal Colón a "Blade Runner" (1492–2019). Mexico City: Fondo de Cultura Económica, 1994.

———. "Individualization and Acculturation: Confession among the Nahuas of Mexico from the Sixteenth to the Eighteenth Century." In Lavrin, Sexuality and Marriage, 96–117.

———. Man-Gods in the Mexican Highlands: Indian Power and Colonial Society, 1520–1800. Stanford: Stanford University Press, 1989.

———. "La 'segunda aculturación': El estado ilustrado y la religiosidad indígena en Nueva España (1775–1800)." Estudios de historia novohispana 8 (1985): 175–201.

Guilhem, Claire. "La Inquisición y la devaluación del verbo femenino." In Bennassar, Inquisición española, 171–207.

Gunnarsdöttir, Ellen. "Religious Life and Urban Society in Colonial Mexico: The Nuns and Beatas of Querétaro, 1674–1810." PhD diss., University of Cambridge, 1997.

Gutiérrez, Ramón. When Jesus Came, the Corn Mothers Went Away: Marriage, Sexuality, and Power in New Mexico, 1500–1846. Stanford: Stanford University Press, 1991.

Hamilton, Alistair. Heresy and Mysticism in Sixteenth-Century Spain: The Alumbrados. Cambridge UK: James Clarke, 1992.

Hampe Martínez, Teodoro. "Recent Works on the Inquisition and Peruvian Colonial Society." Hispanic American Historical Review 31, no. 1 (1996): 43–65.

Haslip-Viera, Gabriel. Crime and Punishment in Late Colonial Mexico City, 1692–1810. Albuquerque: University of New Mexico Press, 1999.

———. "The Underclass." In Hoberman and Socolow, Cities and Society, 285–312.

Henningsen, Gustav, and John Tedeschi. The Inquisition in Early Modern Europe: Studies in Sources and Methods. De Kalb: Northern Illinois University Press, 1986.

Hernández Sáenz, Luz María. Learning to Heal: The Medical Profession in Colonial Mexico, 1767–1831. New York: Peter Lang, 1997.

Hoberman, Louisa Schell, and Susan M. Socolow. Cities and Society in Colonial Latin America. Albuquerque: University of New Mexico Press, 1986.

Holler, Jacqueline. "I, Elena de la Cruz: Heresy and Gender in Mexico City, 1568." Journal of the Canadian Historical Association 4 (1993): 143–60.

———. "'More Sins than the Queen of England': Marina de San Miguel before the Mexican Inquisition." In Giles, Women in the Inquisition, 209–28.

———. "The Spiritual and Physical Ecstasies of a Sixteenth-Century Beata: Marina de San Miguel Confesses before the Mexican Inquisition." In

Colonial Lives: Documents on Latin American History, 1550–1850, ed. Richard Boyer and Geoffrey Spurling, 77–100. New York: Oxford University Press, 2000.

Hordes, Stanley. "The Inquisition as Economic and Political Agent: The Campaign of the Mexican Holy Office against the Crypto-Jews in the Mid-Seventeenth Century." *Americas* 39 (1982): 23–38.

Huerga, Alvaro. *Historia de los alumbrados (1570–1630)*. 4 vols. Madrid: Fundación Universitaria Española, 1978–88.

Imirizaldu, J. *Monjas y beatas embaucadoras*. Madrid: Editora Nacional, 1977.

Israel, J. I. *Race, Class, and Politics in Colonial Mexico, 1610–1670*. London: Oxford University Press, 1975.

Iwasaki Cauti, Fernando. "Mujeres al borde de la perfección: Rosa de Santa María y los alumbrados de Lima." In Millones and Maza, *Una partecita del cielo*, 71–110.

———. "Vidas de santos y santas vidas: Hagiografia e imaginarios en Lima colonial." *Anuario Estudios Americanos* 51, no. 1 (1994): 47–64.

Jaffary, Nora E. "Deviant Orthodoxy: A Social and Cultural History of *Ilusos* and *Alumbrados* in Colonial Mexico." PhD diss., Columbia University, 2000.

———. "El tratado espiritual de María Josefa de la Peña." In Lavrin and Loreto López, *Diálogos espirituales. Letras femeninas hispanoamericanas, siglos XVI–XIX*. Puebla, Mexico: Benemerita Universidad de Puebla, forthcoming.

———. "La percepción de clase y casta en las visiones de los 'falsos místicos' en el México Colonial." *Signos históricos* 8 (July–December 2002), 61–88.

———. "Virtue and Transgression: The Certification of Authentic Mysticism in the Mexican Inquisition." *Catholic Southwest: A Journal of History and Cultura* 10 (1999): 9–28.

Jantzen, Grace M. *Power, Gender, and Christian Mysticism*. Cambridge: Cambridge University Press, 1995.

Jiménez Montesserín, Miguel. *Introducción a la Inquisición española: Documentos básicos para el estudio del Santo Oficio*. Madrid: Nacional, 1980.

Jiménez Rueda, Julio. *Herejías y supersticiones en la Nueva España: Los heterodoxos de México*. Mexico City: Imprenta Universitaria, 1946.

———. *Historia de la cultura en México*, vol. 2: *El Virreinato*. Mexico City: Editorial Cultural, 1960.

———. "La secta de los alumbrados en la Nueva España." *Boletín del Archivo General de la Nación* 16, no. 1 (1945).

Johnson, Lyman, and Sonya Lipsett-Rivera, eds. *The Faces of Honor: Sex, Shame and Violence in Colonial Latin America*. Albuquerque: University of New Mexico Press, 1998.

Kagan, Richard. *Lucrecia's Dreams: Politics and Prophecy in Sixteenth-Century Spain*. Berkeley: University of California Press, 1990.

Kamen, Henry. *Inquisition and Society in Spain in the Sixteenth and Seventeenth Centuries.* Bloomington: Indiana University Press, 1985. Rev. ed. issued as *The Spanish Inquisition: A Historical Review.*

———. *The Spanish Inquisition: A Historical Review.* New Haven: Yale University Press, 1998.

Karchmer Krivitsky, Samuel. "La ginecología y la obstetricia." In *Contribuciones al conocimiento médico,* ed. Hugo Aréchigal and Juan Somolinos Palencia, 279–85. Mexico City: Secretaría de Salúd, 1993.

Katzew, Ilona. *New World Orders: Casta Painting and Colonial Latin America.* Exh. Cat. New York: Americas Society Art Gallery, 1996.

Kicza, John E. "Life Patterns and Social Differentiation among Common People in Late Colonial Mexico City." *Estudios de Historia Novohispana* 11 (1991): 183–200.

———. "La mujer y la vida comercial en la ciudad de México a finales de la colonia." *Revista de ciencias sociales y humanidades* 11, no. 4 (1981): 39–59.

———. "The Social-Ethnic Historiography of Colonial Latin America." *William and Mary Quarterly* 45, no. 3 (July 1988): 453–88.

Klein, Herbert S. "The Demographic Structure of Mexico City in 1811." *Journal of Urban History* 23, no. 1 (November 1996): 66–93.

Knox, R. A. *Enthusiasm: A Chapter in the History of Religion.* New York: Galaxy, 1961.

Konetzke, Richard. "La emigración de mujeres españoles a América durante la época colonial." *Revista Internacional de Sociología* 3 (1945): 123–50.

Lafaye, Jacques. *Quetzalcóatl and Guadalupe: The Formation of Mexican National Consciousness, 1531–1813.* Chicago: University of Chicago Press, 1974.

Laikin Elkin, Judith. *Imagining Idolatry: Missionaries, Indians, and Jews.* Providence RI: John Carter Brown Library, 1992.

Lanning, John Tate. *The Royal Protomedicato: The Regulation of the Medical Professions in the Spanish Empire.* Ed. John Jay TePaske. DurhamNC: Duke University Press, 1985.

Laqueur, Thomas. *Making Sex: Body and Gender from the Greeks to Freud.* Cambridge MA: Harvard University Press, 1990.

Larkin, Brian. "The Splendor of Worship: Baroque Catholicism, Religious Reform, and Last Wills and Testaments in Eighteenth-Century Mexico City." *Colonial Latin American Historical Review* 8, no. 4 (Fall 1999): 404–42.

Lavrin, Asunción. "Ecclesiastical Reform of Nunneries in New Spain in the Eighteenth Century." *Americas* 22, no. 2 (October 1965): 182–202.

———. "Indian Brides of Christ: Creating New Spaces for Indigenous Women in New Spain." *Mexican Studies* 15, no. 2 (Summer 1999): 225–60.

———. *Latin American Women: Historical Perspectives.* Westport CT: Greenwood Press, 1978.

———. "La riqueza de los conventos de monjas en Nueva España: Estructura y evolución durante el siglo XVIII." *Cahiers des amériques latines* (1973): 91–117.

———, ed. *Sexuality and Marriage in Colonial Latin America*. Lincoln: University of Nebraska Press, 1989.

———. "Unlike Sor Juana? The Model Nun in the Religious Literature of Colonial Mexico." In Merrim, *Feminist Perspectives*, 61–86.

———. "Values and Meaning of Monastic Life for Nuns in Colonial Mexico," *Catholic Historical Review* 58, no. 3 (1972): 367–87.

———. "La Vida femenina como experiencia religiosa: Biografía y hagiografía en Hispanoamérica colonial." *Colonial Latin American Review* 2, no. 2 (1993): 27–52.

———. "Women and Religion in Spanish America." In *Women and Religion in America*, vol. 2: *The Colonial and Revolutionary Periods*, ed. Rosemary Radford Ruether and Rosemary Skinner Keller, 42–78. San Francisco: Harper and Row, 1983.

———. "Women in Convents: Their Economic and Social Role in Colonial Mexico." In *Liberating Women's History: Theoretical and Critical Essays*, ed. Bernice A. Caroll, 250–77. Urbana: University of Illinois Press, 1976.

Lavrin, Asunción, and Rosalva Loreto López, eds. *Diálogos espirituales. Letras femeninas hispanoamericanas, siglos XVI–XIX*. Puebla, Mexico: Benemerita Universidad de Puebla, forthcoming.

———, eds. *Monjas y beatas: La escritura femenina en la espiritualidad barroca novohispana, siglos xvii y xviii*. Mexico City: Universidad de las Américas, AGN, 2002.

Lea, Henry Charles. *A History of the Inquisition of Spain*. 4 vols. 1906. Reprint, New York: AMS Press, 1966.

———. *The Inquisition in the Spanish Dependencies*. New York: Macmillan, 1922.

León, Nicolas. *La obstétrica en México*. Mexico City, 1910.

Leonard, Irving. *Baroque Times in Old Mexico: Seventeenth-Century Persons, Places, and Practices*. Ann Arbor: University of Michigan Press, 1966.

Lewis, Laura A. *Hall of Mirrors: Power, Witchcraft, and Caste in Colonial Mexico*. Durham NC: Duke University Press, 2003.

Liebman, Seymour B., trans. and ed. *The Enlightened: The Writings of Luis de Carvajal, el Mozo*. Coral Gables FL: University of Miami Press, 1967.

Llorca Vives, Bernardino. *La Inquisición española y los alumbrados (1509–1667)*. Salamanca, Spain: Universidad Pontificia, 1980.

Lockhart, James. *The Nahuas after the Conquest: A Social and Cultural History of the Indians of Central Mexico, Sixteenth through the Eighteenth Centuries*. Stanford: University of Stanford Press, 1992.

López Austin, Alfredo. *The Human Body and Ideology: Concepts of the Ancient Nahuas*. 2 vols. Salt Lake City: University of Utah Press, 1988.

Loreta López, Rosalva. "The Devil, Women, and the Body in Seventeenth-Century Puebla Convents." *Americas* 59, no. 2 (2002): 181–99.

———. "Familial Religiosity and Images in the Home: Eighteenth-Century Puebla de Los Angeles, Mexico." *Journal of Family History* 22, no. 1 (1997): 26–49.

Lynch, John. *Spain under the Habsburgs.* Oxford: Basil Blackwell, 1981.

MacCormack, Sabine. *Religion in the Andes: Vision and Imagination in Early Colonial Peru.* Princeton: Princeton University Press, 1991.

Mannarelli, Maria Emma. "Inquisición y mujeres: Las hechiceras en el Perú durante el siglo XVII." *Revista Andina* 3, no. 1 (1985): 141–56.

Maravall, José Antonio. *Culture of the Baroque: Analysis of a Historical Culture.* Minneapolis: University of Minnesota Press, 1986.

Márquez, Antonio. *Historia de los alumbrados (1570–1630).* Madrid: Fundación Universitaria Española, Seminario Cisneros, 1978–94.

———. *Los alumbrados: Orígenes y filosofía, 1525–1619.* Madrid: Taurus, 1972.

Marshall, Sherrin. *Women in Reformation and Counter-Reformation Europe: Public and Private Worlds.* Bloomington: Indiana University Press, 1989.

Martin, Luis. *Daughters of the Conquistadores: Women of the Viceroyalty of Peru.* Albuquerque: University of New Mexico Press, 1983.

Martin, Norman F. "Pobres, mendigos, y vagabundos en la Nueva España, 1702–1766: Antecedentes y soluciones presentados." *Estudios de Historia Novohispana* 8 (1985): 99–126.

Martínez Alier, Verna. *Marriage, Class and Colour in Nineteenth-Century Cuba: A Study of Racial Attitudes and Sexual Values in a Slave Society.* Ann Arbor: University of Michigan Press, 1974.

Mathes, W. Michael. "Libros novohispanos de medicina durante el siglo de la Ilustración, 1700–1821." *Colonial Latin American Historical Review* 4, no. 1 (Winter 1995): 55–69.

Maza, Francisco de la. *Catarina de San Juan, princesa de la India y visionaria de Puebla.* 2nd ed. Mexico City: Consejo Nacional para la Cultura y las Artes, 1990.

———. *La ciudad de México en el siglo XVII.* Mexico City: Secretaria de Educación Pública, 1985.

———. *La decoración simbólica de la Capilla del Rosario de Puebla.* Puebla, Mexico: Ediciones Altiplano, 1971.

———. *El Guadalupanismo mexicano.* Mexico City: Fondo de Cultura Económica, 1981.

———. *Los retablos dorados de Nueva España.* Mexico City: Ediciones Mexicanas, 1950.

Mazzoni, Christina. *Saint Hysteria: Neurosis, Mysticism and Gender in European Culture.* Ithaca: Cornell University Press, 1996.

McDonnell, Ernest. *The Beguines and Beghards in Medieval Culture, with Special Emphasis on the Belgian Scene*. New York: Octagon Books, 1969.

McKnight, Kathryn Joyce. *The Mystic of Tunja: The Writings of Madre Castillo, 1671–1741*. Amherst: University of Massachusetts Press, 1997.

McNamara, Jo Ann. "The Rhetoric of Orthodoxy: Clerical Authority and Female Innovation in the Struggle with Heresy." In *Maps of Flesh and Light: The Religious Experience of Medieval Women Mystics*, ed. Ulrike Wiethaus, 9–27. Syracuse: Syracuse University Press, 1993.

Medina, José Toribio. *Historia del tribunal del Santo Oficio de la Inquisición en México*. Santiago, Chile: Imprenta Elzeveriana, 1905. Reprint, Mexico City: Consejo Nacional para la Cultura y las Artes, 1991.

Megged, Amos. "Magic, Popular Medicine and Gender in Seventeenth-Century Mexico: The Case of Isabel de Montoya." *Social History* 19, no. 2 (May 1994): 189–207.

Méndez, María Agueda. "Ilusas y alumbradas: Discurso místico o erótico?" *Caravelle* 52 (1989): 5–15.

Mendiola Gómez, Jaime. "Historical Synthesis of Medical Education in Mexico." In *Aspects of the History of Medicine in Latin America*, ed. John Z. Bowers and Elizabeth F. Burcell, 88–96. New York: Josiah Macy Jr. Foundation, 1997.

Merrim, Stephanie. *Feminist Perspectives on Sor Juana Inés de la Cruz*. Detroit: Wayne State University Press, 1991.

Meyer, Michael C., and William H. Beezley, eds. *The Oxford History of Mexico*. Oxford: Oxford University Press, 2000.

Micale, Mark S. *Approaching Hysteria: Disease and Its Interpretations*. Princeton: Princeton University Press, 1995.

Milhou, Alain. "Gregorio López, el iluminismo y la Nueva Jerusalem americana." In *IX Congreso Internacional de Historia de América*, vol. 3: *Europa e Iberoamérica: Cinco siglos de intercambios*, ed. Sarabia Viejo and María Justina, 55–83. Seville, 1992.

Millar Carvacho, René. *Inquisición y sociedad en el virreinato peruano: Estudios sobre el tribunal de la Inquisición de Lima*. Santiago: Instituto Riva-Agüero, Pontificia Universidad Católica de Perú, Instituto de Historia, Ediciones Universidad Católica de Chile, 1998.

———. *Misticismo e Inquisición en el virreinato peruano: Los procesos a los alumbrados de Santiago de Chile, 1710–1736*. Santiago: Ediciones Universidad Católica de Chile, 2000.

Miller, Beth. *Women in Hispanic Literature: Icons and Fallen Idols*. Berkeley: University of California Press, 1983.

Millones, Luis, and Gonzalo de la Maza. *Una partecita del cielo: La vida de Santa Rosa de Lima narrada por D[o]n Gonzalo de la Maza a quien ella llamaba padre*. Lima: Editorial Horizonte, 1993.

Moreno de los Arcos, Roberto. "New Spain's Inquisition for Indians from the Six-teenth to the Nineteenth Century." In Perry and Cruz, *Cultural Encounters*, 23–36.

Morgan, Ronald J. "Saints, Biographers and Creole Identity Formation in Colonial Spanish America." PhD diss., University of California, Santa Cruz, 1998.

———. *Spanish American Saints and the Rhetoric of Identity, 1600–1810*. Tucson: University of Arizona Press, 2002.

Mörner, Magnus. *Race Mixture in the History of Latin America*. Boston: Little, Brown, 1967.

Muir, Edward, and Guido Ruggerio. *Sex and Gender in Historical Perspective*. Baltimore: Johns Hopkins University Press, 1990.

Muriel de la Torre, Josefina. *Conventos de monjas en la Nueva España*. 2 vols. Mexico City: Editorial Santiago, 1946.

———. *Cultura feminina novohispana*. Mexico City: Universidad Nacional Autónoma de México, 1981.

———. *Hospitales de la Nueva España*. Mexico City: Jus, 1960.

———. *Las mujeres de Hispanoamérica: Época colonial*. Madrid: Editotrial Mapfre, 1992.

———. *Los recogimientos de mujeres: Respuesta a una problemática social novo-hispana*. Mexico City: Universidad Nacional Autónoma de México, 1974.

Myers, Kathleen. " 'Redeemer of America': Rosa de Lima (1586–1617), the Dynam-ics of Identity, and Canonization." In Greer and Bilinkoff, *Colonial Saints*, 251–75.

———. "Testimony for Canonization or Proof of Blasphemy: The New Spanish Inquisition and the Hagiographic Biography of Catarina de San Juan." In Giles, *Women in the Inquisition*, 270–95.

———. *Word from New Spain: The Spiritual Autobiography of Madre María de San José (1656–1719)*. Liverpool: Liverpool University Press, 1993.

Myers, Kathleen, and Amanda Powell. *"A Wild Country out in the Garden": The Spiritual Journals of a Colonial Mexican Nun*. Bloomington: Indiana University Press, 1999.

Nebel, Richard. *Santa María Tonantzín, Virgen de Guadalupe: Continuidad y transformación en México*. Mexico City: Fondo de Cultura Económica, 1992.

Nieto, José C. "The Franciscan *Alumbrados* and the Prophetic-Apocalyptic Tradi-tion." *Sixteenth-Century Journal* 8 (1977): 3–16.

———. "The Heretical Alumbrados Dexados: Isabel de la Cruz and Pedro Ruiz de Alcaraz." *Revue de Littérature Comparée* nos. 2–4 (1978): 293–313.

Numbers, Ronald. *Medicine in the New World: New Spain, New France, and New England*. Knoxville: University of Tennessee Press, 1987.

Osowski, Edward W. "Saints of the Republic: Nahua Religious Obligations in Central Mexico, 1692–1810." PhD diss., Pennsylvania State University, 2002.

Pagden, Anthony. "Identity Formation in Spanish America." In *Colonial Identity in the Atlantic World, 1500–1800*, ed. Nicholas Canny and Anthony Pagden, 51–93. Princeton: Princeton University Press, 1987.

Palmer, Colin. *Slaves of the White God: Blacks in Mexico 1570–1650*. Cambridge: Harvard University Press, 1976.

Paz, María. "Spanish Spirituality's Mid-Sixteenth Century Change of Course." In Alcalá, *Spanish Inquisition*, 421–30.

Pérez Villanueva, Joaquín, and Bartolomé Escandell Bonet. *Historia de la Inquisición en España y América*. 3 vols. Madrid: Biblioteca de Autores Cristianos, Centro de Estudios Inquisitoriales, 1984–2000.

Perry, Mary Elizabeth. "Beatas and the Inquisition in Early Modern Seville." In *The Inquisition and Society in Early Modern Europe: Studies in Sources and Methods*, ed. Gustav Henningsen and John Tedeschi, 147–68. De Kalb: Northern Illinois University Press, 1986.

———. *Gender and Disorder in Early Modern Seville*. Princeton: Princeton University Press, 1990.

Perry, Mary Elizabeth, and Anne J. Cruz. *Cultural Encounters: The Impact of the Inquisition in Spain and the New World*. Berkeley: University of California Press, 1991.

Petroff, Elizabeth. *Body and Soul: Essays on Medieval Women and Mysticism*. New York: Oxford University Press, 1994.

———. *Medieval Women's Visionary Literature*. New York: Oxford University Press, 1986.

Phelan, Cr. J. L. *The Millennial Kingdom of the Franciscans in the New World*. Berkeley: University of California Press, 1970.

Poole, Stafford. *Our Lady of Guadalupe, 1531–1797*. Tucson: University of Arizona Press, 1995.

Quezada, Noemí. "Alumbrados del siglo xvii: Análisis de casos." In *Religión en Mesoamérica*, ed. Jaime Litvak King and Noemí Castillo Tejero, 581–86. Mexico City: Sociedad Mexicana de Antropología, 1972.

———. "Concepciones tradicionales sobre embarazo y parto." *Anales de Antropología* 14 (1977): 307–26.

———. "Dioses, Santos y Demonios en la curación colonial." In *III Coloquio de Historia de la religión en Mesoamérica y áreas afines*, ed. Barbro Dahlgren Jordan, 106–119. Mexico City: Universidad Nacional Autónoma de México, 1993.

———. *Enfermedad y maleficio: El curandero en el México colonial*. Mexico City: Universidad Nacional Autónoma de México, 1989.

Ragon, Pierre. "Les images miraculeuses du diocese de Mexico au milieu du XVIIIe siecle." *Histoire Economie et Société* 14, no. 3 (1995): 445–60.

Ramos Medina, Manuel. *Imagen de santidad en un mundo profano*. Mexico City: Universidad Iberoamericana, 1990.

———. *Místicas y descalzas: Fundaciones femeninas carmelitas en la Nueva España.* Mexico City: Condumex, 1997.

———. *El Monacato femenino en el Imperio Español: Monasterios, beaterios, recogimientos y colegios.* Mexico City: Condumex, 1995.

Ranft, Patricia. "A Key to Counter Reformation Women's Activism: The Confessor-Spiritual Director." *Journal of Feminist Studies in Religion* 10, no. 4 (Fall 1994): 7–26.

Ricard, Robert. *The Spiritual Conquest of Mexico.* Trans. Lesley Byrd Simpson. Berkeley: University of California Press, 1966.

Risse, Guenter B. "Medicine in New Spain." In *Medicine in the New World: New Spain, New France, and New England,* ed. Ronald L. Numbers, 12–63. Knoxville: University of Tennessee Press, 1987.

Rodríguez, Martha Eugenia. "La medicina científica y su difusión en Nueva España." *Estudios de Historia Novohispana* 12 (1992): 181–93.

Rodríguez G. de Ceballos, Alfonso. "Uso y funciones de la imagen religiosa en los virreinatos americanos." In *Los siglos de oro,* pp. 89–125.

Rodríguez, Marta Eugenia. "La medicina científica y su difusión en Nueva España." *Estudios de historia novohispana* 12 (1992): 181–93.

Rubial García, Antonio. "Espejo de virtudes, sabrosa narración, emulación patriotica: La literatura hagiográfica sobre los venerables no canonizados de la Nueva España." In *La literatura novohispana: Revisión crítica y propuestas metodológias,* ed. José Pascual Buxó and Arnulfo Herrera, 89–110. Mexico City: Universidad Nacional Autónoma de México, 1994.

———. "Josefa de San Luis Beltrán, la cordera de Dios: Escritura, oralidad y gestualidad de una visionaria del siglo XVII Novohispano." In Lavrin and Loreto López, *Monjas y beatas,* 161–77.

———. *La santidad controvertida: Hagiografía y conciencia criolla alrededor de los venerables no canonizados de Nueva España.* Mexico City: Universidad Nacional Autónoma de México, 1999.

———. "Tebaidas en el paraíso: Los ermitaños de la Nueva España." *Historia Mexicana* 44, no. 3 (1995): 355–83.

———. "Tierra de prodigios: Lo maravilloso cristiano en la Nueva España de los siglos XVI y XVII." In Nelly Sigaut, ed. *La Iglesia Católica en México.* Zamora, Michoacán, México: El Colegio de Michoacán, 1997.

Sacristán, María Christina. *Locura y disidencia en el México ilustrado, 1760–1810.* Mexico City: El Colegio de Michoacán, Instituto Mora, 1994.

———. *Locura e inquisición en Nueva España, 1571–1760.* Mexico City: El Colegio de Michoacán, 1993.

Sampson Vera Tudela, Elisa. *Colonial Angels: Narratives of Gender and Spirituality in Mexico, 1580–1750.* Austin: University of Texas Press, 2000.

Sánchez Lora, José Luis. *Mujeres, conventos y formas de la religiosidad barroca.* Madrid: Fundación Universitaria Española, 1988.

Scott, Joan. *Gender and the Politics of History.* New York: Columbia University Press, 1988.

Seed, Patricia. *To Love, Honor, and Obey in Colonial Mexico: Conflicts over Marriage Choice, 1574–1821.* Stanford: Stanford University Press, 1988.

———. "The Social Dimensions of Race." *Hispanic American Historical Review* 62, no. 4 (November 1982): 569–606.

Seminario de Historia de la Educación en México. *Historia de la lectura en México.* Mexico City: El Colegio de México, 1997.

Seminario de Historia de las Mentalidades. *Del dicho al hecho . . . : Transgresiones y pautas culturales en la Nueva España.* Mexico City: Instituto Nacional de Antropología e Historia, 1989.

———. *Familia y poder en Nueva España: Memoria del tercero simposio de historia de las mentalidades.* Mexico City: Instituto Nacional de Antropología e Historia, 1991.

———. *Familia y sexualidad en Nueva España.* Mexico City: Fondo de Cultura Económica, 1982.

———. *Introducción a la historia de las mentalidades.* Mexico City: Instituto Nacional de Antropología e Historia, 1979.

———. *La Memoria y el olvido: Segundo simposio de historia de las mentalidades.* Mexico City: Instituto Nacional de Antropología e Historia, 1985.

———. *El Placer de pecar y el afán de normar: Ideologías y comportamientos familiares y sexuales en el México colonial.* Mexico City: Joaquín Mortiz, Instituo Nacional de Antropología e Historia, 1986.

———. *Seis ensayos sobre el discurso colonial relativo a la comunidad doméstica.* Mexico City: Instituo Nacional de Antropología e Historia, 1980.

Sigaut, Nelly. *La iglesia Católica en México.* Zamora, Michoacán, Mexico: El Colegio de Michoacán, 1997.

Los siglos de oro en los virreinatos de América: 1550–1700. Exh. Cat. Madrid: Sociedad Estatal para la Conmemoración de los Centenarios de Felipe II y Carlos V, 1999.

Silverblatt, Irene. "New Christians and New World Fears in Seventeenth-Century Peru." *Comparative Studies in Society and History* 42, no. 3 (2000): 524–46.

Stallybrass, Peter, and Alison White. *The Politics and Poetics of Transgression.* London: Methuen, 1986.

Stern, Steve J. *The Secret History of Gender: Women, Men, and Power in Late Colonial Mexico.* Chapel Hill: University of North Carolina Press, 1995.

Surtz, Ronald E. *The Guitar of God: Gender, Power, and Authority in the Visionary World of Mother Juana de la Cruz (1481–1534).* Philadelphia: University of Pennsylvania Press, 1990.

———. *Writing Women in Late Medieval and Early Modern Spain: The Mothers of Saint Teresa of Avila.* Philadelphia: University of Pennsylvania Press, 1995.

Tambs, Lewis A. "The Inquisition in Eighteenth-Century Mexico." *Americas: A Quarterly Review of Inter-American Colonial History* 22 (1965): 167–81.

Taylor, William B. "Between Global Process and Local Knowledge: An Inquiry into Early Latin American Social History, 1500–1900." In *Reliving the Past: The Worlds of Social History*, ed. Olivier Zuns, 115–90. Chapel Hill: University of North Carolina Press, 1985.

———. *Magistrates of the Sacred: Priests and Parishioners in Eighteenth-Century Mexico*. Stanford: Stanford University Press, 1996.

———. "Mexico's Virgin of Guadalupe in the Seventeenth Century: Hagiography and Beyond." In Greer and Bilinkoff, *Colonial Saints*, 277–98.

———. "The Virgin of Guadalupe in New Spain: An Inquiry into the Social History of Marian Devotion." *American Ethnologist* 14 (1987): 9–33.

Thomas, Keith. *Religion and the Decline of Magic*. New York: Charles Scribner's Sons, 1971.

Toussaint, Manuel. *Colonial Art in Mexico*. Austin: University of Texas Press, 1967.

Tovar de Teresa, Guillermo. *México Barroco*. Mexico City: SAHOP, 1981.

Twinam, Ann. *Public Lives, Private Secrets: Gender, Honor, and Illegitimacy in Colonial Spanish America*. Stanford: Stanford University Press, 1999.

Ulrich, Laurel Thatcher. *A Midwife's Tale: The Life of Martha Ballard, Based on Her Diary, 1785–1812*. New York: Knopf, 1990.

van Deusen, Nancy E. *Between the Sacred and the Worldly: The Institutional and Cultural Practice of Recogimiento in Colonial Lima*. Stanford: Stanford University Press, 2001.

———. "Defending the Boundaries of Virtue: The Discourse of *Recogimiento* in Seventeenth-Century Lima." *Journal of Family History* 22, no. 4 (October 1997): 373–89.

———. "Defining the Sacred and the Worldly: *Beatas* and *Recogidos* in Late Seventeenth-Century Lima." *Colonial Latin American Historical Review* 6, no. 4 (Fall 1997): 441–77.

Vargaslugo, Elisa. "La obra de arte como móvil de la experiencia mística." In Colegio de San Ildefonso, *Arte y mística*, 117–24.

Veith, Ilza. *Hysteria: The History of a Disease*. Chicago: University of Chicago Press, 1965.

Velasco, Shelly M. *Demons, Nausea, and Resistance in the Autobiography of Isabel de Jesús*. Albuquerque: University of New Mexico Press, 1996.

Villa-Flores, Javier. " 'To Lose One's Soul': Blasphemy and Slavery in New Spain, 1596–1669." *Hispanic American Historical Review* 82, no. 3 (2002): 435–68.

Villaseñor Black, Charlene. "St. Anne Imagery and Maternal Archetypes in Spain and Mexico." In Greer and Bilinkoff, *Colonial Saints*, 3–29.

Viqueira Albán, Juan Pedro. *Propriety and Permissiveness in Bourbon Mexico*. Trans. Sonya Lipsett-Rivera and Sergio Rivera Ayala. Wilmington DE: Scholarly Resources, 1999.

Voekel, Pamela. "Peeing on the Palace: Bodily Resistance to Bourbon Reforms in Mexico City." *Journal of Historical Sociology* 5, no. 2 (1992): 183–208.

Warner, Marina. *Alone of Her Sex: The Myth and the Cult of the Virgin Mary*. New York: Vintage, 1976.

Weber, Alison. "Between Ecstasies and Exorcism: Religious Negotiation in Sixteenth-Century Spain." *Journal of Medieval and Renaissance Studies* 23, no. 2 (1993): 22–34.

———. *Teresa of Avila and the Rhetoric of Femininity*. Princeton: Princeton University Press, 1990.

Weckman, Luis. *The Medieval Heritage of Mexico*. New York: Fordham University Press, 1992.

Weinstein, Donald, and Rudolf Bell. *Saints and Society: Two Worlds of Western Christendom, 1000–1700*. Chicago: University of Chicago Press, 1982.

Weismann, Elizabeth Wilder. *Art and Time in Mexico: From the Conquest to the Republic*. New York: Harper and Row, 1985.

Weithaus, Ulrike. *Maps of Flesh and Light: New Perspectives on Medieval Women Mystics*. Syracuse: Syracuse University Press, 1992.

Index

Page numbers in *italics* indicate illustrations.

tests for detecting the, 152–53. *See also* demonic

diabolism. *See* devil

Diario Curioso de México (Robles), 50–51

Diego, Juan, 115

disease. *See* epilepsy; gonorrhea; hysteria; illness

doctors, 146, 147–48, 151, 155, 158, 161

doctrine. *See* Council of Trent; Counter-Reformation, theology during; Mexican Provincial Councils

domestic violence, 2, 68

Double Mistaken Identity, 172

Echagaray, Barbara de, 132, 144, 146, 162

ecstasy, 39–40, 63, 64, 65, 68

Edicts of the Faith (edictos de la fe), 23; and creating deviancy, 33–34; defining *alumbradismo* by, 29, 30, 34

Elements of Medicine (Brown), 158

elites: living conditions of, 50; racial attitudes of, 54–55

embusteros, 105, 189–92

encomenderos, 52

Enlightenment, 18, 98–99, 155–64

epilepsy, 140, 143, 146–48, 151, 155–57, 160, 219n10

Erasmus, Desiderius, 26, 28

Erickson, Kai, 193n8

ermitaños. See hermits

Eucharist, 77, 111, 137, 169; miracles, 68–69, 119; visions of 121–22, 124

faith: in colonial society, 14, 119; of mystics, 14, 15, 17

familiares, 22, 24

Farfán, Agustín, 148–49

—Works: *Tractado breve de medicina*, 148–49

fasting, 68, 73, 133

Felipe de Jesús, Saint, 7, 87

femininity: colonial ideal of, 7–8, 9–11, 61–63, 94–97, 129

Flores, Beatriz de Jesús las, 68, 91–92

food, 68–70, 89, 133–34, 158, 159

Franciscans, 28, 29, 39, 56, 89, 91, 93

Francisco de Jesús María, 83, 104–6

Franco, Jean, 12–13, 14, 131

Fuente, Alonso de la, 32

García de Arias, Pedro, 75, 89, 93, 173–74; theology of, 25, 85, 93–94; writings of, 70–71

gender: challenges to roles of, 2, 8, 9–11, 70–73, 94–97; in the Counter-Reformation, 59–63, 91; maintenance of, roles, 7–8, 61–63, 90–91; and proscribed spiritual activities, 70–73, 94–97. *See also* femininity; honor; masculinity; men; sexual practices; women

Giles, Mary E., 8, 101

Godínez, Miguel, 40, 57, 83, 84, 88, 94, 201–2n80

—Works: *Practica de la teología mystica*, 57, 83, 88

Gómez, Juan, 9, 25, 93

gonorrhea, 148

Greenleaf, Richard, 22, 26

Gregory IX (pope), 86

Guadalcázar, marquis of, 62

Guadalupe Rivera, María, 84

Guía espiritual (Molinos), 199–200n42, 212n69

Guilhem, Claire, 35

Guillamas, Ana de, 32, 33, 36, 84

gynecology, 158

Hamilton, Alistair, 30

healers. See *curanderas*

hechicería, 104–5

heresy, 80, 84–86. *See also alumbrados*; deviancy; idolatry; Islam; Judaism; Lutheranism; Molinos; Protestantism; quietism

hermits, 4, 88, 90–94, 107

heterodoxy, 83–84, 86–90, 174. *See also* deviancy

Hidalgo y Costilla, Miguel, 21

Holler, Jacqueline, 96

Holy Feast and Holy Fast (Bynum), 134

Holy Office. *See* Inquisition

honor: female 7, 9, 61–63, 90–91, 94–97; male, 7, 10

Horta, Pedro de, 156–57

humoral theory, 146, 155

hysteria, 138, 141, 143, 144, 146, 151, 155, 156–64

idolatry, 39, 44, 104–5

patrons: inquisition's suspicion of, 96, 168; supporting mystics, 9, 14, 29, 55–59, 77, 89
Paula Rosa de Jesús, 150, 152–53
Paul V (pope), 152
Pelagianism, 71, 207–8n109, 212n71
Peña, Luis, 57
Peña, María Josefa Rita de la, 73, 74
Pérez de la Serna, Juan, 62
Perry, Mary Elizabeth, 60, 61
peyote, 67, 77, 102–3, 127
Philip II (king), 20–21
Philip IV (king), 62
physicians. *See* doctors
Picazo, María Manuela, 55, 68, 75, 94–95, 115–16
pipilzintli, 105, 214n105
Plata, Juan, 31–32, 58, 106
poetry, 71
poverty: in Mexico, 52–53, 129; mystics and, 53–54, 93, 173–74; women and, 52–53, 88, 162
Practica de la teología mystica (Godínez), 57, 83
Prado y Obejero, Bernardo, 151
prayer, 74, 75
pregnancy, 132, 171
pride, 154–55
proselytism of Mexican Indians, 28, 38–39
prostitution, 53
Protestantism, 38, 62, 63, 168; associated with *alumbradismo*, 30, 33, 107; as Iberian heresy, 5, 28
Provisorato del ordinario, 20
pulque, 69
purgatory: miracles involving, 66–67; 102–3

quietism, 30, 35, 98, 98, 107, 169
quiestismo. *See* quietism

race: demographics of, 21, 49–50; and deviancy, 5, 100–106; and sanctity, 97, 100–101; and social hierarchy, 6–7, 54; in visions and miracles, 48, 109, 113, 133–36. *See also* blacks; *castas*; Indians; whiteness
Raggi, Maria, 210n17
Ramos, Alonso, 100–101
Rangel, Angel, 53, 66, 99, 127–28, 130, 171

reading, 70, 212n65
Real Pragmática, 6, 194n14
recogimiento: as an institution, 8; as a theological concept, 28, 29, 168
Reformation, Protestant, 28, 31. *See also* Luther; Lutheranism
resistance: historiography of, 11–14; mysticism and, 5–6, 8–9, 10–11, 12–13, 26
retablos, 165
revolts, 105
Richelieu, Cardinal, 66
Riverius, Lazarus, 155, 159
Robles, Antonio de, 50–51
—Works: *Diario Curioso de México*, 50–51
Rocha, Diego Manuel de la, 56, 66–67
Rodríguez de Castro y Aramburu, Ana de. *See* Aramburu, Ana de
Rodríguez Juárez, Juan, 115
Rodríguez Juárez, Nicolás, 122; *Transveración de Santa Teresa*, 122
Romero, Teresa, 13–14, 104, 132, 171
Romero sisters, 34, 56, 132. *See also* Bruñón de Vertiz, José; Josefa de San Luis Beltrán; María de la Encarnación; Romero, Teresa
Rosa de Santa Rosa. *See peyote*
Rose of Lima, Saint, 87; and *criollo* identity, 42, 62; as role model for mystics, 6; *Las tentaciones de Santa Rosa*, 120; in visions, 127–28
Rubial García, Antonio, 42
Ruiz de Alcaraz, Pedro. *See* Alcaraz, Pedro Ruiz de

Sahagún, Bernardino de, 105
saints, cult of the, 42, 105
Salmerón, Pedro, 144–45
sanctity: demographics of, 86–87; perception of, 5–6, 11, 15. *See also* orthodoxy
San Juan de la Penitencia convent, 58–59
Santiago Matamoros, 61, 206n70
Santo Oficio. *See* Inquisition
Satan. *See* devil
sermons, 116–17, 173
De Servorum Dei beatificatione (Benedict XIV), 87
sexual practices: and the devil, 128, 150–51; and hysteria, 138–39, 150–51, 159, 161,

and men, 79–80; suspicion of female, 48, 60–61, 90, 95, 100, 132
Sigüenza y Góngora, Carlos de, 82
—Works: *Parayso occidental,* 82
souls, 102–3
spell-making. See *hechicería*
stigmata, 2, 81

Tercer abecedario espiritual (Osuna), 28
Teresa de Jesús, Santa. *See* Teresa of Avila, Saint
Teresa of Avila, Saint: ecstasies of, 122; miracles of, 117, 122; popularity of, 61; as role model for mystics, 6, 40, 74, 76; in visions, 37, 69, 150; view of the body, 88–89, 210n36; writings of, 74
—Works: *Libro de la vida,* 122; *Moradas,* 74
tertiaries, 91, 198n31
tobacco, 69–70, 77, 102–3
Tomás de Villanueva, Saint, 28
tonalli, 102–3
Torres, Juan Luis, 147–48
torture, 24, 80
Tractado breve de medicina (Farfán), 148–49
Tribunal del Santo Oficio. *See* Inquisition
Trinity, 69, 84, 110, 115

Urban VIII (pope), 87

Valdés, José Eugenio, 82
—Works: *Vida admirable y penitente,* 82
Valdés, Fernando de, 28–29
—Works: *Index of Prohibited Books,* 28
Valle de México, marqués de, 56, 204n49
van Deusen, Nancy, 198n27
Vanegas, Juan Manuel, 158
—Works: *Compendio de la medicina práctica,* 158
Vargaslugo, Elisa, 115
Vázquez, Aacutengel, 57
Vega, Juan Manuel de, 47, 57
viceroys, 51, 106. *See also* Albuquerque, duque de; Linares, duque de;

Victoria, Salvador, 70, 85, 93
Vida admirable y penitente (Valdés), 82
vidas, 40, 71, 75
Villa Alta, José de, 23–24
Villalpando, Cristóbal de, 110, 111, 115, 118–19; *Bautizo de la Virgen,* 111; *La Mística Ciudad de Dios,* 112
Villarejo, Eusebio, 10, 137–38, 162
Villaseñor Black, Charlene, 43
virginity, 7, 61–63, 117–19, 125–33, 161, 163, 169
Virgin Mary. *See* Mary, Saint
Virgin of Guadalupe, 115–16, 215n13; and *criollo* nationalism, 42, 61–62; cult of, 61–63; in visions and art, 116
Virgin of Immaculate Conception, 62–63, 110–11, *112*
virtues, 94–97, 147, 151, 159–60
visions, 63–70; art and, 115–16; challenges to orthodoxy in, 9, 109–36, 169
vomiting, 103
vows, 91, 94, 167; disobedience to, 59

wealth: and the colonial church, 6–7; as motivation for mysticism, 13–14, 88–89
whiteness: attitude toward, 54–55, 61, 62, 100–101. See also *limpieza de sangre*
will, 85, 154
women: accusations against, 60–61; Catholic church's views of, 28–29, 60–61, 88, 94–97, 131; control of, 59–63, 91; inquisition's views of, 48, 161–64; nature of, 88; occupations of, 90, 91, 95; participation in male religious activities, 70–73; and poverty, 52–53, 88, 162; rates of conviction of, 90; religious practices of, 63–64; religious status of, 48. See also poverty, women and
writing, 71–72, 74, 85, 93–94, 95–96, 113

Zárate, Luis de, 149
Zayas, Ana de, 9, 169; writings of, 71–72, 85, 95–96, 151–52
Zumárraga, Juan de, 20

Milton Keynes UK
Ingram Content Group UK Ltd.
UKHW012112250124
436597UK00013B/284

9 780803 218406